Copyright Acknowledgments

The author and publisher gratefully acknowledge permission for use of the following material:

Excerpts from Nathaniel Micklem, *National Socialism and the Roman Catholic Church* (London: Oxford University Press, 1939), by permission of Oxford University Press.

Excerpts from Nathaniel Micklem, *The Theology of Politics* (London: Oxford University Press, 1941), by permission of Oxford University Press.

Excerpts from Leslie Weatherhead, *Thinking Aloud in War Time: An Attempt to See the Present Situation in the Light of the Christian Faith* (London: Epworth Press, 1941). Copyright 1941. Used by permission of Abingdon Press.

Excerpts from Leslie Weatherhead, *This Is Victory* (London: Hodder & Stoughton, 1940). Copyright 1940. Used by permission.

Excerpts from William Temple, *Some Lambeth Letters*, ed, F. S. Temple (London: Oxford University Press, 1962), by permission of Oxford University Press.

Excerpts from T. E. Jessop, *Has the Christian Way Failed?* (London: Epworth Press, 1941), by permission of SCM Press.

Excerpts from William Temple, *The Hope of a New World* (London: SCM Press, 1940), by permission of SCM Press.

Excerpts from T. G. Dunning, *Settlement with Germany* (London: SCM Press, 1943), by permission of SCM Press.

Excerpts from William Temple, *Thoughts in War-Time* (London: Macmillan, 1940), by permission of Macmillan General Books.

Every reasonable effort has been made to trace the owners of copyright materials in this book, but in some instances this has proven impossible. The author and publisher will be glad to receive information leading to more complete acknowledgments in subsequent printings of the book and in the meantime extend their apologies for any omissions.

To the British people of 1940 to 1941—

The "finger in the dike"

Contents

Foreword *by Richard V. Pierard*   xi

Preface   xiii

1   Introduction: The Legacy of the Great War   1

2   1939: War Again?   7

3   Dealing with Pacifism   23

4   The Enemy: Fascism–Nazism   51

5   The Decline and Fall of Liberal Humanism   79

6   The War for Christian Civilization   97

7   1945: A New Order?   121

8   Reflections   135

    Selected Bibliography   139

    Index   145

Foreword

Richard V. Pierard

World War II was the most extensive conflict in human history. Never before had so many nations in so many parts of the world engaged in a struggle of such titanic proportions. Neither had the loss of life and property as the result of a war ever been greater. It changed the entire course of global development by bringing an end to European imperial and economic hegemony and ushering in the age of American dominance. Thereafter conflicts were more limited in scope, and even the struggle between communism (in its various forms) and Western democracy never erupted into a global war, which in the nuclear age would have meant the total destruction of humanity.

No other topic is the subject of so much scholarly and popular literature as this one. The two-volume *Handbook of Literature and Research on World War II*, edited by Loyd E. Lee and published by Greenwood Press in 1997 and 1998, provides the best overview of the scholarship on the conflict available today, but it is inconceivable that anyone will ever produce a bibliography encompassing all the millions of relevant literary works that have appeared in various languages. Still, the unceasing flow of books, articles, films, videos, and other materials on World War II bears testimony to the continuing grip it has on the public.

Although a torrent of literature has been produced on the military, political, and social aspects of the war, writers have devoted much less attention to its religious dimensions—a point I make in my chapter on Christianity and the war in the *Handbook*. Gerald L. Sittser has filled the gap in our understanding of the situation in the United States with *A Cautious Patriotism: The American Churches and the Second World War* (Chapel Hill: University of North Carolina Press, 1997), and in this volume A. J. Hoover does likewise with respect to the attitudes of the British clergy.

He has examined the mountain of published sermons, tracts, essays, articles, and even unpublished items that clerics from various traditions generated during the war years. He finds, as Sittser did of the American clergy, that the support for the British cause was solid and unwavering while at the same time elements of caution and ambiguity were present. They firmly supported the Allies and were implacably hostile to Nazism and fascism, but the quality of the response was much different from that found in World War I. The assessment of their country's position and attitude toward the enemy population was more sophisticated and compassionate. They even saw distinctions between the Nazi leaders and their ideology and ordinary Germans.

One thing that contributed to the changed situation was the disillusionment brought about by World War I and the intense pacifism that was so prevalent in church circles in the 1930s. Another was the ecumenical movement, which was characterized by liberal optimism and brought together Christian leaders from various nations. This produced more understanding of the complex political situations and awareness that many German churchmen opposed the totalistic claims of Nazi paganism and the regime's efforts to gain control of the churches. Because of their own ambiguous attitude toward war in general, the British clergy trod more gingerly as they threw their support behind the nation and the struggle to preserve Western Christian civilization.

Hoover approaches his subject with a sense of understanding drawn from his studies of Christian apologetics and clerical nationalism in earlier times. He recognizes the cultural backgrounds of the actions and statements made, and he pulls no punches in criticizing those aspects of modern society that he dislikes. Some readers will not like his explanations, but they will also find themselves obliged to reexamine their own assumptions. Hoover's assessment of the British clerical response to World War II calls into question views widely held today. Thus, his account is both insightful and inspiring, and one that challenges us in our present situation.

Preface

Even since my days in graduate school, I have been fascinated by the topic of nationalism, particularly clerical nationalism, and particularly the patriotic preaching of Christian ministers in wartime. This volume will be my third book on the topic of clerical nationalism. The first, *The Gospel of Nationalism: German Patriotic Preaching from Napoleon to Versailles* (1986) examined the nationalism of the German Protestant clergy in three wars: the Napoleonic Wars (1806–1815), the Franco–Prussian War (1870–1871), and the First World War (1914–1918). The second, *God, Germany, and Britain in the Great War: A Study in Clerical Nationalism* (Praeger, 1989) compared the nationalism of German and British clergymen in World War I.

The present volume looks at the wartime preaching of the British clergy in World War II (1939–1945). My materials come from several religious groups: the Church of England, the Church of Scotland, the Roman Catholic Church, and the Free Churches (Baptists, Methodists, Congregationalists, and Quakers). A variety of documents are examined: sermons, articles, books, pamphlets, tracts, speeches, and addresses, as well as letters and other private papers, especially the papers of the two Anglican archbishops during the war, Cosmo Gordon Lang and William Temple. We look at a variety of churchmen, from vicars and canons to bishops and archbishops; we even look at some articulate Christian laypersons such as T. S. Eliot and Dorothy Sayers. Some non-British theologians like Reinhold Niebuhr, Fulton Sheen, and Karl Barth also are included in our analysis because they influenced British clerical opinion so deeply in this world crisis.

I shall make no apology for my obvious pro-British stance in this book. As Mark Twain would say, I'm prejudiced on this topic, and I would be ashamed if I weren't. I think Churchill was exactly right when he said we shouldn't be neutral between the fire and the fire department. I hope the world will long remember the valiant stand that Britain took against the Nazi war machine in the dark days of 1940 and 1941, before the Soviet Union and the United States entered the war. If Britain had fallen to Hitler, there would have been no Normandy invasion in 1944, because there would have been no base of operations from which to launch it. If there had been no Normandy invasion, then Hitler might have conquered all of Europe, from the Atlantic to the Urals and even beyond. We can thank the British for holding a finger in the dike, as it were, until help could arrive to counterattack and overthrow fascism in Europe. I count it a great privilege to dedicate this book to the British people who held out in those fateful years of 1940 and 1941.

If we ask *how* the British were able to hold out, I think we shall have to say that a part of the credit must go to the nation's spiritual leaders, the British clergy—Protestant and Catholic, Anglican and Free Church. They all supported the war and gave a vigorous critique of fascist ideology, depicting it as a modern form of idolatry—a pagan worship of leader, race, and state. They attacked Nazi racism as a ghastly violation of Christian equality and universalism. Already in the 1930s their Christian "reflexes" were working well as they detected violations of Christian principles in National Socialist Germany. We can be sincerely grateful that they were not addicted to the modern vice of cultural relativism or multiculturalism, which sees no difference between ideologies.

I wish to express my deep appreciation to Canon Alan Wilkinson of Portsmouth Cathedral for his kind encouragement during my research on this project. His many writings on the clergy and war have recently earned him the well-deserved degree of Doctor of Divinity from the University of Cambridge. His sane and balanced treatment of all issues involving Christianity and warfare brings to mind the warning of George Bell, Bishop of Chichester (1929–1957), that "the Church is not the State's spiritual auxiliary," a warning we all need to take to heart. I am also grateful to Edmund and Jane Haviland of Thursley, who showed exemplary British hospitality to my wife and me while traveling in England; Edmund also gave me the benefit of some of his research in the parish journals.

This is now the third research project that I have accomplished with the assistance of the Research Council of Abilene Christian University. I owe a great debt of gratitude to Dr. Carley Dodd and the members of the Council for funding my trips to England in the summers of 1995, 1996, and 1997. My wife, Gloria, accompanied me on these research trips and not only helped me to locate some of the sources but did research on her own in some of them. She is the perfect scholar's wife.

CHAPTER 1

Introduction: The Legacy of the Great War

During the 1960s the United States fought a long, costly war in Vietnam; it was the most unpopular and divisive military conflict in American history. The ambiguities of the conflict led to a high degree of domestic unrest in the country. Young antiwar protesters devised a pithy slogan called "Give peace a chance!" The antiwar groups in Great Britain in the 1920s and 1930s preached a similar message to the British people: *Give peace a chance*. Perhaps no period in world history has witnessed more talk and organization for peace than the period of 1919 to 1939. For many moral, sensitive people, the Great War of 1914 to 1918 had brought history to a head. Millions took seriously the claim that it was a "war to end all wars" and went to work to build a new world without military conflict. If we now chide such people for their "unrealism," we must remember that their determined optimism seemed eminently justified at the time.[1]

Hopes for peace were usually associated with the new League of Nations, sired by President Woodrow Wilson, though rejected by his own U.S. Senate. In Britain the League of Nations Union became the most influential society for peace during the 1920s. Every Armistice Day, Christians were encouraged to support the League and work for international understanding and reconciliation. Old-fashioned patriotism was frowned upon as the cause of the Great War and the enemy of internationalism. Clergymen used the Bible and their pulpits to stress the doctrine of universal love, and its political corollary, internationalism.

Actually the British people and Christian clergy were not all that "international" before the First World War. The clergy "painted themselves into a corner," as it were, with their sermons against Imperial Germany during the conflict. They identified many "sins" of Germany, but the one they stressed the most was what we may call the "Doctrine of the Amoral State." This tenet went by many names: Kaiserism, Bismarckism, Prussianism, *Realpolitik*, the Gospel of Force, or simply, Might Makes Right. Whatever its name, it referred to the notion that morality did not apply to the state. Personal morality is binding on the individual because the group will enforce it, but the state has nothing above it, and thus must be the judge in its own cause. Since there is no tribunal above the state, war is the only possible court of appeal. For decades various German leaders and intellectuals had articulated this doctrine, and thus it was taken in Britain to be a basic tenet of the new German Empire.[2]

During the Great War British churchmen of all faiths expressed deep shock that a great, cultured nation in the modern, civilized world would have the temerity to seriously suggest the barbaric idea that mere power determined the right between nations. Arthur Winnington-Ingram called it "the Pagan Doctrine of the State" and claimed that "the entire theory is a legal, philosophical, metaphysical falsehood, the most disastrous piece of false thinking still surviving on earth."[3] Clergymen and spokesmen for all churches joined in this critique of the barbaric doctrine of *Realpolitik*. Archbishop of Canterbury Randall Thomas Davidson staked out the moral high ground for the Allies when he affirmed, "We believe, with an intensity beyond words, that there does exist exactly what our opponents deny, a higher law than the law of the state, a deeper allegiance than can be claimed by any earthly Sovereign, and that in personal and national conduct alike we have to follow higher and more sacred principles of honour than any State law can enforce."[4]

By contradicting the notion of nationalistic relativism for four years, the clergymen had committed themselves, by implication, to a doctrine of absolutism and universalism—to the idea of an international ethical code, a standard of morality among the powers, a Tao for the nations. Thus we are not surprised that the clerical imagination was seized by the idea of a league of nations, a supranational agency empowered to keep the peace. As Albert Marrin observed, "Men were moved as if by a vision of the Beyond."[5] They treated the coming of Wilson with almost as much reverence as the coming of Christ; Wilson was bringing a "new deal" in diplomacy, because the old had obviously failed to prevent the near suicide of Western civilization. In a book called *God and the Allies: A View of the Grand Entente*, Rosslyn Bruce, vicar of Saint Augustine's in Edgbaston, urged that the alliance was not an accident of history but "a practical link in the chain of Divine purposes, working through the human means of friendly nations, to the establishment of an international understanding throughout the whole of civilized society."[6] In February 1918, the Upper House of Canterbury Convocation passed this resolution:

That this house notes with special satisfaction the prominent place recently given by prominent statesmen among the Allies to the proposal of a League of Nations. We desire to welcome in the name of the Prince of Peace the idea of such a League as shall promote the brotherhood of man, and shall have power at the last resort to constrain by economic pressure or armed force any nation which should refuse to submit to an international tribunal any dispute with another nation. Further, we desire that such a League of Nations should not merely be regarded as a more or less remote consequence of peace, but that provision for its organization should be included in the conditions of a settlement.[7]

The churches of Britain were one of the strongest supporters of the League in the interwar period. The Revised Prayer Book of 1928 contained a collect for the international body. Lord Robert Cecil, a devout Anglican and president of the League of Nations Union, wrote to his wife, "I have had a great feeling that I have been 'called' to preach the League spirit on public affairs and there seems to be so much in the Bible about that kind of thing." In 1933, the Archbishops of Canterbury and York and thirty-five bishops and leaders of other churches appealed to governments to work through the League and urged Christians to join the League of Nations Union.[8]

Since war was in general disrepute, people tended to fall for conspiracy theories about its origins. In America some politicians and intellectuals charged that wars were usually started by newspaper editors (partly true of the Spanish–American War in 1898) and armaments manufacturers. In Britain they added other culprits: the military officer class and the imperialist politicians. If you accept this hypothesis, you will then agree with the suggestion that simple structural change will remove all the causes for war. This reminds us of the strange theory of Baron d'Holbach (1723–1789), that utopia would come when "every king is strangled with the guts of every priest." One also recalls the Marxists, who believed that utopia will come with the mere abolition of private property and the profit motive.

Positive feelings about the League of Nations were accompanied by increasingly negative feelings about the diplomatic agreement that ended the war, the Treaty of Versailles. The ink on that Treaty was hardly dry before most people began to feel that it was a flawed document, negotiated in hatred and haste. David Lloyd George was returned to the office of Prime Minister as a result of the notorious "Khaki Election" of 14 December 1918, which John M. Keynes called the most unfortunate election in modern British history. Lloyd George took to the stump, promising to make Britain a "country fit for heroes to live in." To get the money to keep his pledge he had to promise that he would go to Versailles and "squeeze the Germans until the pips squeak." One of the most popular slogans in this pivotal election was "Hang the Kaiser!"

It was amazing how soon most Britons repented of their rash actions in the Khaki Election. Already by 1919 Keynes had released his *Economic Conse-*

quences of the Peace, a most learned indictment of the treaty, written by a former treasury official and an economist who would become the most important economic thinker of the century. Keynes pointed out that Germany was the economic heart of Europe; thus to cripple Germany was to cripple all Europe, a very foolish move, especially if you expected these same Germans to pay reparations. Keynes' book was very popular with the younger generation, who were usually pacifists and convinced that the same old guard that had caused the war had devised a disastrous peace.

Meanwhile, across the channel, Adolf Hitler, an evil but astute man, could tell that there was a certain "guilt feeling" about Versailles in Britain. By the mid-1930s the Treaty was so discredited the German leader could be almost certain that no war would be fought against Germany for trying to revise it. The British people were thoroughly convinced that Germany had legitimate grievances against the Versailles settlement. As long as Hitler demanded only German territory, there would be no opposition, because such a move could easily be justified by the sacred principle of national self-determination, disclosed by the messiah himself, Woodrow Wilson, in his sacred revelation, the Fourteen Points. Not until Hitler seized the rump of Czechoslovakia in 1939—after declaring "We want no Czechs!"—did it become evident that he had merely been using the principle to cloak his aggressions. A few clear-headed Britons, who were not blinded by romantic notions of essential human goodness, saw early that revisions, even of a flawed treaty, should never be accomplished as a result of force, especially force wielded by a moral nihilist like Hitler.

Many people, however, did not know about Nazism's moral nihilism until it was too late. It was easy in the early days to reject negative interpretations of Nazism as hostile conservative propaganda. Fascism in general was admired by many people in Britain, who were impressed with its "dynamism," which contrasted favorably with the slow methods of democracy. Hitler was often commended for his bold solutions to problems like unemployment. Mussolini and Franco were deeply appreciated by many Roman Catholics in Britain. In fact, "almost all vocal English Roman Catholics," writes Wilkinson, "supported Franco in the Spanish Civil War."[9]

This rosy view of the Fascist dictators sounds almost criminal to our ears today, but we must recall that between the wars there was in Britain a strong desire to atone for the bashing given the Germans in the sermons of the Great War. It was embarrassing to read the patriotic homilies from 1914 to 1918, referring to the Germans as "huns," "beasts," "devils," "barbarians," and the "antichrist." Four years of preaching hate, many argued, led to the hateful Versailles Treaty with all its injustices. There was a strong, perhaps unconscious, urge to construe German policies in a favorable light in order to avoid the hostility and antagonism that might lead to another war.

Another war? "Don't even think of it! It was so horrible it must never—repeat never—be allowed to recur!" That was the feeling of most Britons, from the common people right up to the throne. Lloyd George confided to his mistress that he heard King George V say in 1935: "I *will* not have another war, I *will not*. The last war was none of my doing, & if there is another one & we are threatened with being brought into it, I will go to Trafalgar Square and wave a red flag myself sooner than allow this country to be brought in."[10] Astute observers saw the new weapons of World War I and projected the horrors of the next conflict. The predictions of F. Holmes Dudden in 1918 were disturbingly accurate:

As you look into the future, can you discern any brighter prospect than that of kingdoms arrayed against kingdoms and continents against continents—gigantic armies grappling with gigantic armies; airships by the thousand raining bombs upon doomed cities, whose inhabitants burrow like rats underground to escape destruction; all the resources of science taxed to the uttermost to furnish effective instruments for this diabolical work of devastation; and the last relics of conventional chivalry and generosity and magnanimity rent in rags and torn to tatters?[11]

The antiwar sentiment penetrated the academy. Both the Cambridge Union (1927) and the Oxford Union (1931) passed motions in favor of pacifism. Then the Oxford Union dropped a special bombshell on 9 February 1933 by debating a resolution worded "that this house will in no circumstance fight for its king and country." The motion carried 275 to 153, which shocked most of the nation. (Fifty years later the same motion was debated again and lost by 416 to 187. A participant of the original debate stood up and tearfully explained the special circumstances surrounding the first vote.) The motion had been introduced by a noted philosopher, C. E. M. Joad. The vote took place just ten days after Hitler came to power. Many people, including many Germans, concluded that the younger generation of Britons would not fight in a future war.

So, if one asks, as many young history students do, how Hitler was so successful in his foreign policy in the 1930s, one would have to reply that he was a devilishly clever politician who skillfully exploited certain auspicious conditions in the diplomatic situation: the guilt feeling over the Treaty of Versailles, the fear of another terrible war, the fear of Soviet Communism, and the desire for peace. But you can manipulate people just so far and then they will turn on you. The British people did indeed give peace a chance—probably too much of a chance. But we are impressed with how quickly they recovered from their illusions in 1939, the year in which our story begins.

NOTES

1. The best account of the Anglican clergy in World War I is by Alan Wilkinson, *The Church of England and the First World War*, 2d ed. (London: SCM Press, 1996). Another good study is by Albert Marrin, *The Last Crusade: The Church of England in the First World War* (Durham, N.C.: Duke University Press, 1974). See also C. E. Bailey, "British Protestant Theologians in the First World War: Germanophobia Un-

leashed," *Harvard Theological Review* 77, 2 (1984): 195–221. See also A. J. Hoover, *God, Germany, and Britain in the Great War: A Study in Clerical Nationalism* (New York: Praeger, 1989).

2. See Hoover, *God, Germany, and Britain*, 21–25; A. J. Hoover, "Waiting for Woodrow Wilson: Internationalism among the British Clergy in the Great War," *Canadian Review of Studies in Nationalism* 20, 1–2 (1993): 87–95.

3. *Christ and the World at War* (London: Wells, 1916), 157.

4. *The Testing of a Nation* (London: Macmillan, 1919), 87.

5. *Last Crusade*, 240.

6. (Birmingham, Cornish Bros., 1915), vii.

7. G.K.A. Bell, *Randall Davidson: Archbishop of Canterbury* (Oxford: Oxford University Press, 1962), 891.

8. See Alan Wilkinson, *Dissent or Conform? War, Peace and the English Churches 1900–1945* (London: SCM Press, 1986), 88.

9. Ibid., 98. For a good analysis of this general topic, see Richard Griffiths, *Fellow Travelers of the Right: British Enthusiasts for Nazi Germany 1933–39* (London: Constable, 1980).

10. A.J.P. Taylor, *Lloyd George: A Diary by Frances Stevenson* (London: Hutchinson, 1971), 309.

11. *The Delayed Victory and Other Sermons* (London: Longmans, Green, 1918), 173.

CHAPTER 2

1939: War Again?

World War II started with Hitler's attack on Poland early on the morning of 1 September 1939, barely twenty years since the end of the Great War of 1914 to 1918. The two decades between the wars had witnessed the rise of Fascism and Communism, the Great Depression, the decline of the League of Nations, and other developments that alarmed good liberals. Britain was now faced with another war on the continent of Europe. This time, however, she had gotten into the war with a clear prewar pledge to fight. On 31 March 1939, Prime Minister Neville Chamberlain informed Parliament of his fateful promise to protect Poland from a German attack, a pledge supported by Britain's closest ally, France. Since Hitler did not believe that Britain and France would fight for Poland, this promise was the thing that touched off the war. It was the first time in her history that Britain had decided for war or peace based on a possible attack, rather than waiting for the war to start and then entering it as she saw fit, judging the balance of power.[1]

The British people had been hammered with earth-shattering events for most of the 1930s, so the outbreak of war was not the total surprise that it had been in August 1914. Yet, though it was no surprise, the war was still a disappointment to many. It made religious people ask, "Why did God let this conflict break out? Why did he subject us to another war?" Some people added the words, "again?" or "so soon?" S. C. Carpenter confessed that the question troubling him most was why God had permitted "such an appalling mass of world-wrecking dynamite to be controlled by one man."[2] The spiritual leaders of the nation are supposed to answer questions like these. What could they say? The task of the hour was philosophical "damage control."

Both world wars raised this question of providence, not only with churchmen and serious thinkers, but also with Christian laypersons, not to mention the quasi-religious and marginal believers. Like the Jews during the Exile, Britons were being forced to ask fundamental questions about their traditional faith, the conventional interpretation of their own history. History was producing new wine that would not fit into the old wineskins.

D. R. Davies put the question in proper perspective by noting that Christianity is the only religion in the world that is really aware of history and that takes seriously the tension between time and eternity, between heaven and earth, the ideal and the real. It is the only other-worldly faith where this world is of decisive significance, where heaven is organically related to earth. Christians do not simply hand over the world to the devil or ignore it as an illusion, as a Hindu or Buddhist might do. Consequently, when a war breaks out, most Christians are genuinely disturbed and feel a need to justify the ways of God in history.[3] War always causes a lot of philosophizing, even among the unphilosophical. It always produces a defense of God, a *theodicy*—a term coined by Leibniz from two Greek words for "God" and "justice."

War is a test of faith. It challenges the simple, childlike trust that everything is O.K., that whatever is, is right, that the portrait of Being has no dark spots. James Russell Lowell spoke for the optimists when he said, "I find great comfort in God. He would not let us get at the matchbox if He had not made the Universe fireproof."[4] Lowell died in 1891, and after viewing the "fires" of 1914 and 1939, thinkers of the twentieth century were beginning to wonder if the world was so fireproof after all. Two world wars in twenty years requires a lot of explaining. Many observers of current history found their deep misgivings accurately expressed in Alex Comford's poem, "We Live in a Blind Time."

> We live in a blind time—blindness is made
> the chief consideration; it is living,
> a way of getting bread. Nobody throws
> money to those who see. To kill with ease
> you must buy blindness. War and actions are blind,
> obedience is blind, soldiers are blind, and history
> now is a blind boulder that rolls and crushes people,
> following the slope that time has cut for it;
> history is a falling stone. The seeing run
> out of its way, out of its way.[5]

WHY DID GOD ALLOW THIS WAR?

History may indeed seem blind, but no Christian can let this pessimistic analysis pass without responding. Most British clergy used the war to make an old point: God has his own plan for history, but we do not know its particulars. It may include war. It may result in disbelief and arrogance, if one gets upset or loses faith because of his ignorance of God's plans. Sidney Berry struck a common chord when he denounced the lust for certainty, the hankering for predictions, the running after astrologers and pseudoprophets who claimed to know the future.[6] Anthony Otter said that to constantly ask "what something is for" is a sort of "rheumatism of the brain."[7]

On the whole the British clergy have always believed in free will, in man's capacity to make history in cooperation with God. As St. Paul told the Romans, "All things work together for good, to them who love God and are called according to his purpose" (Rom. 8:28), or, better, "In all things, God works for good." C. H. Dodd translated this verse: "With them that love God, He cooperates in all things."[8] That is, God labors with humans in the shaping of historical events. True, God has determined the general shape of history and the final triumph of good, but man nevertheless determines a part of the story; he can do things that will cause God to modify His plans. He can "make a difference." John Hadham put it nicely in saying that when God gave us free will he gave us the gift of complicating his plans.[9]

If free will *is* a reality, then we can see that perfect knowledge of the future might be a threat to the moral life. If the future is fixed, there is no free will, and a totally-determined universe would logically paralyze action. If you feel that the future is fixed and immutable, you will lapse into resignation and simply wait for the inevitable to happen. But the attitude of strong men, concluded Berry, is to help shape the future and not merely to study it, "to play their part to the utmost of their powers and to trust in God to bring their hopes and efforts to a victorious fulfilment."[10]

God does not stand aloof from man in his struggles with evils like war. God somehow causes war and directs war to the realization of his plans; he is not the author of evil, but he uses evil once it starts by the free choice of man. The Bible shows war to be very normal, and it is not afraid to make God a participant in wars, revolutions, and human suffering. God takes his stand with man, wherever man happens to be. He shares man's strange, mixed, terrible situation. He is immanent in His creation; thus when you ask, "Why does God let this happen?" you should finish the question with, "Why does He let it happen *to Himself*?" Our patient God treads his own *via dolorosa* and asks us to share His patience and sorrow. It is all a glorious and incoherent picture, but it is vain for the rationalist to tidy it up and make it all sound logical. The believer must walk by faith and live with the incoherence. Action takes precedence over reasoning in wartime, trust over understanding. When Christ died on the Cross he did not say to his father, "Father, thank you, it is all clear, I now *understand* everything," but rather, "Father, into thy hands I *entrust* my spirit" (Luke 23:46).[11]

One could simply fall back on absolute trust or "blind faith," but as a matter of fact the religious people of Britain did not—they usually defended God by pointing to evil conditions that made war necessary or inevitable. Dorothy L. Sayers expressed it succinctly: "War is a judgment that overtakes societies when they have been living upon ideas that conflict too violently with the laws governing the universe."[12] Just as politics is individual action writ large, so war is individual human sin writ large. If war occurs you know for sure that evil has reached critical mass, to borrow a metaphor from physics. "It is simply impossible," asserted Fulton J. Sheen, "to have millions of men in the world living according to their pagan principles, and not produce the modern chaotic world in which we live."[13] Alec R. Vidler confessed he was not at all surprised that "man's most ambitious attempt at an apostate civilisation should have produced a state of confusion, demoralization, and bewilderment without precedent in the world's history."[14] Nathaniel Micklem, principal of Mansfield College, Oxford, said it was foolish to ask why God allowed this war: "When we ponder the acknowledged moral decay in France, the repudiation of Christianity in Germany, the secularism that dominated the pre-war age here as in Europe, the social injustices, the godlessness, the flaunting wickedness, we might more wisely ask how we could not believe in God, if He did not bring such rottenness down in destruction."[15]

Defending God dovetails nicely with refuting Fascism because the central issue is human freedom. God stands vindicated, argued Glasgow, if we simply remember that man is partly divine. He is free and moral; if he were stone, tree, or plant, he would not inflict these horrors on his fellows. "Being men, endowed with the supremely mystical gift of a critical free will, *they can do what they will*. If God could refuse to 'allow' them to do what they do they would not be free. They would be as cabbages."[16] Glasgow referred to people who want both free will and no war as "squallers." Berry said such people want God to become the Supreme Leader and take things into his totalitarian hands, overriding the decisions of men, making men the ciphers they are under Fascism. "The fact that He does not take that way is the clearest proof that it is only along the road of freedom that His purposes in creation can be fulfilled. And it is that Divine order of life which makes the struggle for freedom a sacred thing."[17] Weatherhead said, "Those who want God to stop the power of a dictator are frequently found to be praying that God would become one Himself. . . . To prevent the *possibility* of war God would not have created man free at all."[18] F. A. Cockin, canon of St. Paul's, asserted bluntly, "This is the kind of world you have asked for; and nothing, not even divine omnipotence, can save you from getting it."[19] Martyn Lloyd-Jones concluded that to ask God to prohibit war is to ask Him to prohibit one of the necessary consequences of sin:

We boast of our free-will and resent any suggestion or teaching that God should in any way interfere with it. And yet, when, as a result of the exercise of that very freedom, we find ourselves faced with the horrors and troubles and sufferings of a war, like peevish children we cry out our protests and complain bitterly against God because He has not used His almighty power and forcibly prevented it! God in His infinite and everlasting wisdom has decided not to prohibit sin and not to restrain altogether the consequences of sin. War is not an isolated and separate spiritual and religious problem. It is just a part and an expression of the one great central problem of sin.[20]

Judas Iscariot, who betrayed Jesus Christ, made the same error. He was in a hurry. He wanted the kingdom to come *now*, regardless of conditions, like the farmer who sowed seed in the winter on unplowed ground. Judas couldn't understand why Jesus waited. Some have suggested that his betrayal of Christ was a way of forcing Christ's hand and compelling him to act. When he saw Jesus working miracles, he must have reasoned within himself, "We could conquer the Romans right now! Look at the power Jesus has! Why does he wait? A man who can raise the dead would never let himself be arrested, would he?" But Jesus had his own methods and his own time-table. He offered a cross, not a crown. He allowed himself to be arrested by Rome and executed unjustly. When Peter tried to defend him with a sword, he told him that he was using the wrong method, that if he wished he could summon twelve legions of angels to save him (Matt. 26:53).[21] When he hung on the Cross, they taunted him with the challenge, "Come down and we will believe you!" (Luke 23:36, 39).[22] It was the same in 1939.

John Hadham felt keenly the need for theodicy in World War II. In a book he wrote in 1941, *God in a World at War*, he painted a picture of God as a thoroughly intelligent and competent personality who knew what He wanted and felt completely capable of carrying out His plans. He gave us free will knowing that it could complicate His plans. He did not allow this war: *We* allowed it, in spite of all His warnings. His war with evil is a real one that has raged for centuries, and evil sometimes wins. He cannot just cry, "Halt!" when he thinks that the wrong side will win or that men have learned their lesson. He lives in a world of realities, not in a world of divine dictatorship.

God thus shows his courage and patience, argued Hadham, when he allows his creatures to spend thousands of years making the most catastrophic mistakes while slowly discovering for themselves the very simplest elements in their progress to perfection. He seems to have plenty of time; He gives like a Father, only when He knows it is needed. He has given us beauty, wealth, and brains and the will to use them, but there is one thing He has not and cannot give us—safety! He will not stop a war we have started by our own evil choices. A deity who would do that would not be our God but a "godling." "No one but a completely self-centered godling would take the line: 'They haven't asked *me*, I'll shove a spoke in their wheel.' What a mean, contemptible little rat such a godling would be, and how different from everything which his world and his own human life have revealed of the God we call 'Father'!"[23]

Once you have cleared God of any blame for war, you can now look on the bright side of things and see positive results in wartime. Weatherhead warned people not to take literally the theology of much of the Old Testament, such as Psalm 91:7: "A thousand shall fall at thy side and ten thousand at thy right hand, but it [evil] shall not come nigh thee." The best refutation of this Pollyannish notion that bad things never happen to good people is Jesus Christ himself, who, though sinless, died by an unjust execution.[24] The second best refutation is the book of Job, whose message warns that good men sometimes must suffer. "How the world is managed I cannot tell," said A. E. Houseman, "but it is no feather-bed for sluggards."[25] "Faith is not the passport to the easy road," said Berry, "God's noblest sons have been called to sterner things than the protected life can show." He asked, "How many men who have lived lives which have been comparatively placid and untroubled have made any lasting contribution to the world?" The heroes thrown up by the war, men like Montgomery, Dobbie, and Wingate, live a simple, stoical lifestyle. War shows the error of materialism and drives us back to the spirit. "It is significant that, after an age in which every clever wit or half-wit made this quality of moral severity the target for his shafts and sallies, the stern demands of the struggle in which we are engaged have brought us back to the note of austerity. The tribe of little men used to make fine play with Cromwell and the breed of his Ironsides, but to-day he is more often quoted by the statesmen than any other great figure in our past."[26]

Canon F. T. Salter related the story of a man named John, whose home had been completely demolished in a German bombing raid. The next morning his wife caught him musing and asked for his thoughts. He replied philosophically, "It's all right my dear. I'm just counting our assets and, in spite of everything that happened last night, I really believe we've still got much more than we've lost. This morning someone came into our dug-out and told me that we had lost everything. It's a lie. Thank God I've still got my health and strength to carry on with my job. I still have you, my dear, and the children. Thank God you're all safe. Hitler hasn't smashed my faith in the love and wisdom of God, nor my faith in the ultimate victory of Right."[27]

Gilbert Russell made the struggle with evil the best proof for Christianity. We are wrong, he argued, if we think our faith is better than other religions because it explains the evil in the world and they do not. On the contrary, Christianity gives men the power to overcome the evil and others do not. "The Christian Church won the Roman Empire not in the debating hall but in the arena. It was not by their better 'explanations' that the early Christians astonished the world. It was by the way they went to meet the lions." Once you have attained this vision of history, you can accept with tranquility almost anything that happens. After the Battle of Britain, Russell posed the question, "Did God know beforehand about all the children who've been killed in air raids during these last six months?" He answered, "Yes, He knew. And—this is the great thing to remember—He still thought it worth while: worth while to create them and send them into the world, though it was only for so short a time and for such a fearful end. God knew what was going to happen to those precious brains—He has always known. . . . [I]t was better that they should live and die—yes, live and die like that—than never live at all. Now they are His forever. They can never die again."[28]

Emile Cammaerts confessed that he became truly religious only when his son, Pieter, was killed in the war. In his sorrow he felt deep anger for awhile, but then concluded that "we may not even question divine justice in sending us pain or joy, because we know neither our worth, nor the motives which prompt God's actions." Life is molded of reality and illusion, but there is no illusion in death. Death is always truthful, always real. "We cannot be sure that we believe in God until we have met Death face to face and overcome despair. It is only when we succeed in preserving our love for God and man after this ordeal, that it deserves the name of love." In the death of his son, he discovered the true meaning of pain: "Pain is either constructive or destructive. It is the trial of the soul. Before meeting it, in this acute form, I merely believed that I believed. I felt exalted by religion in the same way as I felt exalted by love, art, music, or literature. It was part of my life, but it did not master my life."[29] Many other religious people testified that war had brought them face to face with God, and they now understood the words of Job: "Surely I spoke of things I did not understand, things too wonderful for me to know. . . . My ears had heard of you, but now my eyes have seen you" (Job 42:3, 5).

Early in the war a powerful voice came across the Atlantic from the American prophet, Reinhold Niebuhr, who was read and admired by many people in Britain. In his book, *Europe's Catastrophe and the Christian Faith*, written the second year of the war, Niebuhr compared Europe's travail to the era of St. Augustine (354–430), when the Roman Empire was falling, and Christians rushed to explain that their faith was not responsible for the tragedy. Augustine's message was simple: "Do not weep for Rome because no City of Man will last forever. Be true to Christ, whose Body, the Church, is the City of God, in the world but not of the world." Niebuhr suggested that modern secularists who preach the doctrine of inevitable progress are just like the worshipers of the Roman Empire; they have deified something temporal. "The Christian derives his sense of life's meaning not from the ordered course of history or from its stabilities. He derives it from his faith in the Lord of history, whose majesty is sovereign over history and whose mercy is involved in the sufferings of history."[30]

People get despondent over war because they have forgotten to read their Bible. The Bible is a realistic, even pessimistic volume—a book for bad times and dark ages. Read your Bible, advised Lloyd-Jones, and "you will not find the notion that God is working with all His might to prevent war or establish eternal peace." We must study the Scriptures to discover exactly what God has promised to do for this world, "instead of projecting our own hopes and desires and wishes into and on to God's plans, and then be surprised and disappointed when we discover that they are not being carried out."[31] George Barclay related that a man came up to him after a punishing air raid and said, "It must be difficult to be a Christian preacher in such times!" I knew what he meant, said Barclay, but, strange as it may seem, his attitude was not at all Biblical: "If we take the Bible seriously it will show us that days of calamity, both personal and national, can be days of growing faith and growing knowledge of God. . . . We are being given a chance to learn the lesson which long ago was taught by the prophets of Israel, the lesson that when history is being made, the living God is being active."[32]

Not only Bible history, but the history of Europe and Christendom is full of cases where God overruled evil and brought good out of it. No one ever really "gets away" with evil in history because God has promised, "Vengeance is mine, I will repay!" (Deut. 32:35). Alexander the Great conquered an empire with immoral force, but his campaign built roads and spread the Greek language, both of which were used for the expansion of the Gospel.[33] Right in the middle of the brutal but efficient *Pax Romana* the Christian Church started and flourished.[34] Great persons in history seldom realize how they may be promoting the plan of God. Davies assured his readers that in the present world war,

Providence is pursuing objects which transcend those of all the combatants. To assume that Providence has accepted our objectives for its own is a terrible national arrogance. There is no human evil which God cannot subordinate in some way or other to His Kingdom. He used Cyrus to defeat Babylon, not to promote Persian imperialism, but to prepare for the coming of Christ. God may be using England and France to defeat Hitlerism, but not to aggrandize British and French imperialism. The defeat of Germany is an item in the preparation for the Second Coming of Christ.[35]

Vidler seemed amused when he found a reference to the British people of the first century by the Jewish historian, Josephus, who made a remark about "the Britons, previously unknown to history." What does that do to the popular song, "There'll always be an England"? Our pride suffers, does it not, when we realize that we once did not exist, that we were considered a barbarian people on the fringe of civilization? We must, therefore, keep open the possibility that great nations of the future will rise and become Christian civilizations.[36] Rupp said it well: "God has His purposes for the nations, purposes misunderstood by those who claim their own history as Revelation."[37]

Harold Nicolson gave Britons this piece of advice: When you're depressed about the current situation, pull out a map of the world—not Europe—but the world. Look at the religions of mankind displayed on a world map. See Christianity spreading into Africa and Asia. Then remind yourself of something Christians tend to forget: Europe is not the same as Christendom! The gospel is not confined to Europe. If a dark night of unbelief should fall over Europe, God will carry on His plan somewhere else. The West may be reevangelized from the East. What a prospect! Yet that is the way it sometimes works out in the mysterious counsels of God. Christ must be saying, "O ye of little faith," to those who seriously think that Hitler and Mussolini could bring down the Church of God.[38]

This process of thought now brings us to a very unpleasant implication, the one that got the prophet Jeremiah thrown into jail when he preached it: *We could lose*! The Axis could win, the Allies could be defeated, and Britain could be invaded and conquered. No matter how much he might love his country, the British Christian could not avoid this possibility, because it is clearly taught in the Bible. An old hymn says, "The Kingdoms of earth pass away one by one but the Kingdom of Heaven remains." We must summon the courage to affirm with Bishop Bell, "The Church . . . is not the State's spiritual auxiliary." Britain may fall but the Church will endure. We must face the stern fact, said Phyllis L. Garlick, that "in the long run God's redemptive purpose may be more truly served by further suffering than by speedy victory."[39] Micklem wrote, "Even if we lose, which is possible, God can do more with a defeated nation dedicated to Him than with a victorious nation that became proud and revengeful."[40] Weatherhead agreed: "Defeat can be a very healthy spiritual condition both in men and nations. . . . God may be able to do more with a defeated nation that was penitent than with a victorious nation that was aggressive."[41]

At this point the simple, unreflective Christian might be thoroughly confused. With all our uncertainty about God's ways, how should we pray? What exactly do we ask God to do? Look at the actual prayer record of the early war, and you will be troubled. The first national day of prayer was 26 May 1940, and in a few days, Sweden signed a trade pact with Hitler, Belgium surrendered, the Germans trapped the British Expeditionary Force on the coast and captured all its equipment—the worst news Britons had gotten in centuries. Cynics jeered, "That shows you how much good prayer does!" But then came the miracle of Dunkirk, and people thought their prayers were obviously answered. So they had a Day of Thanksgiving for Dunkirk and prayed for France; but then came the news that France had surrendered to Hitler. All this led to the quip that the best thing Archbishop Lang could do was to ordain a Day of Prayer for Hitler![42]

Actually, things are never as bad as they seem. We must remember that God has His own timetable for events, and your particular prayer might not fit his timing. Glasgow reminded folks that the forces of evil often seem to win in the first round, but "in the end the forces of evil are bound to be defeated, for God is supreme."[43] Barry drew out the lesson that ad hoc days of prayer are dangerous, because they make prayer look like primitive magic; we think that if we all pray in unison we will get the goods delivered on the spot. God becomes our cosmic bellhop, not the Father who knows what we need before we ask, as Christ said (Matt. 6:8).[44] William Temple tried to strike the proper balance between God's providence and human effort:

I have seen it said that the deliverance at Dunkirk may have been an answer to prayer but was more certainly due to the devotion, enterprise, courage and discipline of Navy, Mercantile Marine, Army and Air Force. Certainly it was due to these, but where do these come from? Those who are accustomed to pray to the "Lord of all power and might" who is "the author and giver of all good things" will not draw any contrast there. All honour to the heroic men through whom that deliverance was wrought; and thanks be to God who inspired and sustained them in their endurance and achievement.[45]

British churchmen thus labored to explain the war and to restore and sustain faith in the Biblical God, the personal, powerful, ethical Yahweh, who created the universe and controls its destiny. No matter what may be occurring right now, the universe is ultimately rational, Being is gracious, and the plans of God will eventually succeed.

A DIFFERENT KIND OF WAR

It has been said that historians of the future will probably look back on the twentieth century and conclude that both world wars were the same war with a twenty-year truce in between, just another Thirty Years War like the one of 1618 to 1648. Both world wars were fought to prevent Germany, Imperial and Nazi, from dominating the European continent. This assertion seems valid if you take territorial expansion as the only aspect to be considered. If you look deeper, however, you will notice some interesting differences between the two wars.

First, there is the matter of prelude. The crisis of August 1914 broke out over Europe with very little preparation, whereas World War II had a lead time of several years. The decade of the 1930s was full of crises that woke people up to the possibility of another war: the Japanese invasion of Manchuria (1931), Mussolini's conquest of Abyssinia (1935–1936), Hitler's foreign policy moves such as the reoccupation of the Rhineland (1936), the *Anschluss* with Austria (1938), and the Munich Crisis (1938). When Hitler violated the Munich agreement and marched onto the rump of Czechoslovakia in March 1939, people began to speak of, "When war comes," not "If war comes."

In the first war the government did not feel compelled to use conscription until January 1916, but already by the spring of 1939 men of twenty and twenty-one were called for military training. Months before Hitler attacked Poland, people were busy getting ready—digging air raid shelters, stockpiling food, training in civil defense, learning to use gas masks, preparing blackout procedures, and establishing evacuation routes. The clergy plunged energetically into these activities, preparing themselves personally, their flocks, and their buildings for use in the war effort. New prayers were published in the summer of 1939 for possible use in times of war or rumors of war.[46]

In 1914 most people were a bit confused and ambivalent about going to war with Germany, a nation they admired in many ways. But the people of 1939 had already had the opportunity to appraise the ideology of Nazism, and most judged it as evil. Several good books and articles had appeared in the 1930s analyzing Fascism and Nazism, the latter usually called "Hitlerism." Consequently, in the second war the government did not need the same low level of jingoistic propaganda that it used in the recruiting drives of World War I. Most people were already sufficiently motivated. The Kaiser was bashed royally in the first war, to be sure, but nothing like Hitler in the second, as we shall see in coming chapters.

Yet, paradoxically, the second war lacked the anti-German hysteria of the first. Perhaps this was because people could see that Nazi Germany was not totally unified; good Christians inside Germany were fighting the Nazi regime, and many had fled to Britain for refuge. George Bell, bishop of Chichester, constantly reminded people that there was a difference between Nazis and Germans. A group of German refugees regularly met in Cambridge under the leadership of Pastor Franz Hildebrandt, who conducted a Lutheran service on Sunday evenings at Holy Trinity Church. When blackout regulations made this late service impossible, Vicar Max Warren and Pastor Hildebrandt worked out a joint service earlier in the day for both Germans and English. "That such a service could be held on the first Sunday of the war," writes Wilkinson, "represented a pledge that the anti-German hysteria of the first war would not be repeated."[47]

In the first war, the German Church was pretty firmly behind the Imperial government; there were very few suggestions that the government was antireligious, and few clerics ever referred to the kaiser as the antichrist. But the Hitler regime split the Protestants into two parts, the German Christians and the Confessing Church, and angered the Roman Catholics enough to elicit a formal papal denunciation of Nazi ideology. Some Christians of both Catholic and Protestant branches fled to England, carrying with them the horror stories of Nazi persecution. It was easier, therefore, in the second war for Britons to say things like "Not all Germans are Nazis," or "I know many good Germans living here in England," or "The good Germans still living in Germany are afraid to speak up."

One of the kindest things many clergy of 1914 did was to explain bad German behavior in terms of temporary insanity. Germans had just "gone bonkers" for awhile; they were "out to lunch." This thesis seemed to imply that sanity would someday return, but the British wondered if the Germans of the 1920s were completely sane, and they really wondered about German sanity after 1933.

What can we say about this? Does insanity come and go with such alarming irregularity? Perhaps careful thinkers saw that temporary insanity would not work a second time as an excuse for bad German behavior. Perhaps it was just a rationalization prompted by the fear of calling a spade a spade, an unwillingness to admit real evil in the world. Hitler was often called a madman, but perhaps this was just too nice—he was simply evil. Whatever may be the case, one finds less analysis (or psychoanalysis) of the springs of German behavior in World War II.

The rationale given for fighting the Germans was different in the second war—more cautious, low-key, subdued, detached, prosaic, and nuanced. The poet Keith Douglas warned that it was dangerous to be sentimental or emotional in these times: "To trust anyone or to admit any hope of a better world is criminally foolish, as foolish as it is to stop working for it. It sounds silly to say work without hope, but it can be done; it's only a form of insurance; it doesn't mean work hopelessly."[48] "Without hope" doesn't mean the same as "hopeless"—one often finds these puzzling distinctions used to describe things in the second war.

Many intellectuals had been "Niebuhrized" in the 1930s. Niebuhr's books debunked simplistic moralizing, stressing the ambiguities of human decisions and the mixed motives involved in individual and collective behavior. Most mature churchmen, like most mature poets, therefore, did not spring to attention when asked to produce propaganda sermons and poems bashing the Germans and eulogizing the British. The war was depicted as a necessary struggle, but a necessary evil, not a crusade. We fight with a heavy heart, refusing to demonize all Germans. We defend the bad against the worse, not the good against the bad. Most clerics flatly refused to simplistically identify the kingdom of God with the British Empire or the Allied cause.

Government propaganda was not accepted with the same degree of trust in the second war as in the first. Part of this was the natural aftermath of a great war; when you watch a propaganda film years after the war, you usually laugh at its artless simplicity. People in the period of 1939 to 1945 still recalled some of the offensive propaganda of the Great War; they had read many books and articles in the 1920s and 1930s analyzing and ridiculing the propaganda of the first war. Furthermore, they had listened to the obvious propaganda distortions coming out of Goebbels's "lie machine" in the Third Reich. Many people had matured between the wars; as your education increases you grow cautious when dealing with government propaganda, even that of your own government. Right in the middle of the war George Orwell said, "All propaganda is lies, even when one is telling the truth."[49]

This caution was especially true of atrocity stories. After reading many books on wartime propaganda, many people were convinced that atrocity stories were almost always to be doubted, just as one nowdays would automatically discount partisan rhetoric during an election. Such caution is admirable and reasonable, but it had one drawback—it caused people in Western Europe to disbelieve stories coming out of Eastern Europe about the systematic extermination of the Jews. These stories were worse than the atrocity tales from Belgium in the first war, so should not one be even more suspicious of them? Surely, many argued, no nation could be so cruel and barbarous.

The Church was more independent in World War II. In World War I Archbishop Davidson would occasionally register mild criticism of the government, but in the second war, George Bell boldly rebuked the government publicly for its policy of saturation bombing of German cities. This courageous behavior, in the tradition of Nathan, Jeremiah, and John the Baptist, probably cost Bell the office of Archbishop of Canterbury when William Temple died in 1944.[50]

The Church did more to protect pacifists and conscientious objectors in the second war. Archbishop Lang took steps early in 1939 to insure that conscientious objectors (COs) were granted proper rights. The Church was still officially opposed to pacifism, but it defended the pacifists' right of freedom of conscience and literally went to court for many of them. There were actually more COs in the second war than the first; but they were treated better, and so their opposition to the war was less of a problem because they did not attract an audience when their rights were not violated. On the whole the British public supported the second war more than the first. The Labour Party was filled with pacifists during the Great War and beyond, but in May 1940, Labour leader Clement Attlee joined Winston Churchill in a coalition government in full support of the war. The failure of appeasement and the shocking demeanor of Nazism had driven the pacifists into the wings of society. Many very prominent people who dissented in World War I supported World War II—men like Bertrand Russell, C. E. M. Joad, Herbert Morrison, and Kingsley Martin.

In the first war there was a considerable distance between those at home and those at the front, in the dreaded trenches. The war was seldom brought home in all its gory reality to the British people. But in the 1930s people slowly awoke to the implications of aerial warfare and realized that England had lost her traditional insular protection. "The airplane always gets through," went a popular saying. All nations with air forces had studied the possibilities of strategic bombing, striking deep into enemy territory to destroy factories, bridges, and other military targets. This new kind of warfare meant that everyone in a sense was now on the front lines.

That included the clergy. They suffered like everyone else in the bombing, and they helped in the aftermath of aerial attacks. No longer could you charge that they did not contribute to front-line action. Clerics opened their churches and homes as bomb shelters and helped minister to the wounded and dying after the attacks. Vicars gave up their chauffeurs and reduced their gasoline allowances. Bishops left their palatial residences or moved into one section of the residence. Some gladly allowed their mansions to be used as shelters for evacuees. The public in general felt that the clergy did its fair share of the work during this war.

World War I, at least on the Western front, was a static warfare of trenches, where the lines did not change more than a few miles for four years. In the 1930s Hitler told his generals to develop a mode of warfare that would not end in trenches, and the result was "lightning war" (*Blitzkrieg*). From 1939 to 1941, Germany conquered most of Europe using this new technique, but then the Allies mastered it and used it to conquer Germany (1942–1945). *Blitzkrieg* allowed huge mechanized armies sweeping over vast areas of land, which was exhilarating for both the servicemen and the patriots at home, who were glued to their radios waiting for word of victory. War became much more mechanized; horses almost disappeared in favor of motorized vehicles. Traditional foot soldiers played second fiddle to the machines.

When you have machines, you can save human beings. British war leaders remembered the high casualty rates of battles like Verdun, the Somme, and Passchendaele and were determined to avoid them in the second war. They used armor instead of men when they could; they used carpet bombing on troops in the field and on German cities, and it worked. British dead were reduced by more than one-half in World War II, from 765,000 to 300,000.

World War I began with excitement. It was supposed to be a short one; soldiers were told they would be home before Christmas. Disillusionment grew during the war, and especially after it, when it appeared to many that all the sacrifices had been in vain. By contrast, World War II began with a grim pessimism, with the realization that it would probably last a long time. It began without burning emotion but with a deep conviction of the justice of the cause, a conviction that persisted and even deepened as the war progressed and especially after the Nazi death camps were opened. Fifty years later this conviction remains unchanged; the second war has been called "the last good war." Millions of people in the world still feel that if there was ever a just war in history it was World War II.

The British clergy supported the government in both wars, but, for various reasons, the public in World War I felt the clergy was uncritical and lacked independence. The reputation of the clergy was restored for the most part in the second war. Churchmen combined a judicious independence with a wholehearted support of the conflict and impressive service to suffering people on all fronts.[51]

Finally, the end was different. The Great War ended with a treaty and a League of Nations that seemed to secure a lasting peace, keeping faith with the wartime slogan, "A war to end all wars." Conversely, World War II ended with the discovery of Nazi death camps and the obliteration of two Japanese cities by atom bombs, which gave the *coup de grace* to humanistic optimism. It ended with the Allies and the Soviet Union at loggerheads over the future of nations like Poland—the Cold War in embryo. The second war was so terribly destructive that even the victors were frightened. The atomic bomb seemed to place the ultimate power of the universe into the hands of a creature that had passed the technology test but had clearly flunked the ethics examination.

NOTES

1. George Glasgow, *Diplomacy and God* (London: Longmans, Green, 1941), 50.

2. *Faith in Time of War* (London: Eyre & Spottiswoode, 1940), 14.

3. D. R. Davies, *Secular Illusion or Christian Realism?* (London: Eyre & Spottiswoode, 1942), 105.

4. Cited in Frederick B. Macnutt, *Four Freedoms: Atlantic and Christian* (Leicester, England: Thornley, 1943), 25.

5. N. L. Clay, ed., *This Half Century: 50 Poems from 1900 to 1949* (London: Heinemann, 1950), 69.

6. *The Great Issue and Other War-Time Studies* (London: Independent Press, 1944), 45.

7. *The World We're Fighting For* (London: SCM Press, 1941), 79.

8. Used by Leslie Weatherhead, *This Is the Victory* (London: Hodder & Stoughton, 1940), 118.

9. *God in a World at War* (Harmondsworth, England: Penguin, 1941), 7.

10. *Great Issue*, 45.

11. This apt illustration is used by Weatherhead, *This Is the Victory*, 153.

12. *Why Work?: An Address Delivered at Eastbourne, April 23, 1942* (London: Metheun, 1942), 3.

13. *Philosophies at War* (London: Blandford, 1945), 63.

14. *Secular Despair and Christian Faith* (London: SCM Press, 1941), 85.

15. *Europe's Own Book* (London: Morrison & Gibb, 1944), 48.

16. *Diplomacy and God*, 132.

17. *Great Issue*, 110.

18. *This Is the Victory*, 94.

19. "The Judgment of God," in *This War and Christian Ethics: A Symposium*, ed. Ashley Sampson (London: Blackwell, 1940), 6.

20. *Why Does God Allow War? A General Justification of the Ways of God* (London: Hodder & Stoughton, 1939), 95.

21. *This Is the Victory*, 211.

22. Ian Macpherson, *The Cross in War-Time* (London: Stockwell, 1941), 7.

23. *God in a World at War*, 59.

24. *Thinking Aloud in War-Time: An Attempt to See the Present Situation in the Light of the Christian Faith* (London: Hodder & Stoughton, 1939), 153.

25. Quoted in Otter, *The World*, 40.

26. *Great Issue*, 20, 25, 107.

27. *Keep Smiling!: Sixteen Tonic Talks on Religion and Life* (London: Muller, 1942), 34.

28. *The World*, 40, 43.

29. *Upon This Rock* (London: Cresset Press, 1942), 108, 109, 128.

30. *Europe's Catastrophe and the Christian Faith* (London: Nisbet, 1940), 31. For the same illustration, see F. R. Barry, *Faith in Dark Ages* (London: SCM Press, 1940), 62.

31. *Why Does God Allow War?*, 88–89.

32. *The Bible Speaks to Our Day* (London: SCM Press, 1944), 10.

33. Weatherhead, *Thinking Aloud in War-Time*, 135.

34. J. M. Murry, *Christocracy* (London: Drakers, 1942), 84.

35. *The Two Humanities: An Attempt at a Christian Interpretation of History in the Light of War* (London: Clarke, 1940), 111.

36. Alec Vidler, *God's Judgment on Europe* (London: Longmans, Green, 1940), 109.

37. *Is This a Christian Country?* (London: Sheldon, 1941), 54.

38. In Barry, *Faith in Dark Ages*, 26–27.

39. *How Shall We Pray in War-Time?* (London: SPCK, 1942), 7.

40. Editorial in *British Weekly*, 12 October 1939.

41. *This Is the Victory*, 116.

42. See Barry, *Faith in Dark Ages*, 49–51; Glasgow, *Diplomacy and God*, 121.

43. *Diplomacy and God*, 121–122. For examples, see Gordon C. Zahn, *Chaplains in the RAF* (Manchester University Press, 1969); Tom Harrison, *Living through the Blitz* (London: Penguin, 1978); Susan Briggs, *Keep Smiling Through: The Home Front 1939–45* (London: Cox and Wyman, 1975).

44. *Faith in Dark Ages*, 51–52.

45. *The Hope of a New World* (London: SCM Press, 1940), 34.

46. See the document, "Spiritual Ministration to the Wounded and Dying as a Result of Hostile Air Raids," released in 1939, long before any air raids (*Lang Papers* 79: 327).

47. *Dissent or Conform? War, Peace and the English Churches 1900–45* (London: SCM Press, 1986), 236.

48. Ibid., 242.

49. Cited in Ian McLaine, *Ministry of Morale: Home Front Morale and the Ministry of Information in World War II* (London: Allen & Unwin, 1979), 137.

50. Ronald C. D. Jasper, *George Bell: Bishop of Chichester* (London: Oxford University Press, 1967), 284.

51. See Wilkinson, *Dissent or Conform?*, ch. 9; Briggs, *Keep Smiling Through*, 68–71; Paul Wesley, *A History of the Church of England 1945–80* (London: Oxford University Press, 1984), ch. 2, 7; Rupert Davies, *The Testing of the Churches* (London: Epworth, 1982).

CHAPTER 3

Dealing with Pacifism

There were not very many pacifists in Britain during World War II, so why should we have an entire chapter on the topic? Because, oddly, though there were few pacifists, there was a great deal of preaching, teaching, and writing on the topic, almost as if the clergy had to keep convincing themselves and their coreligionists that fighting a war was indeed permissible. There was a similar phenomenon in World War I.[1] Montgomery Belgion was correct when he observed, "In the course of two thousand years the Church has been unable to produce agreement among its members regarding whether Our Lord condemned war or whether he left it to individual Christians to decide if a given war was just or not."[2]

This problem sometimes leaves the clergy in a precarious position. Belgion relates an interesting episode from the life of King Henry VIII, who in 1513 dispatched troops to fight in France, but then found himself shortly thereafter listening to an antiwar sermon from the eminent classical scholar and theologian, John Colet. Colet declared that soldiers violate the law of love when they fight in a war. Henry called Colet for a conference, and they had a very private talk about the problem—Erasmus heard the sermon and reported on the meeting. Both Henry and John finally agreed that no war is ever totally just, but war is still a necessary evil.[3] It was not the last time that a pacifist would face the wrath of a government at war.

Pacifism was the original position of the Church on the question of war. For the first three centuries of our era, Christians considered it a sin to fight. Those who take the apostolic Church as a fixed, eternal pattern say that settles the matter—war is always wrong! The activists argued that times had changed, and the Church had to change with them. Early Christians were pacifists because the Roman state persecuted them and they could hardly be expected to fight for such a pagan government. Furthermore, all the wars in the Roman Empire were internal or civil wars, not wars for defense. But when the barbarians flooded in during the fourth century, Christians saw anarchy for the first time and learned the value of the state. After Constantine (280–337) Christians began to serve in imperial armies. We find pacifistic sentiments in Origen and Tertullian but not in Augustine, Ambrose, or Gregory.[4]

In the Middle Ages the Church had to deal with Germanic barbarians, whose very religion was warfare. Germans felt that warfare was a normal, natural, and noble occupation for man, an activity that was to be interrupted only by short intervals necessary for rest and preparation for the next war. Gradually Christian theologians developed the just war theory, which Maurice Reckitt, editor of *Christendom*, called "the legacy of the Church to Europe."[5] The Church slowly convinced the Germans that war was something evil and that it must be considered as a last resort. The Church bound the fighting nobility with agreements like the Peace of God and the Truce of God, which forbade war on unarmed people and excluded war from certain times and places. Gradually the barbarian was tamed and transformed into the Christian knight of the High Middle Ages, a gentleman who fights according to the rules.

The just war theory did not abolish war; it just caused the combatants to engage in a propaganda campaign to make the conflict look legitimate. War continued, often with appalling destruction of persons and property. Right in the middle of the terrible Thirty Years War, Dutch jurist Hugo Grotius published his book, *De jure belli et pacis* (The Law of War and Peace) and took up once again the problem of limiting war. Then, for nearly three hundred years, Europe experienced wars that were limited, wars that did not slaughter the civil population. After the wars of the French Revolution and Napoleon (1789–1815), Europe enjoyed a century of relative peace (1815–1914), which coincided with tremendous progress in technology, education, arts, and sciences. During the Victorian Era the intellectuals, humanists, and optimists were predicting the elimination of war from the planet. Then came the Great War with its horrendous casualties and its terrible new weapons: submarines, tanks, machine guns, poison gas, and the bombing airplane. More men died in the first three weeks of World War I than during the entire Napoleonic era. The bombing airplane brought its own morality with it and renewed the possibility of slaughtering civilians as part of military strategy.

The horrors of the Great War made many people in western Europe determined to abolish warfare forever. "Never again!" they exclaimed. They built the League of Nations, held disarmament conferences, and signed the Kellog–

Briand Pact (1928), which abolished war as a means of national policy. Pacifism seemed to have the moral high ground again, just as in the first centuries of the Christian era. What were the arguments for pacifism?

THE CASE FOR PACIFISM

Nathaniel Micklem, a nonpacifist, admitted that if we look to the spirit, intention, and logical implication of Scripture, the pacifist interpretation is "strong if not overwhelming."[6] The pacifists seem to be closer to the spirit of Christ; they always detect a noticeable uneasiness among the activists when they defend war, as can be seen in the statement of Goudge: "When we justify a just war, we must not forget how sorely war always needs justification."[7] War sorely needs justification because our ethical model, Jesus Christ, clearly repudiated the methods of violence, instructing his disciples to "resist not evil," "turn the other cheek," and "love your enemies" (Matt. 5:38, 44). He said that peacemakers were to be congratulated (Matt. 5:9). He refused to let Peter defend him with the sword and turned down the assistance of legions of angels when falsely arrested. His method was obviously nonviolence and nonretaliation; his trial and execution were compared to a lamb, led to the slaughter without a protest (Isa. 53:7). If God is love, then the deepest force in the universe is on the side of the person who practices nonviolence. Christ followed the path of love and was victorious in the long run; God exalted him *after* he had emptied himself (Phil. 2:9).

In 1914, a group of 130 pacifists met in Cambridge and formed the International Fellowship of Reconciliation. It soon spread to Holland and America and by 1919 became a worldwide fellowship, publishing a journal, *The Christian Pacifist*. On the back cover of the journal was a succinct statement of the pacifist creed:

The Fellowship of Reconciliation believes that the Kingdom of God on Earth is the true alternative to the present world-system and the only permanent form of human society. In its establishment it seeks in the name of Christ to unite with one another people of every class and nation. Therefore, to belong to the Fellowship means to be a part of an international brotherhood within which there can be no thought of war, and whose members refuse to take part in any war for any cause whatsoever. The Fellowship sees in the characteristic methods of the present social system a contradiction of the law of the universe which is the spirit that was in Jesus, and summons men to create, in place of this decaying society, one which expresses the brotherhood of all men. To do this means willingness to suffer rather than inflict suffering.

Even the Lambeth Conference of 1930 had asserted, "War as a method of settling international disputes is incompatible with the teaching and example of our Lord Jesus Christ."[8] If wars could be subdivided into "loving" and "cruel," the activist might have a case, but war is *essentially* cruel in all its forms. "War is hell," as the American Civil War general, William T. Sherman, once said.

"You cannot qualify war in harsher terms than I will; war is cruelty and you cannot refine it." At the base of Sherman's equestrian statue, Henry van Dyke placed this couplet:

> *This is the soldier brave enough to tell*
> *The glory-dazzled world that war is hell.*[9]

To the argument that a bad peace can be worse than war, Erasmus responded, "A disadvantageous peace is better than the most just war." The honest religious pacifist, as opposed to the "war Quaker," who uses pacifism to evade military service, says, "I must follow the command of Christ to love all men regardless of the consequences." There is no way you can love your enemy and kill him. If it is God's will that evil should triumph and rule the world for awhile, then so be it. In the end, if not in this world then in another, we shall see the victory of good over evil, and those who have had suffering inflicted upon them by evil people will find full compensation.

As war approached in 1939, many solid pacifists began to waver. One can see the internal struggle going on in Gerald Vann, whose book, *Morality and War*, was published in 1939 shortly before war broke out. Vann was obviously torn by the arguments for and against pacifism. He respected the opinion of the Holy Father, Pope Pius XI, that the coming crisis involved Christian culture, but he wondered if the Pope might be exaggerating. He deplored the atmosphere of hatred which modern propaganda aroused in wartime, but admitted that in turning the other cheek, he might be turning others' cheeks; that is, he could be delivering many children to fascist control. After several pages of torment, he finally admitted that the coming war may be a duty, but "the deepest anguish of mind" arises when "the Christian finds himself faced with a situation in which he is convinced that war is a duty, but the methods of war which will be used, a crime." It was a case of "good cause, bad weapons." He specified aerial bombing as the bad weapon, a method of warfare which strikes directly at the "innocent and poor," the very folks that Jesus will ask us about in the Judgment (Matt. 25:31–46).

Vann's book leaves the reader in a quandary—the war is just but the methods are evil. If we decide not to fight, then God "will not desert us because we have chosen rather to be faithful to the purity of the Gospel than to risk making a compromise with evil and bringing Christianity to dishonour." Perhaps the world is waiting for just such a "Christ-nation" to redeem it from its "vicious circle of injury and counter-injury and mutual hatred and distrust."[10] The "great soul" from India, Gandhi, asked Britons to become such a "Christ-nation."

I appeal to every Briton to accept the method of non-violence instead of war for the adjustment of relations between nations. I appeal for the cessation of hostilities, not because you are too exhausted to fight, but because war is bad in essence. I want you to fight Nazism without arms. You will invite Herr Hitler and Signor Mussolini to take what they want of the countries you call possessions. Let them take possession of your beautiful island, with your many beautiful buildings. You will give all these, but not your souls or your minds. You will refuse to owe allegiance to them.[11]

Leslie Weatherhead described in dramatic terms his conversion from pacifism to activism. He said the question that bothered him most was, "How can anything be right for a Christian about which he cannot pray?" It seemed impossible for him to pray this prayer: "O God, help me to shoot straight, to kill or maim my brother German. Help me to hold my bayonet steady when I drive it in, and twist it round and tug it out in the way I have been shown. Help me to drop my bombs accurately and kill as many as possible of my brothers for whom Christ died. In the name of Christ the loving and merciful Saviour, I make my prayer.—Amen."[12]

Yet this same Leslie Weatherhead two pages later says he changed and gave up his pacifism. He confessed that he was too tired by that time to think any more, but he knew he was moving to the other position. He began to see that force was always necessary, "else you hand life over to the criminal classes." Who were these Fascists, the "criminal classes"? Why did their beliefs and behavior cause pacifists like Weatherhead to change? We deal with that question in Chapter 4.

THE REFUTATION OF PACIFISM

Before we give the case for activism, we should note that many (and probably most) British clerics spoke warmly about the pacifist witness and insisted that pacifists be protected from government persecution. The archbishops of the war led the way in fighting for this position. Archbishop of Canterbury Cosmo Gordon Lang wrote that he had said repeatedly in the House of Lords, "I do not agree with the position of the complete Pacifist, but I respect his conscience."[13] William Temple insisted that the difference between pacifist and activist, "however important at the present time, is a difference about the interpretation to be given to a Gospel which both have received and which they are united in proclaiming."[14] He felt that Christian unity was more important than victory; he wrote to Cyril F. Garbett, Archbishop of York, that "the maintenance of the spiritual fellowship of all Christians is for the church a concern that takes precedence even of the military defeat of Nazi-ism."[15]

Temple loved to use the example of St. Francis, who abandoned all his worldly goods but did not insist that everyone had to follow his way. "I believe that there are Christians who are called to personal pacifism and to give the special witness which this carries; but if they go on to say that *all* Christians ought to be pacifists, I believe that they are involved in profound theological error."[16] Monks and nuns are not useless, he noted, but we don't want everyone to become one.[17] As archbishop, Temple had a policy of not writing introductions to books, but he made an exception in the case of Stephen Hobhouse's *Christ and Our Enemies*, a pacifist essay, and he explained to the author, "I want to do it exactly because I am, as you know, not non-pacifist but anti-pacifist; and I value every means of expressing unity with pacifists for that very reason."[18] Like most British clerics, Temple thought that war against Fascism was necessary. "I have been urged to receive the evil of the Nazi regime into my own soul as a redemptive sacrifice, instead of resisting it. But no one has told me how I can do this."[19]

The first thing the activist must do is to contest the pacifist claim to Scripture. The pacifists act as if the Bible were totally on their side, but this claim can be challenged. Most British clerics would have agreed with Karl Barth: "The Christians who do not realize that they must take part unreservedly in this war must have slept over their Bibles as well as over their newspapers."[20]

War is mentioned a great deal in the Bible, especially in the Old Testament—a situation which causes pacifists to make an unwarranted distinction between the testaments. They argue that the Old Testament is outdated, with its vengeful Jehovah who is always making war, in contrast to the loving Father of Jesus described in the New Testament. Pacifists therefore commit the ancient heresy of the gnostic Marcion, who rejected the Old Covenant. But this is contrary to the orthodox doctrine of the Trinity, argues W. W. Lucas in his carefully documented *War and the Purposes of God: A Survey of Scripture Teaching*. He says it would be ridiculous to argue that Christ had sworn off war, since Christ is the same as the Jehovah of the Old Testament who causes wars, guides wars, and uses wars in his plan.[21] To say the New Testament is pacific in contrast to the Old ignores such passages as Hebrews 11:32–34, where the ancient heroes of faith are extolled for conquering kingdoms, becoming powerful in battle, and routing foreign armies. Lucas observed, "It would be a mistake to suppose that only irreligious and unconverted men and hypocrites are responsible for wars. In the Old Testament the moral philosophical and religious leaders were responsible for some of the wars sent by God."[22] Alfred Zimmern asked, "Is there not an element of Pharisaical self-sufficiency in failing to realize that a soldier can be at peace in the trenches or in forgetting that some of those on whom the Church has bestowed the title of Saint have followed the profession of arms?"[23]

At his trial, Jesus told Pilate, "My kingdom is not of this world. If it were, my servants would *fight* to prevent my arrest by the Jews" (John 18:36) (italics added). Pacifists use this verse to prove that Jesus did not approve of war, but actually it proves no such thing. On the contrary, Jesus was saying simply that war could not advance *his* kingdom; by implication he taught that force was necessary and good in a normal worldly political kingdom. "You must never fight—physically—for Christianity," argued Temple, "because you can always serve it better by another method, namely martyrdom. Moreover, Christianity exists only where it is freely accepted; the use of force on behalf of it is therefore a betrayal of it." But the same cannot be said of a "Christian civilization," a political entity that has been molded for centuries by the deep influence of the

Christian faith. Most clerics followed Temple in this distinction: we are not fighting for the Church or for Christianity, but for Christian civilization.[24]

It is significant that the New Testament mentions three godly centurions from the armies of Rome who were commended for faith and were never told that they should retire from the army. When certain soldiers asked John the Baptist what they should do to repent, he answered: "Don't extort money and don't accuse people falsely—be content with your pay" (Luke 3:14). If the occupation of a soldier had been inherently sinful, John would have told them to get another job, would he not? Can you imagine Christ telling a brothel keeper, "Be content with your pay?"[25]

Temple maintained that when pacifists argue from the commandment, "Thou shalt not kill," they obfuscate the issue, because the original in Exodus 20:13 really means "Thou shalt do no murder." There are several words for "kill" in Hebrew but the word used in the sixth commandment relates specifically to "murder." Temple defined murder as the taking of a man's life for private ends; thus legal execution would not be the same as murder. He gives a careful argument to show that in wartime the commandment against murder does not apply:

Now to take another man's life is normally as great an invasion of his personality as can be conceived. But if two nations have entered into a dispute and have referred it to the arbitrament of war, the soldiers and, in a less degree, the citizens of those nations stand over against each other as representatives and agents of their countries. A soldier of necessity offers his life to be taken; he does not aim at being killed—he aims at killing; but in the process he offers his life. If it falls out that his offer is accepted, his personality is not thereby violated; it is fulfilled in his self-sacrifice, or at least carried forward towards its fulfilment.[26]

Pacifists argue eloquently from the principle of love, but the activists counterattack with the argument from "tough love." The same Jesus who said offer the other cheek made a whip and lashed the greedy moneychangers out of the Temple (Matt. 21:12). If his own actions are any kind of guide, when he said "resist not evil" he obviously did not mean "submit to evil." He resisted evil men in Israel, men who desecrated the Temple with their greedy commercialism, who taught false doctrines and misled simple people. "But," replies the pacifist, "this involved no physical force, only verbal attacks." But surely using a whip is physical force![27]

The question is not how to love the Germans, reasoned Temple, but how can we show love to Frenchmen, Poles, Czechs, and Germans all at once? Once you consider all sides of the complex question, you see that to resist the Germans by force was a way of showing love to them and to all the others. The law of love sometimes commands fighting, which "becomes an expression of love only because every alternative is worse." In respect for Christ's command to "resist not evil," you might let a killer kill you personally, but you should not allow a brute to kill a child if you could prevent it, even to the point of killing the brute. You are under obligation "and that obligation is rooted in love." The issue then is, "Is the Nazi threat to civilization so serious that the evil of allowing it to develop is greater even than the monstrous evil of war?"[28]

L. J. Collins, dean of Oriel College, Oxford, used an Old Testament passage effectively in making the same point. When Jehu, King of Israel, was asked by Joram, "Have you come in peace, Jehu?" he replied, "How can there be peace as long as all the idolatry and witchcraft of your mother Jezebel abounds?" (2 Kings 9:22). Usually people do not talk about peace when absolute values are involved; pacifism in this case means betrayal.[29]

Our problem, said many churchmen, is that we have developed a mushy, sentimental, unbiblical view of love. Charity means more than just being nice to people. You love a person when you sincerely and steadily concern yourself with his welfare. Parental love may require discipline, not coddling. Loving Hitler would include stopping him in his mad career, just as Christ loved the Pharisees he drove out of the Temple.[30] Micklem illustrated the issue with this question: What if the Good Samaritan had reached that man on the Jericho Road just as the bandits were doing their evil work? The Samaritan was a loving person—precisely what actions would have been demanded by his love? Would you say he should just wait until the bandits had thrashed the poor man, since love can only work after evil has done its work? Would the pacifist try to prevent injury? How could he do this without using force? It would appear that by refusing to fight, we too are "passing by on the other side," just like the priest and the Levite condemned in the parable (Luke 10:25–37). "War is an unspeakable evil," concluded Micklem, "but passivity may well seem a greater evil. To spare the Germans is to refuse to help the impotent and needy; it is to keep our own hands 'clean' at the cost of the degradation of men, women and children in soul and body."[31] Micklem branded pacifism as a form of blasphemy. "To disclaim responsibility for maintaining the liberties of our people, hardly won by our forefathers through centuries of struggle and sacrifice, and to be willing to submit to a ruthless and mind destroying alien domination in order to avoid suffering and even death—that is blasphemy, and it is the final treachery to the human race. It is blasphemy, for it is the denial of God."[32]

T. E. Jessop was so disturbed at the pacifist distortion of love that he wrote a book called *Has the Christian Way Failed?* We have confused love with sentimental love, he said, and as every novelist knows, the latter can change suddenly into hate, which would never happen to genuine love. "There can scarcely be a more grotesque caricature of love," he declared, "than to identify it with seeing black as white, with cajoling evil instead of standing against it, with hesitation, indecisiveness and fear of firm action." To love your enemies does not require that you sacrifice your friends to them, as we have done with Germany. "It is incredible to me that a spirit that has shown itself so inept in the presence of obvious evil on an obviously large scale can fairly claim to be called Christian." He blamed the foreign policy reverses of the 1930s on this false kind of love:

It is because they were faced with so much charity in this sense, that the ablest set of political scoundrels of modern times have found it relatively easy to clamber into power and fully thrust their way through the greater part of the Continent. . . . There is nothing Christian in moral blindness and moral timidity, in refusing to call foul things by their proper names, imagining, as well as finding, excuses for those who are doing the foul things, and in nervously yielding to them instead of boldly binding them to a better way. . . . [O]ur extraordinary tolerance of the vilest forms of political evil in the international field requires for its explanation either sheer indifference or else an unconscious assumption that eventually God will clear up the mess for us.[33]

Pacifists loved to use Gandhi's action in India as an argument, but the activists judged this a big mistake. Gandhi's method of nonviolence worked in India because India was ruled by Great Britain, a nation with a Christian conscience, albeit weakened in modern times. He succeeded because he appealed to the "good side" of Britons, the same way Edmund Burke defended the American colonists in the 1770s. If India had been ruled by Nazi Germany, Gandhi's method of nonviolence would have failed miserably because that regime had no conscience and no public opinion to exert moral pressure on the government. When they asked Hitler how he would handle the problem of India, he replied bluntly: "That's simple, first shoot Gandhi!" Weatherhead recalled that in 1934 Bishop Barnes of Birmingham had urged a policy of disarmament, claiming that "no great nation would so shock the conscience of the world as to use aeroplanes against a country that had rendered itself incapable of retaliation." What Bishop Barnes called impossible is exactly what Mussolini did to Abyssinia and Hitler did to Poland! Obviously some pacifists do not know the evil we are dealing with, concluded Weatherhead.[34]

But force never really settles anything, continues the pacifist. "Just look at all the wars of history! All of them were futile and unnecessary. History proves that war just breeds more war with no real resolution of conflicts." To say that war never solves anything betrays an ignorance of military history; one may point to many military campaigns that settled outstanding international questions, some for several decades and even centuries. The Congress of Vienna (1815) gave Europe a century of relative peace from 1815 to 1914. Goudge asked, "What can be more preposterous than to forget all the just wars of the past and the good they effected, to involve in one common condemnation Judas Maccabaeus and Tamburlaine, King Alfred and Louis XIV, Joan of Arc and Mussolini?"[35]

What about the bad effects of war? You may consider yourself better than your enemy, but in fighting him you become like him. In fighting Fascism, we will become like the Fascists. Lewis Mumford jumped on this objection with passion: "One might as well say that an honest householder who confronts a burglar with a revolver will in turn become a burglar if he shoots. Indeed, a fascist must have invented that slippery phrase, and grinned in triumph when it went the rounds among democratic peoples who wanted an excuse for inaction."[36]

Niebuhr dealt with a similar objection from pacifists: "Let him who is without sin cast the first stone." This verse, taken out of context (John 8:7), would destroy civilization if applied in a wooden literal sense. If applied consistently, only a sinless judge could ever judge anyone, which would lead to "the abolition of the whole judicial process in society." We cannot find a perfect judicial system, but we must keep on judging; we would not be so stupid as to allow love to abolish our—admittedly imperfect—judicial system. "We must contend against evil, even though we know that we are ourselves involved in the evil against which we contend."[37]

Many people are moved by the argument, "I just can't imagine Jesus putting on a soldier's uniform and fighting in a war and actually killing someone!" Micklem responded by quoting Jesus's statement, "Man, who appointed me a judge or an arbiter between you?" (Luke 12:14). This verse might suggest that Jesus was totally unconcerned with justice, since he refused to be a judge. But did that suggest that none of his followers could be a judge? Obviously not. Temple pointed out to a pacifist that asking what Jesus could or would do is pointless—he never married, but we do not proscribe marriage on that account. "While it is true one cannot picture him as a soldier, it is also true that one cannot picture him as a lawyer or as a professional member of an orchestra."[38]

A pacifist might say, "I did not bear my son to be killed by a German bomb." Dorothy L. Sayers responded, "No? And what particular death had you in mind for him when you bore him? Meningitis or cancer, pestilence or a broken neck, pneumonia or tuberculosis, death at the hand of a drunken lout in a road-accident, or the creeping doom of senility?" She suggested that the pacifist had made life into an absolute and worshiped it rather than the God who gave life and decree that it must end in death. "Like every other temporal absolute, life takes revenge on those who make it a god."[39]

When you go to war, you kill mostly the innocent people who really did not want the war. The leaders of the enemy nation escape unharmed, which is a great injustice. This argument may be true, but it is ultimately irrelevant. If the Germans insist on fighting for Hitler, they are involved in the evil he perpetrates. Temple wrote, "The moral duty is to resist the force of Germany directed as it is directed now; all German citizens are in some degree involved unless they are rebels, and then they are in concentration camps and not in the army." While the war lasts, we must presume "the identity of the State with the whole body of its citizens." The main principle of any future peace must be "no peace with Hitler or with those who have been his colleagues; but with the German people guided by a trustworthy Government a peace honourable to them as truly as to us, freely negotiated in a Congress of European nations."[40]

There was a new wrinkle in the pacifist–activist dialogue in World War II, which one could call the "Niebuhr Syndrome." We recall Vann's argument, based on the dictum of St. Thomas, that "a man may not commit one sin in order to avoid another." Another way of saying it would be that God would never place us in a situation where we would have to do wrong to do right, or, God would never get us into a predicament where we would have to make a choice between two evils. This is precisely the dictum that Niebuhr denied, and he carried a good section of the British clergy with him when he wrote the books explaining his position, *Why the Christian Church is Not Pacifist* and *Europe's Catastrophe and the Christian Faith.* He argued with considerable verve that the Church must not at this crucial juncture of history be misled by pacifist perfectionism, the idea that only sinless people can judge and fight. "The fact that all men are sinners does not absolve us of the responsibility of making a stand against injustice, tyranny and persecution."[41]

Although Niebuhr never used the designation, the logical fallacy being committed here is called "the argument of the beard." Its name comes from the old question, "How much hair does it take to make a beard?" Would a slight five o'clock shadow do? Or do you need a prophet's beard reaching to your waist? We know what a beard is, and we know what cleanshaven means, but we have trouble precisely defining a beard. You commit the fallacy if you reason that "since we can't define a beard, there is really no difference between bearded and clean-shaven."[42] The pacifist commits it when he reasons that "since all humans are sinners, you would need to be sinless to judge or fight another human." This would stop all wars, to be sure, but it would also stop all courts, all police, and all parenting! The same reasoning would prove that there is no essential moral difference between Hitler and St. Francis, since Francis was not perfectly good and Hitler was not totally evil. The person committing this logical error is "shade blind"; he is so impressed by the continuum of small differences that he misses the real differences. He equates a manure pile with a mountain merely because they have the same shape.

Most pacifists display a perverse preference for tyranny over war. Tyranny is peace, and that is all that seems to matter. They like to assert that many democratic states have tyranny of a sort, an observation that really disturbed Niebuhr: "It is sheer perversity to equate the inconsistencies of a democratic civilization with the brutalities which modern tyrannical States practise. . . . If we cannot make a distinction here there are no historical distinctions which have any value."

Niebuhr asks us to face the sad fact that no one is perfect, that even the most saintly life "is in some measure a contradiction of 'love thy neighbor.'" This is true on the personal level but especially true on the political level, when we act as states. "Political controversies are always conflicts between sinners and not between righteous men and sinners." Yet from this fact, that justice is never totally free from vindictiveness, the pacifist draws the erroneous conclusion that "we ought not for this reason ever to contend against a foe."[43] Pacifism is just a contemporary form of Christian perfectionism, and such people all through Christian history have rejected the political dimension, because it requires compromise, a choice between evils. The perfectionist is freed from any responsibility for social justice; he can let the world go to the devil while he works on his personal holiness. Niebuhr calls this notion "an absurd idea"— that "perfect love is guaranteed a simple victory over the world."[44] The American prophet gave this advice to the morally perplexed: "When the Christian does the best thing he can in the circumstances in which he actually finds himself, after he has sought the guidance of God and the advice of his fellow-Christians, he cannot be said to be 'compromising' his standards: if he is doing what he honestly thinks is God's will to the best of his ability, that is no compromise but the right thing for him to do at that moment."[45]

Lewis Mumford preached a similar message in his books, *Men Must Act* (1939) and *Faith for Living* (1941). He, too, accused liberals of the argument of the beard: "Those who cannot see any difference between the sins of the British Empire and the sins of Nazi Germany are incapable of making elementary distinctions." He cited with approval the actions of Lincoln in the Civil War, who suspended the writ of habeas corpus and closed down some newspapers. "Democracy must at least have the resolution to ensure its survival." Liberals are paralyzed by their perfectionist theology: "To be too virtuous to live is the characteristic moral perversion of liberalism in our generation."[46]

Mumford pointed to the cases where fascism attacked liberalism (democracy). What happened? "Facing a war waged mercilessly by fascism against all his ideals and hopes, the liberal shows himself more concerned over minor curtailments of private liberty . . . than he is over the far more ghastly prospect of permanent servitude if fascism finally covers the earth." Liberals defend freedom of speech, even for fascists, while their freedom is being taken away by fascists! Once this war against fascism is won, we can return slowly to persuasion, "but to sacrifice the very existence of democracy to the rational principle of persuasion is itself a highly irrational act." Like Niebuhr, he blamed the fascist victory of the 1930s on liberal pacifism: "A world-wide holocaust has taken place because the courage to exert force, with rational purpose, on behalf of a moral principle was lacking in the statesmen and parties in power in the western democracies. This includes the United States."[47]

British churchmen echoed this complex, Niebuhrian defense of the war. Temple wrote to a young man that Pastor Hildebrandt of Cambridge had made the common error of pacifism, which was "a neglect of the relative values of justice in insistence upon the absolute claims of love." It was a sin to enter the war, he admitted, but a greater sin to refuse to enter a just war. "So here nothing is perfectly good except what directly expresses love of God and man; but in this wicked world the first step towards love is justice and the maintenance of freedom, without which the expression of love becomes impossible." To a young man asking to be excused from military service, he defended Britain's entry into the war by affirming that "our motives were mixed, as is always the case with every human action" but that did not alter the fact that "the course we took was right even though we took it partly for reasons not wrong but less than perfect."[48]

Weatherhead quoted with approval the remarks of the Dean of St. Paul's in the *Spectator* of 10 February 1939: "Christianity for good or evil has consented to play the game of civilisation, and it must play the game out." Christians thus are under a constant tension and can never escape it in this life. Our choices are nearly always between partial goods, not absolute evils. Given our centaur nature, we can never do what is absolutely good. Paradoxically, it is sometimes right to do wrong. For example, in 1915 when the *Lusitania* was sunk, a crazy man tried to get into a crowded lifeboat, which would have capsized the boat and drowned everyone. The passengers kicked him back into the water—he had to be sacrificed.[49]

Vidler commended Niebhur's phrase, "the relevance of an impossible ethic," in negotiating the claims of the government on the individual Christian. He admitted that it is not within our power to construct a final, totally consistent harmony between love and justice, between the kingdom of God and the world. We trust to the mercy and forgiveness of God when we err, and we must err. Few men stated the Niebuhrian position so bluntly as Vidler: "What we have to do in concrete situations is to find out what is the best sin we can commit, and then to go and commit it with a good conscience."[50]

Obviously not everyone liked this position. Farmer voiced the natural objection from the standpoint of the soldier: How can I put my whole heart into something that is sinful? It is a strange doctrine that we must fight and then ask for forgiveness.

So many young soldiers, who have something of Christian sensitivity, feel the whole thing to be so utterly beastly and degrading that to ask God's forgiveness in the very act of putting the maximum of their own efficacy into it strikes them as being on the verge of blasphemy. Like Studdert-Kennedy [a famous World War I chaplain] they feel that if it is really God's will . . . that they should do this, if He has made a world where, even as corrupted by sin, there is no option, in order to secure good, save to mow men down with molten lead or blow them to pieces with high explosives, then they are not merely anti-war but anti-God.[51]

Criticism of the Niebuhrian dialectic came also from the military. Temple got a letter in 1944 from Air Marshal John Salmond, taking him to task for his critical remarks on the bombing of Luebeck and Rostock. Temple had written that war was a "hideous evil," but Salmond said that this position was exactly what got us unprepared for this war. Now that the Allies are preparing for the great invasion, this is no time to disillusion the troops.

Our forces have to be hardened to the necessity to kill and to kill at once or pay with their lives. They are trained to be tough, to be hard and to count their own, and other lives, cheap. . . . Why is it necessary in the name of Christianity to teach them to look upon with regret the inevitable results of at length putting their training into execution? If you succeed the result will be a sapping of strength of the offensive will. This is total war and the public are in it as much as the training fighting man, consequently public opinion and that of the fighting man should be carefully fostered along the same line, namely to become hard and ruthless in a hard and ruthless task.[52]

Phyllis Bottome summed up the great activist discovery: "We have learned in this war that tanks minus morals can overpower flesh and blood minus tanks. But we have not yet fully learned that tanks plus morals can overcome tanks minus morals; since flesh and blood (which after all direct the tanks) can do *more* with morals than without them."[53] Sidney Berry said that this simple truth went back to Oliver Cromwell, who once told his navy men, "Trust God and keep your powder dry!"[54] Any way you express it, many Christians, in the face of fascist evil, had to give up pacifist perfectionism. Like Temple, they did not want to call the war a "crusade," since that term had offensive connotations from the deplorable Crusades of the Middle Ages. But a just war it surely was—a war against an obvious evil. Leo spoke for thousands of Christians and churchmen when he said, "No Christian can be a pacifist in action at this juncture of history."[55]

There was one pacifist point that stuck: the warning about becoming like the enemy as you fight him. Many, many churchmen ignored the complaints of the military and warned about the *spirit* in which British soldiers must fight. John Middleton Murry claimed that the worst thing that could happen would be to fight Nazism only to discover we had become Nazis ourselves. W. R. Matthews noted that the only protection against the hardening of combat is that "the individuals who compose the nation should guard the ideals of justice, freedom, and mercy in their own souls." Temple replied to Marshal Salmond that warning about the horrors of war should not diminish military resolve; he claimed that Britain had largely avoided the deterioration of war since 1914 because of the "steady witness given to Christian principles."[56] Britain was fortunate that it had a prime minister who warned against revenge; Churchill said vengeance was not only a vice, it was not even a good war aim.[57] The Church used prayers such as the following to inculcate the proper attitude:

Almighty God, Father of all, help us to remember when we suffer through the war, that vengeance belongeth to Thee, and that Thou has committed all judgment to Thy Son; deliver us from hatred and turn the hearts of our enemies to Thyself that their rulers and people may see what Thou wouldest have them do and have grace and power to do it; through Jesus Christ our Lord. Amen.

Almighty God, who by Thy holy apostle hast taught us that we fight not against flesh and blood but against the powers of darkness enslaving the souls of men, help us, in this time of war, so to remember our high calling that we may fight manfully under Thy banner for the establishment of Thy Kingdom of truth and love, of righteousness and faith; and crown our efforts with good success; through Jesus Christ our Lord. Amen.[58]

Bishop Bell always warned his fellow churchmen that no matter how necessary the war, it is the function of the Church to remain the Church. The Church should never allow itself to be considered the state's "spiritual auxiliary." "It must not hesitate, if occasion arises, to condemn the infliction of reprisals, or the bombing of civilian populations, by the military forces of its own nation. It should set itself against the propaganda of lies and hatred. It should be ready to encourage a resumption of friendly relations with the enemy nation. It should set its face against any war of extermination or enslavement, and any measures directly aimed to destroy the morale of a population."[59]

Certain Christian groups with an antiwar history found themselves during the war struggling to appear patriotic. The Methodist Church held a conference in Leeds on 25 July 1942, at which the new president, W. H. Armstrong, brought up the topic of commitment to the war. He deplored the general impression in some quarters that the Methodist Church had committed itself to pacifism: "I want to say in my own judgment the vast majority of the Methodist people are wholeheartedly behind the Prime Minister in the great task that is ahead." He explained that the Church in recent statements had simply declared its intentions not to forsake its conscientious objectors. He reassured people by saying, "We are fighting against a doctrine which is in direct antagonism to Christian ideals—a doctrine which if victorious, would strike a deadly blow at our spiritual convictions and social aspirations." The conference eventually passed the following resolution: "The Conference believes it to be a great responsibility and high privilege that the British Commonwealth of Nations is charged with the duty of securing, by the blessing of God, the triumph of righteousness, truth, and freedom, brutally outraged at the present time. The Conference is confident that Methodist people will steadfastly uphold this sacred cause until its complete victory has been achieved by the attainment of a righteous and lasting peace."[60]

Meanwhile, over in the United States, the American Baptist Church met in Atlantic City, New Jersey, and passed with a 5 to 1 ratio the following cautious endorsement of the war: "We will not bless war, but we will not withhold our blessing from our sons who fight and from our country's cause in which they with the sons of the Allied Nations now engage."[61]

Even the Quakers backtracked a notch. H. G. Wood, a distinguished Quaker theologian, introduced an interesting distinction in an article for *The Friend* (7 June 1940) between the "Quaker Absolutist" and the "Quaker Alternativist."

In the present crisis, when the British people cannot withdraw from the conflict and make peace with Hitler except by the complete surrender of honour and independence, Friends, in my judgment, cannot rightly remain neutral in their sympathies and cannot rightly engage in any form of political pacifist propaganda. Our testimony against all war is not a testimony in favour of any and every kind of peace, and we do wrong to cry "Peace, peace," where there is no possibility of a peace which a Christian can approve.[62]

In summary, it was very difficult to find an official Christian group that opposed Britain's participation in World War II or that wanted to appear neutral in the war against Fascism.

DEALING WITH PACIFISTS

Dealing with pacifism as an ideology is one thing; dealing with real, flesh-and-blood pacifists is another. The Church of England hierarchy found its patience and ingenuity sorely taxed in dealing with various groups within the nation during the war.

First, there were the Jehovah's Witnesses, a cult from America that refused to salute the national flag or fight in national wars. Minister of Information Duff Cooper wrote Temple in 1942 that even if the group could not be regarded as subversive, "its proselytizing work tends to direct attention from the national war effort."[63] Cooper commissioned research into the group's beliefs. It turned out that they believed Christ had returned to Earth in 1914, when the dispensation of Satan had ended, and the present war was the battle of Armageddon in which Jehovah would defeat the enemies of the theocracy. The war would mean the destruction of everyone except the Witnesses, who would rule with Jehovah in the theocracy. All Witnesses claimed exemption from military service on conscientious grounds. Given their dogged evangelistic activities, there was a fear that they might infiltrate the military services. They imported a great deal of material from the United States, on which they made a handsome profit. The government had already reduced sharply the amount of bulk paper material they were allowed to import.

Temple told Cooper that the Witnesses were "for the most part simple rather foolish people who are impressed by this farrago of nonsense," but he conceded that "the organization is exerting a degree of influence that begins to amount to a public danger." He admitted that they had been wronged by the government in being imprisoned more than once for the same offence. He wrote to Ernest Bevin that they were "extremely difficult folk. They are of course regular cranks with whom it is peculiarly hard to deal. . . . I think their propaganda is most objectionable." He wrote to the Archbishop of Birmingham that "the movement itself seems to me to be pernicious to the last degree and it seems to be quite scandalous that the Government has I understand just given it a very large supply of paper for its propaganda. But no doubt a great many of the young folk who come under its influence are sincere and entitled accordingly to respect and appropriate treatment, and I agree with you that renewed imprisonment for what is not a new offense but only constancy of conviction is both a hopeless policy and open to objection on moral grounds."[64]

Lang and Temple were usually sympathetic with COs in general, except when they demanded things like the guarantee of the old job they lost because of their convictions. Lang reminded them that he would defend their rights to their convictions, but he would also defend the rights of their employer to hire whom he wished. He also expressed agreement with parents who did not wish their children to be taught by COs. Several times in his letters on the topic, Temple quoted Dr. Johnson: "The Roman Government had every right to kill the Christian martyrs and they had every right to be killed!"[65]

The Church of England was also continually concerned about the status of its own clergy during the war. On 4 September 1939, the Ministry of Labour informed Lang that the government had decided to follow the precedent of the year 1916 and exempt from liability to be called up for service in the Armed Forces of the Crown, any "man in Holy Orders or a regular minister of any religious denomination." Lang received several letters from ordinands who were nearing the end of their seminary training and were fearful they would be called up since they were not yet strictly clergy. Lang reassured them that in his opinion the government would never hassle an ordinand whose ordination would have been completed that autumn.[66]

Not all Britons were happy with this clerical exemption. In May 1940, Lang received a letter from the Southgate Labour Party, penned by the general secretary, C. R. Goodchild, informing him that in his ward the following resolution was carried after much heated discussion: "As this is a Christian country, and we are supposed to be fighting against German paganism, why should a 'man in holy order, or a regular minister of any religious denomination' be exempt from Military Service under the National Service Act, 1939? Should they not be fighting in the front line?" The same Goodchild wrote again in July explaining that the feeling of the ward was that since this war was being fought "by Christians against Pagans," the clergy should "before advising others to take up arms, be prepared to do so themselves and stand in the front lines of the fight for Christianity" and not just pray for the souls of the soldiers who are fighting.[67]

Some churchmen endeavored to slip through loopholes in the law. The heads of theological colleges petitioned Sir John Anderson to let off candidates from their militia training, not only during their university course but altogether. The Bishop of Coventry wrote Lang that he was ashamed at such a request, however anxious the theological colleges may be to keep their colleges open. "Why should these men be exempted from what every other young man will have to do? They would be all the better for doing their training."[68]

Special attention had to be given to a parareligious body know as the "Oxford Group." The government had a "Schedule of Reserved Occupations" that defined men who did not have to go to war. The Oxford Group appealed for such a classification inasmuch as they were religious, even evangelistic, but not regular clergy. They called themselves "lay evangelists." On their first application, Ernest Bevin ruled that the work of the group was social, not religious; thus they did not quality for the exemption. This decision removed almost their entire staff. The group asked Lang to petition Bevin once again; he did so reluctantly. Bevin replied that he was getting many letters about the group but sadly must maintain his original ruling.[69]

The Church of England had a small pacifist group who called themselves the Anglican Pacifist Fellowship. The letterhead on the Fellowship's stationery contained this declaration: "We, Communicant members of the Church of England, believing that our membership of the Christian Church involved the repudiation of modern war, pledge ourselves to take no part in war, and to work for the construction of Christian peace in the world." In 1940 this group asked Lang for a special meeting in which they could discuss the question, "What was the point at which the Church would rather see the war lost than won by methods it deplored?"

At first Lang declined the offer for a meeting, informing the group that no useful purpose would be served by a such a gathering; they would only rehash old arguments. Paul Gliddon, the secretary, acted very hurt in his response: "If we cannot turn to our Archbishop at a time like this, to whom can we turn?" Lang relented and agreed to a meeting, but then Gliddon asked if they could bring some of the priests in their council, fourteen in all, along with a stenographer who would make a shorthand account of the meeting. Lang consulted with Temple, who agreed that the group should not be allowed to make a verbatim report of the meeting, which would be like "letting these tiresome people blow off their steam in our faces." "I am inclined," continued Temple, "to let them also have a condenser and container for it if they like! We are only seeing them at all to prevent them from feeling 'frustrated' as one says nowadays, so I am inclined to let them have what they want."

Lang replied to Gliddon that they could use a shorthand secretary and even make a verbatim report, but only for making a summary of the meeting. He insisted that he did not want anything officially published about the meeting; that would in effect make it a public meeting, and every word might be publicized. The meeting finally took place, and the Fellowship submitted its report to Lang on 13 June 1940. Lang quickly informed them that the summary was longer than he had anticipated. He could not approve it until he knew how it would be used. Gliddon said he would cut it down to twelve hundred words but would like to be free to circulate it generally among his people. Lang sent the report to Temple, complaining that some of the phrases were out of context and misleading. Temple agreed that no full report should be allowed to go out, only a summary; he said he did not recall saying some things just the way they appeared in the report. He warned, "I do want to show these people as much personal sympathy as possible, but I do not want to have utterances of ours available which might be used as halfway towards pacifist propaganda."

The whole episode petered out when Lang informed Gliddon that only the shorter report could be used as a record of the deputation. We must keep in mind that all this happened in the spring and summer of 1940, when France was falling and Britain was bracing herself to face the Nazi juggernaut. Lang and Temple must have wondered about people who would dicker over a deputation when such an enemy was at the gates.[70]

Temple had trouble in 1942 with one of his pacifist clergy, the Bishop of Birmingham, who simply skipped the prayers for the armed forces in the House of Lords. A certain M.P. Simon asked him about it, and the Bishop said he did not like the usual prayer. Simon said, "I suppose that those of us who want to pray for those fighting must do it privately." Simon appealed to Temple on the grounds that he chose the rota of bishops, and the prayer was prescribed by Archbishop Lang.

Temple contacted the Bishop with the complaint, and they tried to work out a new prayer that would be acceptable to both. Temple proposed a draft, but the Bishop replied that he was troubled by references to "the cause they serve" and "the common cause," since these phrases suggested that Britain was in no way to blame for the war: "I remember what we did and failed to do in the five years that followed the armistice of 1918, and hesitate over any form of wording which might be held to imply that Divine Providence has forgotten our failures." They finally agreed on the following cautious petition:

Almighty God, our Heavenly Father, we commend into Thy hands our country in this time of war, beseeching Thee to guide all who bear rule or command, that they may have vision, steadfastness and courage; be with all who serve in the forces or as civilians, giving them protection from evil of body or soul; uphold the spirit of our whole people and make us worthy of victory; look in mercy on all who suffer through the war in every land—the sick and wounded, the anxious and bereaved, the prisoners and exiles, those whose homes have been destroyed; and bring us out of strife to a true peace based upon freedom, justice and good will; through Jesus Christ our Lord. Amen.[71]

SPECIAL PROBLEMS: REPRISALS AND BOMBING

Friedrich Nietzsche observed that bad music and bad arguments always seem to sound good in wartime. That is because war short-circuits the human reason; patriotic propaganda dulls the critical intellect. Temple knew this better than most and used his office to combat crazy ideas that popped up in Britain during the war—ideas like reprisals.

Hubert A. Nicholls wrote Temple berating him for a public statement he had made on loving and forgiving the Germans: "Is there *no* doubt in your own mind on this point, no possible thought that you may be wrong, and that you are asking your people to love something so utterly evil and utterly anti-Christ that you may be guiding them against the simple truths and teaching of the Bible?" Temple wrote back and said that "however carefully one expounds these things the Press omits three-quarters of what one says." He explained that the word "love" misleads people; Christ loved the people he whipped out of the temple. Forgiveness means a readiness to receive people back into fellowship, but it does not take effect until they have changed their outlook. So, forgiving the Germans while they were still Nazis would be impossible. But to suggest, as some do, that there must be some kind of "balance of suffering" whereby the Germans get "whacked proportionally" is nonsense. The Doctrine of Atonement is flatly against such an idea.[72]

The suggestion of "proportional whacking" came also from K. Jakubovic, who urged Temple to lend the authority of his office to a declaration. The declaration was directed toward the Germans and said that from now on the

German people, not the Nazi government, would be regarded as responsible for the murder and ill treatment of every innocent being, and that after the war, we will kill the exact number of Germans! The cost of this project would be limited to the mere price of the leaflets spread over Germany. Temple's response was appropriate:

That we should then take a number of Germans to be killed, as they have killed from among the Jews, irrespective of whether the individuals have had a share in this horror or not, would be to my mind as great an abomination as the thing the Germans are now doing, and I am sure and am also thankful to think that it would be psychologically impossible: British troops ordered to carry out such mass executions would mutiny. I perfectly understand the horror admitting impotence, but I think that is better than deliberately adopting the level of wickedness which the Germans have now reached.[73]

Far more disturbing was an article in August 1944 by D. R. Davies on the lead page of the *Sunday Express* entitled, "It Is Time for Reprisals!" Germany had just begun using the V-1 and V-2 flying bombs against England. Davies was livid, claiming that such a weapon was sheer terror caused by frustration, having no military value at all. It was "the beserker rage of a powerless criminal." Any nation that would use such a weapon proved itself to be a "nation to which it is utterly futile to appeal in any terms of existing law." Nazi Germany had "hoisted the flag of hell," thus placing "herself outside all law, a self-created pariah among the community of nations." To tolerate this slaughter of our people would be criminal.

What we must do, insisted Davies, is retaliate! Compel the Germans to pay ten lives for every British life by bombing them. "Reprisal bombing of German towns not yet touched will paralyze the flying bomb." "What's the good of wasting air power on concrete platforms built by slave labour? Use it on the living flesh of the nation, whose consent, active or passive, alone makes their use of this weapon possible. Thereby you save your own people by making the price of killing them too high to pay."

Temple received a few letters from Christians about this shocking article by Davies, who was the Vicar of Emmanuel, West Dulwich, and a contributor to the *Church of England Newspaper*. He answered one letter as follows: "It suggests to me that he has got personally rattled. . . . I will try to get the opportunity of influencing him a little about it." Temple wrote Davies and chided him for the article, noting that there was no fundamental distinction between British indiscriminate bombing of Germany and the flying bomb. Davies disagreed: "Strategic bombing, for all its ghastliness, still keeps warfare within a framework of law. The flying bomb . . . abandons all pretense to law." If we do not do something drastic, he predicted, the Nazis will start using things more terrible—gas, germ warfare, even monster bombs.[74]

Temple always walked a tightrope between the hard-liners and the Quakers, between those who said, "Stick it to the Germans," and those who said,

"Get out of the war completely." Until the summer of 1944, he had talked in general terms of "punishing" Germany in some way, but he announced in his foreword to Hobhouse's book that he had changed. He now felt that the course of the war had inflicted "overwhelming punishment." After Temple's death, Hobhouse wrote in December 1944 to Canterbury, asking whether there had been any evidence of the archbishop having changed his view that Germany had been "punished enough" by Allied bombing. Mrs. Temple and Mr. White-Thomson, the secretary, together said they felt that that was his final judgment, and later reports of flying bombs and Nazi atrocities had not altered it.[75]

Saturation bombing of German cities became the issue that almost split the activists in World War II. We recall Vann's objection that the war was a good cause fought with bad weapons. When the Anglican Pacifist Fellowship in 1940 asked Lang at what point the Church would rather see the war lost than won by methods it deplored, Lang replied that that point would be the "bombing of open towns." Three years later the fellowship sent a letter to Temple, asking for another deputation, reminding him that Lang's "point" had been reached. Would the Church now take a stand against the war? Temple answered politely that the pressure of time was so great that he could not have a meeting anytime soon. He said he thought anything relevant could be put in a letter, leaving it to him to judge if anything would be so novel "as to justify me in setting aside time for a Deputation when my other engagements would make that possible."[76]

Obviously worried, Temple fired off a letter to Archibald Sinclair of the Air Ministry, complaining that he was receiving urgent questions about a change in bombing policy from limited to total bombing. He said he keeps telling people that this is not true and the government's previous statement still holds. "But I should be very grateful if you could let me have a line to assure me that this is correct." Archibald assured him there had been no change in policy: "It is no part of our policy wantonly to destroy cities—regardless of military objectives—as the German Air Force attempted to do in the 'Baedeker' raids." But he added an important proviso: "What we cannot undertake to do is to refrain from attacking an important military objective because it is situated near old and beautiful buildings."[77]

Five days after Archibald's reply, Temple got a letter from George Bell asking him if he could bring up this matter in the House of Lords. Bell suggested that the question read, "To ask His Majesty's Government whether, without detriment to the public interest, it can make a statement as to its policy regarding the bombing of towns in enemy countries, with special reference to the effect of such bombing on civilians as well as objects of non-military and non-industrial significance in the areas attacked." Temple replied that he would rather leave the problem of bombing in Bell's charge: "I am not at all disposed to be the mouthpiece of the concern, which I know exists, because I do not share it." He told Bell of Sinclair's assurance that the policy had not changed and said he would use this response when questioned about the policy.[78] Reading between the lines, one gets the feeling that Temple had decided not to press the government on the issue, even if the policy had changed; if the government lied, then he could not later be faulted for taking Sinclair at his word.

Bell pressed the issue. By February 1944 it was obvious there had been a change in bombing policy, and Bell wrote, "There is no concealment of the fact that it is now the obliteration of whole towns that is intended; there is no concealment of the fact that Hamburg and Berlin are actually marked out section by section." Are we now dedicated to the notion, he asked, that the ends justify the means, that anything will do to win? Temple answered that it was regrettable that Bell's position was taken by some as representative of all the bishops. He reminded him that even Mervyn Haigh, bishop of Canterbury, whose city had been destroyed by the Luftwaffe, said that the Germans were right, from a military standpoint, to use this kind of obliteration bombing; it was a policy that worked.[79]

Churchill complicated things for Temple. In July 1943 he made a speech to the U.S. Congress in which he referred to "laying the cities and other military centres of Japan in ashes, for in ashes they must surely lie before peace comes back to the world." Immediately the London Society of Friends sent a copy of Churchill's statement to Temple, asking if this signified a change in bombing policy. Temple wrote several letters trying to explain away Churchill's unfortunate statement, pointing out that the phrase "cities and other military centres" implied that cities were targeted only when they were clearly military centers.[80]

Pleas came from the nations being bombed. Nicodim, patriarch of Rumania, sent Temple a fervent letter asking "your grace to use his great influence in order to stop the terrible massacres among the flock entrusted to our care." The patriarch testified that "many thousands of innocent women and children have been killed and many cultural and religious institutions destroyed," far from any military objectives. "We cannot believe that Englishmen and Christians can approve these unnecessary horrors particularly against a nation which has never had anything but friendly relations with Britain."[81] (The main targets in Romania were the Ploesti oil fields, which supplied about one-third of Hitler's petrol. These fields certainly qualified as military targets, as one can see from the fact that the German tanks ran out of gas in the closing days of the Battle of the Bulge in January 1945.)

Then came a protest from Belgium, from Cardinal van Roey, the archbishop of Malines, long regarded as the leading spirit of Belgian resistance to Nazism. Cardinal Roey issued a strongly worded pastoral letter protesting that allied bombing raids were "sewing death and destruction over Belgium." Vast destruction was spread over cities like Malines, Louvain, Liege, Brussels, Ghent, and Charleroi. The RAF dropped bombs and incendiary devices blindly and at random. Of course, they warned people to stay away from railroad lines but the archbishop asked, "Where in a population as dense as ours are we to take refuge in a land riddled with railroad lines?"[82]

There was a subtle shift in Temple's defense of RAF bombing, which may have been unconscious on his part. For awhile in 1943 he accepted the government's statement that only military sites were targeted and defended the bombing as necessary in spite of unfortunate ancillary damage. He insisted on the distinction between intending something directly and causing it incidentally. But then he began to stress that whatever we may do to stop the German war machine will shorten the war; if this is the guiding principle, then certain distinctions tend to get blurred. By April 1944 he was explaining that stopping munitions productions was "more effectively done by the total dislocation of the whole community engaged in the work than by attacks upon the factories themselves, which can be repaired with astonishing rapidity." He compared the bombing to the general shelling of a town under siege. This parallel is very revealing, because in a siege, the fort and town were virtually one—to shell the fort was to shell the town. With this parallel Temple seems to have abandoned completely any distinction between military and civilian targets.[83]

Bishop of Oxford Kenneth Escott Kirk supported the policy of saturation bombing. Asked about the devastation of Hamburg, he said its ghastliness was slight in comparison to the cold-blooded tortures inflicted by the Germans on Russians, Poles, Czechs, and Jews. Asked about the possible bombing of the Eternal City in Rome, the headquarters of the Church, Kirk answered,

If it will shorten the war even by a day, and so be the cause of prolonging some thousands of human lives which otherwise would be cut short, let it be destroyed, tragic though we all recognize the necessity to be. The human race for which it perishes can rebuild the city in even more glorious shape than before. But if by sparing it we have taught men to think of human life as in no higher scale of values than material things, we have turned our back once for all not merely on reason but on the Christian religion itself, and that way nothing but chaos lies.[84]

We now know that the shift to unlimited bombing was made in February 1942. We also know that the British government lied about the change, and the Ministry of Information was a party to the deception. Sinclair gave out many false statements on the policy because he did not wish to provoke the nation's religious leaders. "Bomber" Harris, the motive force behind the new policy, told everyone that he was going to bomb "any civilian who produces more than enough to maintain himself." The whole affair became an insane, Byzantine tangle of lies, weasel words, and pseudojustifications. If you condemn the Germans for three years of terror bombing, it is not easy to find reasons to start using the same tactic yourself. Home Intelligence found out that, in spite of all the guile, there was widespread public knowledge of the shift in bombing tactics; some of the initial attacks were greeted by the public with great enthusiasm.[85]

Temple often said that once you decide to fight, the worst thing you can do is to fight ineffectively. If the die is cast—if war is unavoidable—then you must give it your best shot. If your best shot includes saturation bombing, then so be it. The same logic led Harry S Truman to drop atomic bombs on the Japanese cities of Hiroshima and Nagasaki. He calculated that the number of people who died would be less than those who would have died if the Allies had been obliged to invade the home islands of Japan. Such is the logic of modern war. One of the central guidelines of the just war theory—one must not make war on civilians—was no longer tenable.

CONCLUSION

The British people went to war in 1939 convinced that the struggle was justified. Many of them converted from a previous position of pacifism, even missionary pacifism, to support the fight against Fascism. Something had scared them badly. What was this system of thought that frightened so many Britons? Chapter 4 addresses that question.

NOTES

1. See Hoover, "The Just War," ch. 7 in *God, Germany, and Britain in the Great War* (New York: Praeger, 1989), 103–118.

2. "Censorship and Propaganda," in *This War and Christian Ethics*, ed. Ashley Sampson (London: Blackwell, 1940), 92. For some good general studies of the Christian views on war, see Roland H. Bainton, *Christian Attitudes toward War and Peace: A Historical Survey and Critical Re-evaluation* (New York: Abingdon Press, 1960); Paul Ramsey, *War and the Christian Conscience* (Durham, N.C.: Duke University Press, 1961); Michael Walzer, *Just and Unjust Wars: A Moral Argument with Historical Illustrations* (New York: Basic Books, 1977); Loraine Boettner, *The Christian Attitude toward War* (Grand Rapids, Mich.: Eerdmans, 1942); Albert Marrin, *War and the Christian Conscience: From Augustine to Martin Luther King* (Chicago: Regnery, 1971); John Ferguson, *War and Peace in the World's Religions* (New York: Oxford University Press, 1978).

3. Belgion, "Censorship and Propaganda," 93–95.

4. H. L. Goudge, *The Case against Pacifism: A Sermon Preached before the University of Oxford, Sunday Morning, January 30, 1938* (London: Mowbray, 1938), 11.

5. "The Ethics of Reprisals," in *This War and Christian Ethics*, ed. Ashley Sampson (London: Blackwell, 1940), 163.

6. *The Theology of Politics* (London: Oxford University Press, 1941), 130.

7. *Case against Pacifism*, 13.

8. Quoted by P. T. R. Kirk, *Revolutionary Christianity: How Peace Can Be Saved* (London: Peace Book Company, 1939), 18.

9. Francis A. Judd, *A Call to Christendom in Reference to the War* (London: New Life Movement, 1941), 17.

10. *Morality and War* (London: Burns, Oates, & Washbourne, 1939), 36, 38, 43, 60, 73.

11. Cited in George Glasgow, *Diplomacy and God* (London: Longmans, Green, 1941), 2.

12. Leslie Weatherhead, *Thinking Aloud in War-Time: An Attempt to See the Present Situation in the Light of the Christian Faith* (London: Hodder & Stoughton, 1939), 20.

13. Letter from Lang to Bentley, 31 May 1939, *Lang Papers* 80: 14.

14. *One Lord, One People* (London: Lutterworth, 1941), 16.

15. Letter from Temple to Garbett, *Some Lambeth Letters*, ed. F. S. Temple (London: Oxford University Press, 1962), 146.

16. Letter from Temple to Derek Fane, ibid., 134.

17. *Thoughts in War-Time* (London: Macmillan, 1940), 28.

18. Letter from Temple to Hobhouse, 26 March 1944, *William Temple Papers* 51: 4. The 4 August issue of *The Friend* carried a review of Hobhouse's book, playing up the fact that the archbishop had broken his rule on writing introductions just this once to show the world that he and Hobhouse still considered each other brothers in Christ, united by the love of Christ (*William Temple Papers* 51: 181). In his autobiography Hobhouse reported that over twenty thousand copies of *Christ and Our Enemies* were distributed from 1944 to 1945. The Army and the RAF distributed it to over three hundred chaplains in Germany. See Stephen Hobhouse, *Forty Years and an Epilogue: An Autobiography (1881–1951)* (London: Clarke, 1951), 202.

19. *William Temple Papers* 51: 29.

20. This statement comes from Barth's "Letter to Great Britain from Switzerland," cited in Alexander Miller, *Biblical Politics: Studies in Christian Social Doctrine* (London: SCM Press, 1943), 47.

21. *War and the Purposes of God: A Survey of Scripture Teaching* (London: Marshall, Morgan and Scott, 1940), 73, 137.

22. Ibid., 154. For a similar approach, see J. R. Coates, *War—What Does the Bible Say?* (London: Sheldon, 1940), 15.

23. *Spiritual Values and World Affairs* (Oxford: Clarendon, 1939), 114.

24. This is taken from Temple's introduction in his book, *Towards a Christian Order* (London: Eyre and Spottiswoode, 1942), 8. See also his letter to a pacifist, 26 April 1944, *Some Lambeth Letters*, 171, and Lucas, *War and the Purposes of God*, 139.

25. Weatherhead, *Thinking Aloud in War-Time*, 30.

26. *Thoughts in War-Time*, 33.

27. See Leo, *Give Christ a Chance* (London: Drakers, 1941), 13; Rom Landau, *We Have Seen Evil: A Background to War* (London: Faber & Faber, 1941), 174.

28. William Temple, *A Conditional Justification of War* (London: Hodder & Stoughton, 1940), 10–12, 22.

29. "A Christian Peace—Is It Possible?" in *This War and Christian Ethics*, ed. Ashley Sampson (London: Blackwell, 1940), 195.

30. W. R. Matthews, *The Foundations of Peace* (London: Eyre & Spottiswoode, 1942), 75.

31. *Theology of Politics*, 138–139.

32. Quoted in *Home Bulletin on the Spiritual Issues of the War* 39 (27 July 1940): 4.

33. T. E. Jessop, *Has the Christian Way Failed?* (London: Epworth, 1941), 8, 12, 16, 18–19.

34. *Thinking Aloud in War-Time*, 34.

35. *Case against Pacifism*, 13.

36. *Faith for Living* (London: Secker & Warburg, 1941), 139.

37. *Europe's Catastrophe and the Christian Faith* (London: Nisbet, 1940), 35, 44.

38. Micklem, *Theology of Politics*, 133; Temple, *Some Lambeth Letters*, 155. See also Micklem's letter to Lang on this argument: "He is our exemplar, but it does not follow that we must wear sandals, still less that we must assume a messianic office. He is our exemplar in following His divine vocation; we must copy him *mutatis mutandis* in following ours." *Lang Papers* 80: 42.

39. *Begin Here: A War-Time Essay* (London: Gollancz, 1940), 135.

40. *Thoughts in War-Time*, 64, 67–68.

41. *Europe's Catastrophe*, 24.

42. See W. Edgar Moore, *Creative and Critical Thinking* (Boston: Houghton Mifflin, 1967), 166–168.

43. *Europe's Catastrophe*, 34–35.

44. *Why the Christian Church Is Not Pacifist* (London: SCM Press, 1941), 11–12.

45. *Europe's Catastrophe*, 47.

46. *Faith for Living*, 78–79.

47. Ibid., 44, 76.

48. *William Temple Papers* 58: 193, 280.

49. *Thinking Aloud in War-Time*, 59, 72.

50. "The Theology of Pacifism," in *This War and Christian Ethics*, ed. Ashley Sampson (London: Blackwell, 1940), 20, 26.

51. "The Good and the Right," in *This War and Christian Ethics*, ed. Ashley Sampson (London: Blackwell, 1940), 79.

52. Temple, *Some Lambeth Letters*, 12.

53. *Our New Order or Hitler's?* (Hammondsworth, England: Penguin, 1943), 87.

54. *The Great Issue and Other War-Time Studies* (London: Independent Press, 1944), 29.

55. *Give Christ a Chance*, 11; see *William Temple Papers* 51: 78; *Some Lambeth Letters*, 25; and *The Hope of a New World* (London: SCM Press, 1940), 65.

56. Murry, *Christocracy* (London: Dakers, 1942), 125; Matthews, *The Moral Issues of the War* (London: Eyre & Spottiswoode, 1942), 40; Temple, *Some Lambeth Letters*, 13.

57. In 1942, J. W. Welch, director of Religious Broadcasting for the BBC, had asked Archbishop Lang to take the lead in heading off feelings of revenge which he detected in certain sectors of the British public, for example, among the merchant seamen whose motto was, "V stands for Victory, for the sailor it also stands for Vengeance." See *Lang Papers* 84: 270–272.

58. These prayers were devised by Norman H. Clarke, canon of Southwark Cathedral. See his *Thine Is the Kingdom: A Book of Prayers for Use in Time of War* (London: Harrap, 1942), 34–35.

59. See Bell's article, "The Church's Function in Wartime" in *The Fortnightly Review* (November 1939), cited in Jasper, *George Bell: Bishop of Chichester* (London: Oxford University Press, 1967), 256–257.

60. Reported in *Spiritual Issues of the War* 90 (24 July 1941): 3. Scott Lidgett, an influential Methodist leader, wrote that "never . . . did a nation take up arms in a more momentous cause then in the present case. . . . If the will of Germany . . . prevails, then all the accepted spiritual values of the Christian faith will be persistently outraged throughout Europe and beyond." *The Methodist Recorder* (28 March 1940).

61. *Spiritual Issues of the War* 242 (22 June 1944): 2.

62. *Spiritual Issues of the War* 33 (15 June 1940): 4.

63. *William Temple Papers* 58: 174, 184, 202–205.

64. Ibid.

65. *Lang Papers* 80: 185; *Some Lambeth Letters*, 49. Lang was rather disturbed when the BBC adopted the policy that nonsupporters of the war could not engage in any broadcasting for the war effort. Welch opposed the policy, noting that it would exclude such giants as George MacLeod, Donald Soper, and Canon Raven. The BBC stated its policy bluntly: "There is no freedom of speech today—for anyone." Lang wrote Welch that he reluctantly agreed with the BBC but "it gives me great disquiet" (*Lang Papers* 80: 210–217).

66. *Lang Papers* 78: 99, 135.

67. Ibid., 280, 316.

68. Ibid., 35.

69. Ibid., Vol. 80: 311, 321.

70. Ibid., 64–70, 84–95, 126–146.

71. *William Temple Papers* 51: 3, 9–14.

72. Ibid., 72–74.

73. Ibid., 83.

74. Ibid., 161–170.

75. Ibid., 150, 180.

76. Temple's reply was given 6 July 1943, *William Temple Papers* 57: 133.

77. Ibid., 135, 138.

78. Ibid., 141–142.

79. Ibid., 164–166. The Bishop of Gloucester supported Bell in this matter. He said saturation bombing meant "the destruction of all the fruits of civilization. The real work of the Air Force is to support the troops in battle to defend our ships and attack those of the enemy." For a short account of Bell's role in the controversy, see Jasper, *George Bell*, 261–264.

80. *William Temple Papers* 57: 145–146.

81. Ibid., 168.

82. Ibid., 178–179.

83. Ibid., 167; *Some Lambeth Letters*, 93–94, 102–103, 106.

84. Eric Kemp, *Life and Letters of Kenneth Escott Kirk* (London: Hodder & Stoughton, 1959), 85–86.

85. See Ian McLaine, *Ministry of Morale: Home Front Morale and the Ministry of Information in World War II* (London: Allen & Unwin, 1979), 159–163.

CHAPTER 4

The Enemy: Fascism–Nazism

For the second time in a generation, the British clergy found itself scrutinizing and analyzing the German people, its mentality, its leaders, and its history, trying to find the magic key to that strange system called fascism. Don't say it doesn't matter what a man believes, declared William Temple: "It obviously matters a great deal to all of us what the Nazis believe. They believe it with great fervour and we are not going to extirpate their beliefs by a mild haze of cautiously held opinions."[1] The clergy usually concentrated on the German version of fascism, National Socialism, Nazism, or Hitlerism. They looked upon Mussolini as a rather pitiful puppet of Hitler, and on Italian fascism as a weaker, less threatening form of fascism. Nathaniel Micklem said that the spiritual home of fascism might be Italy, but "its superlative logical development has been in Germany."[2]

As previously noted, many clergymen during the Great War developed the generous thesis that the Germans were afflicted by "temporary insanity," but the clergy of 1939 to 1945 seldom suggested this idea. If they delved into collective psychoanalysis at all, the latter usually suggested that the Germans had a permanent problem, like a special innate tendency to cruelty, or militarism, or blind obedience to authority. Many agreed with Carl Jung, who described the Germans's periodic madness as "furor teutonicus." Rom Landau expressed the feelings of many when he charged that "in the last seventy-five years alone the Germans have started five wars, besides four near misses. If they had had their way there would have been a war every eight years for the last three-quarters of a century."[3] George Glasgow lamented that the "fanatical lack of balance in the German character is one of the problems of the century. . . . It cannot be true twice in living memory that a whole race of people should be dominated against their better will or judgment by one man, mad or sane. There must be, at any rate, some predisposing susceptibility. . . . It is a manifestation of patriotism and racial complex that amounts to dementia. There is something peculiar, and something alarming, about such a race of people."[4] Duff Cooper and Sir Robert Vansittart were on record as believing that the Germans were "genetically flawed."[5] Clemenceau was very quotable on the dark side of German character: "You must never negotiate with a German—you dictate to him!" or "Unfortunately for the rest of us, the Germans are in love with death."[6]

More moderate thinkers excused the Germans by stressing that they had gone through some unfortunate historical experiences. William Paton said Germany had cut herself off from the western tradition: "She has not had the same historical training and discipline as the British, the French and the Americans." D. R. Davies was more precise—he said the Germans had never enjoyed the blessings of being penetrated by Greek (i.e., Greco–Roman or classical) civilization; they remained barbarians for a long time after they brought down the Greco–Roman Empire. Rom Landau stressed that Britain got its gospel from Rome, whereas the Germans did not. Prussia, for example, did not receive Christianity until the thirteenth century. Hilaire Belloc argued that German crudity is "the mark of barbarism," which is typically Prussian, "for the Prussian is above all, immature." Alfred Zimmern emphasized that Germany was the victim of history and geography. She was late in unification and had no boundary with either the Atlantic or the Mediterranean, thus insuring a conservative isolation.[7]

Many clerics pointed to Luther and Lutheran Erastianism as one major root of Germany's problems. The German Church struggle would have been impossible in a Calvinist country; it could occur only in a nation where the Church had abdicated its function and turned over its control to the state. When Luther declared the secular prince to be the *summus episcopus* (primary bishop) of the German territories, he "sowed the dragon's teeth of Nazism," asserted Davies—a great irony that one who had revolted against authority in the Church should make it absolute in the state. Temple concluded that Hitler, on Luther's premises, had the right to control the Church in Germany. Zimmern said that "once Christianity has given Caesar marching orders to conduct affairs according to his own standard, what is there to restrain him?" "How thankful the Führer must be to the reformer," said T. G. Dunning, "for a doctrine which gives the appearance of divine sanction to a doctrine and policy that are really derived from his, the Fuehrer's, insensate lust for power."[8]

It seemed a long time ago to many, but William Steed called on his compatriots to remember the "good genius of Germany"—the philosophy of Kant, the humanism of Goethe, the plays of Schiller, the music of Beethoven and Bach, and the political ideals of the German liberals of 1848.[9] Ian McLaine pointed out that we have a contradiction in our propaganda if we say that the Germans once conformed to a universal standard of European culture, and then say that they have never truly been a part of European Christendom.[10]

Most clerics declined to engage in this historical analysis of the roots of current German behavior; it was a dark and bloody ground which to this day separates historians into warring schools of thought. Nearly all clerics, however, seemed eager to participate in the analysis of Nazism, for in it lay the key to the enemy's highly motivated war against the Allies. Most of them stood in awe of its psychological dynamism.

THE ANATOMY OF NATIONAL SOCIALISM

G. K. Chesterton once observed that whatever starts wars, the thing that sustains wars is something in the soul, something akin to religion. "It is what men feel about life and death. A man near to death is dealing directly with an absolute; it is nonsense to say he is concerned only with relative and remote complications that death will in any case end. If he is sustained by certain loyalties they must be loyalties as simple as death."[11]

A Competing Religion

The British clergy agreed with Chesterton that the followers of Adolf Hitler must be sustained by a religion of some kind. One of their most common observations was that Nazism was a religion in its own right—a surrogate religion, a competing religion. It was far more than a simple political philosophy. Reinhold Niebuhr called it "the most primitive of all religions."[12] Most philosophers would say that any secular ideology like fascism or Communism is at best a quasi-religion, but many students of religion agree that modern secular ideologies have some striking similarities to traditional religions. If religion is defined as man's efforts to attain the highest possible good by aligning his life with the strongest and best power in the universe, then Nazism surely came across as a religion to many contemporary observers. It seemed to have all the right elements: personal faith, gods and devils, ritual, worship, scriptures, the elect and the damned, good and evil, heaven and hell. Lewis Mumford saw the parallels clearly: "Fascism is a diabolical religion, a religion of Yahoos . . . and this means that it has the capacity of every living religion, to integrate action, to create a spirit of willing sacrifice, to conjure up in the community that possesses it a sense of its collective destiny which makes the individual life significant, even in the moment of death."[13]

Man is *homo religiosus*. He must have some religion. If his soul is emptied by secularism it will be filled by something religious. Several churchmen used Christ's parable of the restless spirit, who, being cast out of a man, decides to return to the house it left. "When it arrives, it finds the house unoccupied, swept clean and put in order. Then it goes and takes with it seven other spirits more wicked than itself, and they enter and live there. And the final condition of that man is worse than the first" (Matt. 12:45). F. R. Barry said this is what happened with Nazism: "The driving power of the Nazi revolution is that it gives young men, dissatisfied with the husks of a secularized social order, the heady wine of a substitute religion. A generation of uncommitted young is the material ripe for its appeal. No secularized non-religious theory of political freedom is strong enough to resist it. The effective answer to a false religion is not religious neutrality but true religion."[14]

V. A. Demant argued that state absolutism (or totalitarianism) was a popular concern because it spoke to a deep need in human nature, a force "evoked by the hunger of the soul which has been starved by the agnostic empiricism of liberal humanism." Fascism satisfies the longing for personal meaning. "It restores to human beings a conviction of significance as conscious agents in process that is in the trend of all things in contrast to the liberal idea of 'Progress,' for which the present moment has only significance for a hypothetical and undated millennium."[15]

How did the clergy prove Nazism was a religion? They argued that it had all the elements of a religion, they noted that it was totalitarian and intolerant of all other worldviews. It persecuted and harassed its competitors, especially Christianity. When an ideology becomes intolerant, that proves it has crossed the philosophical Rubicon and become metaphysical. Just as Herod the Great recognized immediately the threat of the Christ-child to his reign (Matt. 2:16), so also Hitler recognized the threat of Christ's Church to his supremacy. The German dictator, said Donald Davidson, is in the direct line of Pharaoh and Herod:

All authority that is based upon might as opposed to right is inevitably the sworn enemy of the rule of Christ. That is why Hitlerism to-day is at war with Christianity. It is simply the clash of an age-old hostility. The two regimes cannot exist side by side. The rule that is founded on love—and Christ's kingdom is love—is hated by the dominion that is founded upon force—and Hitler's kingdom is force. . . . To-day the gates of Hell, the principalities, the powers, the rulers of the darkness of this world, are still pitting their strength against the Christ of Bethlehem. But they shall not prevail. Pharaoh, Herod, Hitler, all come at last to their hideous end, but Christ lives. His kingdom stands and grows for ever.[16]

The clergy proved Nazism a religion by citing statements from German sources.[17] Most useful to them were the remarks of Alfred Rosenberg, the so-called "philosopher of National Socialism," whose convoluted writings even Hitler could not understand. Rosenberg brought out a little pamphlet by Theodor Frisch called *God and Nation: A Soldier's Creed*, which ran 180,000 copies. It promoted Nazism as a competing religion: "To-day the question is not to weaken Catholicism, to strengthen Protestantism, but to replace a religion which is foreign to us by a faith born from the depths of the German soul. . . . Two ages, two signs confront each other to-day: the Cross and the Sword. . . . We cannot live two different faiths. In our heart there is room for only one faith, one creed: Germany! . . . I believe in the strong God and His Eternal Germany."[18]

In 1930 Rosenberg had published his magnum opus, *The Myth of the Twentieth Century*, a strange collection of musings on blood, race, and soil, which very few people read and which has never been translated in its entirety. At the Nuremberg rally of 1937, Hitler decided to honor the Nazi philosopher with a "national prize," the German equivalent of a Nobel prize. A few weeks after receiving this honor, Rosenberg made a speech (October 11), which was reprinted in the party newspaper, *Völkischer Beobachter*. He defended Nazism as a full-fledged *Weltanschauung*, worthy of intellectual consideration by all the world, worthy of taking over complete control of the education of the next generation. "Germany was not saved by the prayers of the Centre-people," he asserted, "but by the sacrificial battle of the National Socialist Labour Party. . . . We are profoundly convinced that, if there be a heaven, one who fights nobly and bravely for Germany will get there before one who goes about to betray his people with a prayer on his lips."[19]

The British Ministry of Information published a weekly sheet called *Spiritual Issues of the War*, in which Nazi sources were frequently cited to show the religious nature of Nazism. One came from *Das Schwarze Korps* (20 January 1940), the official publication of the SS (the Schutzstaffel or "blackshirts"). The writer claimed that, "to assert in the Third Reich that Christ's birth was an infinitely more important event than anything the Fuhrer [*sic*] claims to have realized is high treason and the last word in political perfidy."[20]

Micklem cited a ritual pledge used by German boys of the Ordensburg Adolf Hitler Schools in 1939: "We, Adolf Hitler pupils, are pledged only to the Führer, but not to the Jewish–evangelical philosophy or church. We cannot serve two causes, the Führer and his greatest enemy. Therefore, I . . . hereby announce my resignation from the Evangelical Church." He also quoted a long article from *Der Stürmer* (March 1937) in which Christ is shown not to be a Jew because "the German people can learn nothing from a Jew." Thus Christianity is one of the greatest "anti-Jewish" movements of all time; the death of Christ was the greatest ritual murder of all history.[21]

Robert Ley, head of the Nazi Labor Front, was quoted several times because of this candid statement: "For us there is only one idea, one outlook, one life, one religion which can bring bliss—and that is the eternal belief in the German *Volk*, in its blood and in its soil and in its Creator. Our religion would not exist if our blood did not exist. . . . The teaching of Adolf Hitler—therein is to be found the Gospel of the German people."[22]

One can learn a lot from a group's writing (or rewriting) of history. Micklem obtained copies of some special educational documents called *Schulungsbriefe* (training letters) in which very specific guidelines were laid down for the Nazi reinterpretation of European history in German schools. For example, the Middle Ages were henceforth to be regarded as a lamentable interlude between the original German heathenism and the rise of National Socialism. The medieval church carried on a reign of terror against the healthy, virile, and innocent barbarians. St. Paul is pictured as the archenemy, whose "Jewish brain" worked overtime to destroy the innocent, unsophisticated minds of the original Germans. The Christian doctrines of grace and original sin are an affront to such a pure, robust race.[23]

Many more examples could be given, but these suffice to show that the leaders of the Third Reich considered Nazism a new religion, no matter how much they might deny it in public. If one had any doubt, it was dispelled by Hitler's treatment of Christian publications. The Führer prevented the printing of the Bible and drove the Scriptures from German schools. By the time war came, the government had suspended 14,000 religious periodicals, which comprised 95 percent of the total number of religious publications in the country, while it suppressed only 20 percent of the secular papers.[24]

Japan was guilty of the same crime. In 1937 William Paton published *Christianity in the Eastern Conflicts*, where he described the conflict between Christianity and Japanese totalitarian nationalism. The Japanese state had its own Oriental version of its absolute sacredness, which conflicted with Christian conviction. Paton mentioned a Christian child being arrested for saying that Christ was greater than the emperor. It seemed that Britain and her allies were fighting the same evil system all over the world.[25] John Drewett concluded that the struggle of the twentieth century was "nothing less than the conflict between Christian values and beliefs on the one hand and a view of life based on belief in the human-collective, race or class, as an end in itself."[26]

Once you realize that Hitler was not just a political ruler but a new "savior" founding a new, competing religion, you view the war in a very different light. Sidney M. Berry called it a clear case of "rival faiths," struggling for control of mankind. Barry said the political history of the next century may be that of "a race between two churches, each claiming to be universal—the pagan world-church of Fascism–Bolshevism and the Holy Catholic Church of Jesus Christ." Leo said that the forces of good and evil are "locked in a conflict upon the outcome of which depends the order of existence for the human race for many generations." Hadham predicted that the victory of Germany would mean "the scientific domination of the world by a deliberately perverted and ruthless religion." Paton thought that "an Axis victory would mean for the Church a life in the catacombs for generations to come."[27]

Paganism

If Nazism is a religion, it must be a false one because Christianity is the true religion. What are its errors? It is a reversion to ancient paganism, specifically to a special version of God or the gods called *pantheism*. Pantheism is a spiritual monism—a worldview which uses the word "god" but denies a transcendent personal God, distinct from the creation and asserts the divinity of everything—hence the prefix "pan." Pantheists must logically deny the doctrine of creation and assert that the cosmos is eternal, without beginning or end. Rosenberg argued that there could be no "revelation" from God to man because the soul is already divine, equal to god. Thus to Nazis, God is merely an impersonal principle, a moral idea that we attribute to the eternal forces of nature, and not a transcendent personal First Cause distinct from the world, a standard of truth and morality. Their view is that a supreme value is within their race and their blood.[28]

Demant quoted a publication of the German faith movement that asked, "Do you worship with all your soul—the Great Spirit of your race?" He preferred the word "vitalism" to describe this belief—similar to the word *Lebensphilosophie* (philosophy of life), used to describe a movement in German thought in the 1920s. This "uncompromising immanence" attempted to place God wholly within an eternal, developing universe. Demant called this "demonism," which means the attempt "to give some element in the temporal order the absolute value which only belongs to the transcendent." We are not surprised when such undifferentiated monism ends in complete relativism: "There is a rigid rejection of any mode of the divine activity which . . . could convict the process of error or evil."[29]

Was Nazism a "reversion" to paganism? A German pastor living in England during the war said no—it was worse. The pagan knows nothing of Christ; he is uninformed and therefore innocent. "But that nation which has once been confronted by Christ can no more fall back on a defense of ignorance, but can only definitely reject Christ as He is revealed to us in Holy Scriptures; it becomes definitely anti-Christian. Therefore, whoever, describes the present German world-outlook as a religion for Germany is not simply pagan . . . he stands on the side of Anti-Christ."[30]

Idolatry

By now one cannot avoid the necessary implication that Nazism is a form of idolatry. The essence of idolatry is the confusion between the Creator and the creation; pantheists, then, by definition are idolaters when they worship the entire cosmos without qualification. St. Paul spoke about such people who "exchange the truth about God for a lie and worship and serve the creature rather than the Creator, who is blessed forever" (Rom. 1:25). The "truth about God" is His difference from the universe; the "lie" is the assertion that all is one—that God and cosmos are the same. One might think that pantheism and polytheism–idolatry are antithetical, but a little reflection will dispel this apparent discrepancy. If God is everything, all of being, then He is necessarily each individual thing. Idols are thus just a local expression of the divine. If one worships a local idol he is worshiping god, albeit only a portion. While the common people worship many gods, the sage or guru knows that at bottom they are all one.

Nazism required worship of the state, the nation, the race, and the leader, Adolf Hitler. Bendiscioli noted that "only superficial minds can fall into the error of speaking of a *national God*, or *national religion*." He quoted the pope in refutation: "Our God is the personal God, transcendent, almighty, infinitely perfect, one in the Trinity of Persons and Three in the unity of the divine Essence, Creator of the Universe, Lord, King and ultimate purpose of the history of the world, who does not suffer and can never suffer any other divinity beside Him."[31] The vain prophets of Nazism will fulfill the scripture: "He that dwelleth in heaven shall laugh at them" (Ps. 2:4).

Especially odious was the incredible veneration of Hitler—a mere man, and not a very admirable man. Steed quoted Hitler as saying, "Mankind, led by the German race, is now in a period of transition, just as it was when man first began to pass from the ape-like into the human stage. Now they are passing from the human into the superhuman stage. I have preceded them. In so far as there is a God in this world, I am he."[32] Dunning contrasted this outrageous claim to the Christian idea that we are meant to be conformed to the image of Christ the Son: "Can human nature be so perverted, enslaved, and fundamentally changed as to make the chief end of man to glorify a *Fuehrer* and be enslaved to him?"[33]

We all need role models. For centuries Christians have spoken of the "imitation of Christ." In the Soviet Union, Lenin had replaced Christ as the ideal; and in the Third Reich, Hitler was being proposed as the new man to imitate. In a radio broadcast on New Years Day 1941, as Hitler's empire stretched from the Atlantic to Moscow, the Führer was praised in these words:

He is the greatest educative force and the strongest type-shaping power of the ages. . . . He is both statesman, general and artist. He is the most complete German living. The qualities of our people have become historically effective in him. . . . The personality and the name of the Fuehrer are a programme. Youth is, however, permitted to bear his name. How great this honour is. But great, too, is the obligation which this fact imposes. His name only may be borne with inner justification by those who proceed on their way through life with the resolution to come nearer to the Fuehrer by their behaviour.[34]

Norman Baynes related an incident involving the Hitler Youth that occurred in Kassel, Germany, in 1937. A choir of eight hundred singers and an orchestra of two hundred were about to perform a requiem, into which the composer had introduced the chorale, "Jesus My Confidence." Immediately the Hitler Youth threatened demonstrations. Such a religious text, they said, was incompatible with their views. The performance was cancelled.[35]

Walter Carey, chaplain of Eastbourne College, late bishop of Bloemfontein, gave this vivid description of Nazi idolatry to British soldiers:

In Germany they are making a god of Race and State. You needn't obey the God of heaven, the Father of all men, of Whom Jesus Christ spoke, the God of Justice and Love. But to make your own folk, your own race, supreme in power and bosses of the world, you must worship the State and the Head of the State as infallible and supreme. You worship an idea and a man. If that man bids you, in the name of the State and the Race, to do *anything*—you do it. No cruelty, no ruthlessness, is too much, if only you obey without question the State and the Man. You'll be slaves yourselves, but you can enslave others.[36]

Moral Relativism

The British clergy made a great deal of the element of *moral relativism* in Nazi ideology. It follows logically from Nazi metaphysics, for pantheism and monism collapse all hierarchies and distinctions, leaving you with a flat universe. Archbishop Lang said that "we must admit the failure to make our civilization truly Christian, and the call to amend our ways. But it is one thing to fall short of an ideal, another thing to repudiate it. The repudiation of Christian standards by the ruler of Germany is open and unashamed."[37]

But it was more than repudiation of Christian standards—it was the repudiation of all standards, of the very notion of standards. The Nazis had enshrined the thesis of Nietzsche that all ethics are merely a matter of perspective; there are no moral facts, only a moral interpretation of the facts.[38] In America, Bishop Fulton J. Sheen had his eyes opened by Pearl Harbor. How can we say that the Japanese "violated the conscience of the world, if the conscience of the world has no other measure than the useful? How can Hitler be wrong?" The idea of relativism had finally reached from the academy to the street: "We had no idea that the philosophy of expedience was so wrong when a professor in a cap and gown taught it from a rostrum, but we began to realize how awfully wrong it was when a Jap practiced it from an aeroplane over Pearl Harbor."[39]

Dorothy Sayers called this relativism "the sin against the Holy Ghost"—a sin which cannot be forgiven because it cannot be recognized or repented. John Armitage defined the sin as "doing wrong and claiming and believing the wrong to be right." Isaiah warned, "Woe to those who call evil good and good evil" (Isa. 5:20). Sayers admitted that we may have denied our faith over and over, but we never wholly abandoned it, like the Germans. "Though we may have despaired of ourselves, we have not really despaired of our European heritage. However blindly and feebly, we still hold on to those great principles that sprang from the eternal values; and when it came to that point, with much distress of mind, with much searching of heart, we were yet willing to die for them." Temple conceded that we had not always honored our principles, "but the first necessity is to save them from extinction; and the success of our enemies would mean their extinction at least for many generations."[40]

Fresh on everyone's mind was the long string of broken promises committed by Hitler in the 1930s. Belloc said, "There is no parallel for such a series of perfidies in the history of mankind." W. R. Matthews said that even savages and barbarians respect the sanctity of the oath, and "to feel horror at the breaking of a promise is the first step towards civilisation." Hensley Henson said Hitler reminded him of the medieval emperor Sigismund, who justified his faulty Latin by the plea that as emperor he was "above grammar." Mumford observed that, "On fascist principles, one might reasonably try to win a football game by poisoning the opposing team before the game began. On those terms, winning would be easy but the meaning of victory would disappear."[41]

Here, as before, thinkers illustrated this moral relativism in Nazism by citations from German sources. Davidson quoted one Nazi leader as saying, "The Germans have no feeling of guilt or that they were born sinners." The Ministry of Information published a translation of a "German Catechism for Godbelievers," which identified an unwritten morality as a voice coming from "our blood," because the blood is "the seat of the divine source of life, the voice is a divine voice."[42] The need for rational deliberation by a conscience is gone, for as Hitler pontificated, "The conscience is a Jewish invention, a blemish like circumcision." He said his task was to liberate men from "the dirty and degrading [ideas of] conscience and morality." He must teach the Germans "to distrust the intelligence and the conscience."[43]

George Barclay, one of Christendom's greatest exegetes, used the Bible effectively to critique the pagan notion that the ruler can do what he pleases. It was quite normal by the canons of Oriental kingship for the ruler, who was usually considered divine, to take any man's wife if she pleased him. But when Israel's King David took Bathsheba and had her husband Uriah killed, he got a visit from the prophet Nathan, who condemned him for his sin (2 Sam. 12:1–14). David left us an account of his anguished repentance (Ps. 51). The point here is that Israel was not a typical Oriental nation, and David was not a typical Oriental king. Israel's people were a chosen people being trained by the righteous God. Because of this training, most Israelites could not simply say "the king can do his will because he is the law." They had to say that the king sinned because he broke the transcendent law of God, a law that governs all men, including the king, who, by the doctrine of creation, is not divine. David was big enough to do what no typical Oriental monarch could do: He admitted that Nathan, one of his subjects, had the right to rebuke him. Nazi Germany has reverted to the pagan system, where the king can do anything he wishes because he is the law.[44]

No one rebuked Nazi relativism with greater erudition than Nathaniel Micklem. In a sermon to a group of young lawyers, he shocked them at the beginning with the assertion that Hitler had never broken any laws! The leader can break no laws when you have a *Führerstaat*, a "leader state." Germany used to have a *Rechtsstaat*, a "state of laws," but the Reichstag changed all that when it passed Hitler's Enabling Act on 23 March 1933, giving the leader carte blanche to legislate without parliamentary participation. Since that time the constitution of Germany had been the will of Hitler, just as when John Lackland said, "The law is in my mouth!"[45]

How different this is from the history of Western civilization! As far back as the Greeks, Europeans have believed in eternal, transcendent law, as Sophocles said through Antigone:

> *Unwritten laws, eternal in the heavens.*
> *Not of to-day or yesterday are these,*
> *But live from everlasting, and from whence*
> *They sprang, none knoweth.*

The Roman Stoics took up the same theme. Cicero spoke of true law as being "right reason, congruent with Nature, universally diffused, constant and eternal." It was a great day, said Micklem, when Christian thinkers identified this stoic law with the Ten Commandments, because this marriage formed the basis of Western Christian civilization, ethically speaking. So then later, the English jurist Blackstone could speak of the law of nature as "being coeval with mankind and dictated by God himself . . . binding over all the globe and in all countries and at all times." Micklem said that while the Nazis seek to disconnect law from religion, "the basis of our civilisation is our respect for law, and our conviction that law must be an expression of eternal Justice. Law is essentially connected with Justice and Justice with the will of God."[46]

Douglas Stewart attacked the popular cliche that all persons have a conscience or an innate standard of good and evil. If ethical standards are innate, then what about fascism or Communism or the murder of the Jews? A vague moral agreement in society proves merely that there are common schools teaching a common culture and tradition. Slavery was once legal, though immoral, but if you as a slave owner compared yourself with your fellow slave owners, you might have concluded that you were "a pretty decent chap." Stewart says we can no longer accept the "conventions" of our times because we are right now involved in a war of the conventions (fascism, Communism, and liberalism). To say that the "English conventions" are right is sheer national prejudice, unless you have an outside standard. Nature is no guide, so where do we turn? We are driven by our struggle with Nazism back to transcendent law: "Man is again being compelled, after the determined secularism of several generations, to look beyond himself and beyond his own institutions in order to find the absolute standard which he has lost. Whenever you begin to do that you are entering upon the much despised territory of religion."[47]

It is rather easy to debunk the immoralist. There is something truly frightening about a person who says that there is no difference between good and evil—if he really means it! Mumford pointed out that the nihilist has the advantage over you in a crisis—when he threatens mayhem, he means what he says, though others do not believe him. He denies even in theory the values that mankind has taken for granted for centuries. You cannot depend on shame to stop him; he doesn't know the meaning of hypocrisy. Such a person reminds you of Lady Macbeth, says Sheen, who before she committed murder called on the evil spirits to fill her with "direst cruelty" and "stop up the access and passage to remorse." Davidson felt that such people were described by St. Paul when he spoke of God sending a "strong delusion" to certain people so they would believe a lie and be damned. That surely sounds unfair, but Paul explains that these people already had demonstrated that they did not love the truth and had "pleasure in sin"—that is, they engaged in Nietzsche's *Umwertung* (revaluation). They inverted the true scale of values—they played the very dangerous game of "beyond good and evil."[48]

Irrationalism

Nazism taught not only ethical nihilism, but also *epistemological* nihilism—the idea that truth is relative or perspectival. The Nazis were against objectivity in general; they reveled in a *Lebensphilosophie* that one could call neoromantic. Life came before mind, instinct before reason, and action before analysis. Mumford spoke of the "dynamic irrationalism" of fascism. Demant said the Nazi revolution represented "an attempt to substitute a biocentric outlook for the logocentric tradition of the civilized west." Niebuhr said the Nazis had only accentuated, in a period of social decay, a truth about the sinful character of all men: man is not primarily a rational creature but a spiritual one. He is "not easily tamed by universal law or universal standards of value." Vidler described this nihilism: "Neither power in the State nor impulse in the individual is restrained by any higher sanction, nor brought under the judgment of an objective criterion. The present crisis discloses the collapse and disintegration of the moral and spiritual tradition which was the foundation of European culture."[49]

It never ceases to amaze us how the great Russian novelist, Feodor Dostoevsky (1821–1881), anticipated so many depressing things about our century. Reading *Notes from the Underground*, Davies discovered this striking precognition of fascist irrationalism and anti-intellectualism: "I should not be surprised if . . . there should suddenly arise from some quarter or another, some gentleman of low-born—or, rather, of retrograde and cynical demeanour, who, setting his arms akimbo, should say to you all: 'How now, gentlemen? Would it not be a good thing if, with one consent, we were to kick all this solemn wisdom to the winds, and to send those logarithms to the devil, and to begin to live our lives again according to our own whims?'"[50]

Fascist leaders stressed the mystical and the irrational because they could not survive very long if people started thinking logically about fascism! Their

Aryan racism is a myth, having little scientific proof—hence they retreat into intuition. They fear educated citizens because their propaganda is preposterous. As K.E.K. Kirk quipped, they hurry to get the world conquered before their creed can really be tested! They dare not allow liberty of mind because cold hard reason operating freely would make a shambles of their ideology. Kirk compared this irrational myth with religious faith: "There are creeds . . . which appeal to the free mind in confidence, because they conform to reason; such creeds breed faith in the truest sense. But the Nazi dare not appeal to reason in support of his claims. At best he must pervert both history and science to prove his case. It is not faith but fanaticism, the fanaticism of the priest of Baal, of the mad Mullah, of the armed dervish of the desert."[51]

To fight fascism, therefore, we must champion reason; we must promote the notion of objective truth; we must restore the idea that we are servants of truth, slaves to reality. Truth, like God, is transcendent and objective. Man does not create truth, as Nietzsche held, he *recognizes* it. Karl Barth testified that a revival of the fundamental notion of objective truth was the thing that allowed the Church to meet the crisis of Nazism "not wholly unprepared." At first men did not see the inherent atheism of Hitlerism because their eyes had grown dim. The contrast between Hitler and Christ became thankfully clear as they studied their objective revelation from God.[52]

S. C. Carpenter quoted the couplet:

> *It comforts me to know*
> *That though I perish, truth is so.*

Dorothy Sayers recalled that the Church had always taught Christ as the Divine Logos, the Eternal Reason. The universe is the product of a rational person, not blind necessity, erratic chance, or purposeless demonic forces. Deep down in our natures, she insisted, we honor reason and protest against the irrationality of our present world. "We are lost and unhappy in a universe that seems to make no sense." Her tribute to a bygone ideal was touching: "The Rational Man is an austere figure, and perhaps a little forbidding to the world in its present mood; but he is essentially noble, and a strong tower of defence against triviality, vulgarity, and mass-hysteria."[53]

Leslie Weatherhead offered his readers this poem to strengthen their faith in the ultimate victory of truth and right:

> *I know that right is right; that givers shall increase,*
> *That duty lights the way for the beautiful feet of peace;*
> *That courage is better than fear, and faith is truer than doubt.*
> *And fierce though the fiends may fight, and long though the angels hide,*
> *I know that Truth and Right have the Universe on their side;*
> *And that somewhere beyond the stars is a Love that is stronger than hate;*
> *When the night unlocks her bars, I shall see Him—and I can wait.*[54]

Racism

Racism was perhaps the easiest article in the Nazi creed to attack, since it constituted such an egregious contradiction to Christian equality and universalism. Davies reminded modern intellectuals that though the Middle Ages was indeed an age of superstition, "Medieval Europe can show nothing so vicious as the Nazi superstition of race." Inge called racism "the most grotesque piece of unscientific balderdash ever crammed down the throat of an intelligent people." S. M. Lehrmann, Rabbi of Liverpool, said that "the Church has no nobler task to perform than to act as the modern St. George to the Dragon of racial hatred."[55]

The Church was already on record against racism. The Ecumenical Conference on Church Community and State, held at Oxford, July 1937, declared that "against racial pride, racial hatreds and persecutions, and the exploitation of other races in all their forms, the Church is called by God to set its face implacably and to utter its words unequivocally." The International Missionary Council meeting at Madras, India in 1939 declared that, "God has made all peoples of one blood. No race can therefore disregard the rights and interests of other races. Racial persecution is particularly abhorrent. The Church should exert its influence on the side of all movements working for the full and equal sharing by all races in the common life of mankind."[56]

Many churchmen cited Julian Huxley's small book, *"Race" in Europe*, in their efforts to refute the myth of Aryan racial superiority. Huxley showed that the Aryan race is a fiction entertained by people whose vanity is tickled at the thought of their own uniqueness, and that it has utterly no foundation in scientific fact. Here Bible and science completely agree: The human race is a unity, and those who deny it are guilty of a grievous error. "If there is any belief which is fundamental in the civilised tradition," said Matthews, "it is this faith in the essential unity of the human race and the need to transcend national and racial divisions." God intended the human race to be like a big family, said Vann, but racism is so divisive, you have a hotel, not a home. Dunning spoke of what John the Baptist told the Jews: Don't boast that you are children of Abraham because God is able to produce children of Abraham from stones (Matt. 3:9). St. Paul said it was not the genes of Abraham but the faith of Abraham that impressed the Almighty (Rom. 3:4). Against the idea of a "master race," Temple wrote, "The God whose Majesty is specially revealed in the act of the Lord washing His disciples feet, will not call His strong nations to lord it over the rest of His family." Canon Peter Green devised an appropriate prayer on this matter:

O God, Who has planted in the hearts of men a deep and enduring love for the country of their birth, yet hast taught us by the holy Apostle that in Christ Jesus all distinctions of race, and speech and custom vanish, deliver the peoples of all lands from a false nationalism. Let there be no rivalry among the nations save the rivalry of service, that all may serve Thee and the common good in peace and harmony, through Jesus Christ, the Saviour of all. Amen.[57]

How far the German Church had drifted into compromise on this principle could be seen in a special letter sent to Archbishop Lang on 28 July 1937 from the Bishop of Schwerin in Mecklenburg, Germany, protesting some things said at the World Conference in Oxford against the German Evangelical Church. The Bishop affirmed that the German Evangelical Church felt itself called to serve the German people in maintaining the "unbroken solidarity" between *Volk*, leader and party: "Whoever insults National Socialism insults the German people and whoever insults the German people insults the German Evangelical Church. This must be said so that you know once and for all. Adolf Hitler, National Socialism, and the German people all belong together and no power on earth will be able to break up this unity."[58] A church so "coordinated" with the state has lost its prophetic role. T. S. Eliot observed that "no one today can defend the idea of a National Church, without balancing it with the idea of the Universal Church, and without keeping in mind that truth is one and that theology has no frontiers."[59]

Both Judaism and Christianity had taught love of the alien or stranger. "The alien living with you must be treated as one of your native-born. Love him as yourself, for you were aliens in Egypt" (Lev. 19:34). "The community is to have the same rules for you and for the alien living among you" (Num. 15:15). St. Paul wrote, "There is neither Jew nor Greek, slave nor free, male nor female, for you are all one in Christ Jesus" (Gal. 3:28). Jesus even taught love of enemies (Matt. 5:44). He gave some of his loftiest teachings to a Samaritan woman (John 4:13–26) and made a Samaritan the hero of his greatest parable (Luke 10:25–37). Here the Nazis strongly disagreed. Rosenberg denounced "universal love" as a "blow at the soul of Nordic Europe." He made the common soul the measure of all values, all thoughts, all actions: "It is useless to attempt to establish a common truth for all, a universal religion; such attempts can be made only by degenerates who have lost the sense of their race."[60]

Back in the 1930s, G. K. Chesterton had ridiculed the notion of honor being a special German virtue, saying it may as well be Icelandic or Finnish. The Germanic fetish of "the ancient Teuton" was humbug—it was the Romans and the Christians who civilized us all.

These great gods, the early Germans of the forests, to whom all "creative" energy is due, did not, of themselves, set up one building that has remained, or carve one statue of even prehistoric value, or express in any shrine or symbol the confused mythology which some would substitute for the radiant lucidity of the Faith. The great German civilisation was created by the great Christian civilisation; and its heathen forerunners left it nothing whatever, except an intermittent weakness for boasting.[61]

Dorothy Sayers noticed how ironic it was that the Treaty of Versailles distributed territory on the basis of nation–race, and then Hitler used it as a weapon against the treaty. The Allies had foolishly assigned an absolute value to nationality, and so Hitler proceeded to beat them over the head with it. The people of Britain were stymied by their own sacred principle of "national self-determination" until Hitler marched into the rump of Czechoslovakia. It then became clear that he attached no real value to the principle but was merely using it. The Führer saw all history as grossly simplified, like a child's picture-book full of "good" and "bad" figures marked in bright colors.[62]

The world is composed of nations, large and small, but the Christian must be concerned with the small nations. They are a problem, and one is sometimes tempted, said Matthews, to agree with Hitler and "absorb" them. But that would be tragic, because much of great value would disappear with them. A way must be found "to preserve the identity and independence of these nations while including them in a larger whole which is capable of defending them." Hadham thought it significant that God in the person of Jesus Christ once lived in a small nation like those conquered by Hitler—Belgium and Poland. He thought it very magnanimous of Great Britain to champion the cause of small nations in two world wars:

It is in such a world that the British peoples, soberly and humbly, conscious of their unworthiness and their need of the strength and guidance of God, have been summoned either to be the last victim or the center of a new hope. We are fighting for our own lives, but we are fighting for far more. On our victory or defeat to-day hangs the fate of generations yet unborn in every continent, as well as in our own land. . . . We have proclaimed ourselves engaged in a crusade for freedom and justice, for the rights of small nations to live. Politicians may find these phrases just suitable means to stir up a national effort for very different and less worthy ends. *God takes them seriously* (italics added).[63]

The issue of racism was so vital to Dunning that he defended the war in apocalyptic terms, calling racism "the inner moral Armageddon of the war." Two absolutes, two ultimates are at war, "one admittedly derived from racial consciousness; the other . . . derived from the Divine idea for the race and all other races." The Germans frankly admit their end is Germanic, but we, like Lincoln, seek to be on God's side; we seek "a more ultimate end." It is not our task to persuade the Germans to become good Britons but rather to become good Europeans and world citizens. Does this mean the end of patriotism? "This need not prejudice true and inspiring patriotism any more than patriotism need weaken love of home and loyalty to all. All true wider loyalties never weaken or antagonise lesser ones."[64]

The Christian walks a tightrope on this issue, struggling to keep his balance between Christian universalism and the hard realities of ethnicity. When the Nazis stress race, the Christian must be true to the Gospel and stress unity, but could one stress unity too much? Yes, answered Reinhold Niebuhr. In a defense of Zionism, he charged that we would be guilty of an "unrealistic universalism" if we did not fight for a Jewish homeland after the war. He chided liberalism for suggesting that history was moving forward to a universal culture that would eliminate all ethnic or cultural particularities. A "collective survival impulse" is just as legitimate as an individual survival impulse. Racism is wrong, but so is an atomistic individualism.[65]

Totalitarianism

The total state is a creation of the twentieth century.[66] Dictators use modern means of communication and transportation—radios, newspapers, motorcars, and airplanes—to control the minds of the masses. *Totalitarianism* obtains when the state declares that politics encompasses everything—that there is no longer a private sphere. Everything is potentially public; even sex and religion come under government scrutiny and regulation. Karl Barth gave a good description of the total state: It assumes divine prerogatives and demands "complete surrender of everything by all, complete allegiance of the conscience, servile submission, the fettering of every word and thought, the abandonment of every shred of independent responsibility and free collaboration by the individual with the community, the bending and breaking of every right apart from the right which finds its sole justification in the will of the ruler and his power to enforce that will."[67]

All British clergymen were united on this topic: *The Church must oppose the total state*. The reasons were obvious: God is the ultimate principle in reality, not the state or the leader of the state. In the total state, said Temple, there is no tension between God and state because the state has become God, and its word is the word of God. The Christian Church will always be a source of trouble for such a state, because it claims to "possess a Revelation, at once unique and final, and universal, which makes the Church a perennial source of difficulty to any state which does not avowedly accept that Revelation as the guide of its own action." Fascists stress that man is merely a citizen, but Demant gave the Christian answer: "Man is more than a citizen; the characteristic modes of his being are super-political, and they may not be subordinated to any political end. Political authority is therefore not absolute." Frederick B. Macnutt said that Christ saves us from "thinking of men as cannon fodder of Nazism, as the soulless factory hands of selfish capitalism, or as cogs in the mechanism of Fascism or Marxian State Socialism."[68]

On 6 June 1944, Temple delivered the William Ainslie Memorial Lecture, called "Christianity as an Interpretation of History," at St. Martin-in-the-Fields. It was D-Day, and the Allies had just launched the Normandy invasion to crack Hitler's "Fortress Europe." The occasion was auspicious. Temple contrasted the Jewish–Christian linear view of history with the Greek cyclical view, where everything is repeated an infinite number of times. Only the "once-for-all" Biblical view of history gives genuine significance to a particular time or person. The archbishop thus made the role of the individual the key to the war, because the totalitarian states counted the individual as a mere episode in the life of the race or state. But if Christianity is true, then "the individual has a dignity and a status greater than that of his state or his race."[69]

When you apply original sin to grand politics, you come up with the Actonian rule, "Power corrupts." One can see the corruption of power clearly in the way the total state arrogates to itself the control of the family. Micklem reported that Wilhelm Frick, Nazi Minister of the Interior, published an ordinance in 1938 stipulating that German parents who were "politically suspect" could be deprived of the direction of their children's education. The children of an "untrustworthy" family could be ascribed to another family of "proved political faith." The total state fears all intermediate communities such as family, village, and church. Paton pointed out that all totalitarian ideologies—fascism, Nazism, and Communism—abolish "the small groupings in which the life-giving diversities of society" are sustained, with the result that "between the atomized man and the omnipotent state there is nothing."[70]

Totalitarianism usually produces a cultural desert. Total states generate no creative art that is worthy of international acceptance. Sayers noted the reason: "The artist lives by and for the free expression of opinion, and that is anathema to tyranny. Let us beware how we persecute the creative artist; he is the expression of our greater selves, and when we have lost him, we have lost everything." Micklem scoffed at the Germans's fear that the unity of their nation or the philosophical basis of their state would be undermined if they studied French art, Greek philosophy, or Hebrew prophecy.[71]

The total state seeks to control the minds of all its citizens; thus it desires complete control of the nation's school system, from kindergarten to university. The Third Reich deprived itself of some of its most talented people: Karl Barth, Thomas Mann, Albert Einstein, Emil Brunner, and Paul Tillich. What irony, said Douglas Stewart, that "the age which has put all its faith in enlightenment has seen its greatest thinkers driven into exile by a half-educated fanatic and in obedience to an utterly irrational racial pride." Pope Pius XI said that if we don't fight fascism, it will be like sacrificing our children to Moloch. Kirk pointed to the way the Nazis took over the schools in Czechoslovakia: "If the Nazis were to rob us of our physical freedom as a nation, they would renew their attack in an even deadlier form, until they had taken from us freedom of mind as well. And that, both in itself and in its consequences, would be the greatest of all catastrophes. It is worth while for any man to give his life if thereby he may save his children from such a fate."[72]

Religious people have had many occasions in history to hail the fall of arrogant rulers and praise the justice of God for crushing evil. "How you have fallen from heaven, O morning star, son of the dawn! You have been cast down to the earth, you who once laid low the nations!" (Isa. 14:12). As Carpenter said, people of faith know that a tyrant is nothing; he may "dominate millions and enforce his will. Newspapers may echo his prejudices, and innumerable persons may be murdered or imprisoned because they will not be fashioned according to his word nor be transformed by the depraving of their mind. Yet he is worthless. In the world of real values he does not count." Kirk said of Hitler, "In the hour of death, the end of the German despot and his dupes will be more pitiable even than the fate of his countless victims."[73]

Many clergymen warned that totalitarianism was a general threat to all modern nations, not just Germany, Italy, Japan, and Russia. Matthews wrote that we deceive ourselves "if we imagine that only in Germany is Leviathan collecting his forces for a final bid for empire. His opportunity arises from the conditions of scientific civilization itself." Murry insisted that the war, if it had any Christian meaning at all, was a struggle against totalitarianism and the supreme aim of Britain "must be to prevent itself from becoming a totalitarian society." Davies felt that Nazism was only a warning symptom of a process of disintegrating consciousness in modern man in general—a way of escape from the burden of freedom described by Dostoevsky. "Nazism can be conquered only by the assumption of civil responsibility by the masses."[74]

Archbishop Lang took steps early on to keep the British government from assuming too much control over clergy of the Church of England during the war. In a "Memorandum on the Clergy in Wartime," dated March 1939, he laid down the guideline that "no clergyman should give any undertaking or pledge which would bring him automatically under the control of any Government Department, or Local Authority without the consent of his Bishop." During the war, the government seemed to invade the Church's domain when it decided to open theaters and cinemas on Sunday, and to give home defense training on Sunday mornings and evenings during hours of divine worship. Temple found out how powerful the government could be when George Thomas, Chief Press Censor for the Ministry of Information, wrote him three letters warning about references in church publications to flying bombs. The Germans could piece together such information and deduce certain valuable kinds of information about their weapons, such as the point of impact. Thomas warned that all such reports were supposed to be sent to the censor before publication. Temple thanked him for the rebuke and sent a letter to all parish magazines warning them to be circumspect about all references to flying bombs.[75]

Utopianism

Many ideologies of the twentieth century have announced that a "new man" is coming, a great evolutionary innovation, caused either by social engineering (liberal humanism), economic manipulation (Marxism), or racial hygiene (Nazism). Herbert Butterfield described the utopian as one who is "unwilling to leave anything to Providence." As one American abolitionist said, "God is too slow!" Vidler listed the four big mistaken assumptions of utopianism: (1)

Man is naturally good, (2) the goal of history will be reached within history, (3) utopia will come about solely by human achievement, and (4) man alone shall be glorified for this achievement. The truth is just the reverse of each optimistic assumption: (1) Man is naturally evil, (2) the goal will be reached outside of history—at the end of history, (3) it will be achieved by God, and (4) He will get the glory He deserves for man's salvation.[76]

Many thought that the British people had been blinded by utopianism in the interwar period. Davidson said that during that time you would have thought that the League of Nations was the only hope for the world and that God did not exist. It was a clear case of crying "Peace! Peace!" when there was no peace. Matthews concluded that the League proved worthless and "those who had trusted in it found themselves in a more hopeless position than they would have been in had they relied on their own defenses." He quoted this verse: "Put not your trust in princes" (Ps. 146:3). Davies poked fun at modernism's pitiful confidence in evolutionary perfection: You start with an amoeba at one end of the tube, and at the other end comes out, without any interference from God, an angelic human being! There is only one problem—the amoeba "got stuck in the bloody mess halfway—and then comes out in the form of beasts."[77]

In 1945 the Third Reich collapsed. It was supposed to last a thousand years but was scarcely twelve years old when the Allies brought it to an end. The end reminded one of what God said of Nineveh: "Everyone who hears the news about you claps his hands at your fall, for who has not felt your endless cruelty?" (Nahum 3:19). Empires do not usually last very long; they are too unstable. But this one had about the shortest life of any empire in history. Was there something terribly wrong with the Brown Paradise? The British clergy thought so. It was weighed in the balance and found wanting. "Unless the Lord builds the house, its builders labor in vain. Unless the Lord watches over the city, the watchmen stand guard in vain" (Ps. 127:1).

FASCISM AND ROMAN CATHOLICISM

Since Fascism began in Italy, many people in Western Europe assumed that the Vatican, and by implication the entire Roman Catholic Church, was comfortable with fascist ideology. In 1929 Mussolini and the Vatican concluded the Lateran Treaty, whereby the Pope recognized the state of Italy with Rome as its capital, while Italy in turn recognized papal sovereignty over the Vatican City and secured the full independence of the Pope. It was said by many that the Holy Father preferred Mussolini and the Fascists to the previous democratic regimes dating back to the Unification. Others reasoned that the Vatican preferred authoritarian to democratic systems because its own polity was hierarchical and authoritarian.[78]

The faithful waited anxiously in the 1930s for some official word from Rome about fascism in general and German Nazism in particular. The Vatican had given fewer explicit condemnations of fascism than Communism. The Russian Revolution was still the big bogey, not just for the Vatican but for most of Western Europe. This was especially true of the British people, who had fallen hard for Goebbel's propaganda line that the Third Reich was a bulwark in central Europe, defending Western Christian civilization from the hordes of the godless, communist Soviet Union. Stalin's sins were plain in the 1930s. Hitler's sins not so plain until the 1940s.

Meanwhile, in Great Britain, a local British Union of Fascists led by Oswald Mosley (1896–1980) appealed to many people of the Roman Catholic faith. One of these, Charles Wegg-Prosser, a young lawyer from a prominent English Catholic family, asked Cardinal Hinsley in the spring of 1936 if a Christian could be a fascist. Hinsley decided that the Holy See was in no position to answer that question clearly and objectively at the time, so he proceeded to give Wegg-Prosser his own considered judgment. Holding that in general the Church is above government forms, he nevertheless made it clear that a Roman Catholic could never agree with a philosophy which taught that the whole man, body and soul, was the property of the state: "No Catholic can be a Fascist if he holds that the State is the be all and end all in Society. . . . If some Catholics . . . belong to the British Union of Fascists, their duty is to make sure in conscience that they do not accept or favour . . . the pagan principle that the State is supreme." As for Mosley's group, "Fascism may be simply a united party to secure by calm measures law and order, justice and charity. But note well that mere Jew-baiting is not law and order nor is it justice and much less is it charity. To one who has joined the British Union of Fascists I speak thus:— I have nothing to say against any political party as such but do you and will you avoid anything that makes the State or government or party supreme master of the personal dignity of man?"[79]

The next year, on Palm Sunday, 14 March 1937, the Pope dropped an ecclesiastical bomb on the German government in the form of an encyclical entitled *Mit Brennender Sorge*, which translates as "with deep anxiety" or "with consuming care." The Holy Father pulled no punches and accused the Nazis of imitating the policy of Julian the Apostate who tried to destroy the Christian Church in the fourth century. He charged the German government of violating the Concordat of 20 July 1933, of abusing the education of young people by planning Hitler Youth meetings to conflict with Church meetings, and of harassing Catholic families and persecuting Catholic priests. Catholic clergymen all over the world were very happy that the Holy Father had cleared the air and spoken so candidly about Nazism. Cardinal H. E. Hinsley recalled the words Pius XI spoke to a gathering of cardinals on Christmas Eve 1937: "We must call things by their right names. We know that there is in Germany a grievous persecution, and more, that there has rarely been a persecution more serious, so painful and so disastrous in its widespread effects. This is a persecution in which neither the exercise of force, nor the pressure of threats nor the subterfuge of cunning and artifice have been spared."[80]

Hinsley's opposition to fascism grew with his understanding of it in the international as well as the domestic field. By 1939 he was able to classify it with Communism as a creed alien to British life, a pagan worship of the state.

On 2 September 1939, he sent a message to Prime Minister Chamberlain, assuring him of the absolute loyalty of the Roman Catholic community and proclaiming his wish to "assist the Government in the prosecution of this just war in any way within my power." When Britain declared war on 3 September, he dispatched a pastoral letter calling on every Roman Catholic to increase the fervor of his spiritual life and insisting "no matter how great our hatred of war we cannot stand idly by and allow our neighbor to be enslaved or ruthlessly done to death."[81]

On the same day, Bishop Kirk of Oxford issued a similar message to the clergy and members of his diocese: "If this robbery, this destruction of freedom, goes on unchecked, all that we have known as Christian civilisation is doomed to perish; honour, truthfulness, confidence, and equity will be forgotten, and nothing will survive except the reign of brute force."[82]

On Sunday, 10 December, Hinsley delivered a talk over the BBC which was later published under the title *The Sword of the Spirit*. "I am convinced," the archbishop affirmed, "that Great Britain has engaged in this war in the main for defence of the things of the spirit. She has taken up arms in the cause of justice and freedom." The immediate causes of the war were "a cynical and systematic disregard for truth, a reckless breaking of the plighted word, the brutality of force and ruthless persecution." He concluded, "I hold my country guiltless." He asked his listeners to look at a globe and find Europe, little Europe, a small peninsula at the end of the Asian landmass. So small yet so weighty. This is the parent of modern civilization. "What has generated so much power, moral, mental, physical, in so small an area? The answer is that our civilization has been nourished and made by our Christian faith, with its reverence for the individual as an immortal soul."[83]

If Pope Pius XII had been as outspoken during the war as Arthur Hinsley, the Vatican might not have the bad reputation it now has for its silence on the Holocaust. When Hitler destroyed the Low Countries, Hinsley was dissatisfied with the Pope's limp denunciation, so he gave one of his own, calling it a "dastardly invasion." All nations living under Nazi oppression, he said, were victims of "the gospel of pride and violent hate." When Italy entered the war, he told the faithful that there would have to be a long struggle between the Christian concept of civilization and the pagan notions of fascism. In a letter to the *Times* (13 July 1940), the cardinal warned all Catholic editors not to give any support to the present Vichy government of France. He warned that the *Osservatore Romano* and Vatican Radio did not necessarily reflect the judgment of the Holy Father as some might think. If anyone was in doubt as to whether the Vatican media accurately reflected the Pope's views, he added, they should contact him or the Apostolic Delegate. In a broadcast to Poland on Easter in 1940, he spoke of Poland as being "crucified between two thieves." Later he founded the Catholic Committee for Poland to help Polish refugees who had fled to the west. He called the Nazis regime there "an ersatz religion, a camouflaged paganism fiercely opposed to Christian civilisation."[84] Of course, it was easier to be courageous and outspoken off the continent.

CONCLUSION: GIVING THE DEVIL HIS DUE

Nazism is a fantastic illusion. When great nations and millions of people suffer such deception one has to ask the obvious question: Why did so many good, intelligent people fall for this error? As noted before, not many British clerics delved into collective psychoanalysis, but the ones who did emphasized the Nazis' success at creating a *Volksgemeinschaft*, a "national community." Dunning noted that Nazism derived its strength from depths that were religious, and only in such depths would Christians find a remedy.[85] Modern life reduced man to a cog in the machine, so that what developed was a "lonely crowd," millions of atomistic individuals running around looking for a *Gemeinschaft* of some kind. J. H. Oldham adapted the insights of Martin Buber's "I and Thou" approach into his study, *Real Life Is Meeting*. Fascism, he reasoned, was a dramatic backlash to the foolish individualism of modern times: "To isolate the individual from the context of mutual dependence and mutual responsibility, in which alone he can become a person, is a disastrous perversion of the truth. We cannot be persons except in relation to other persons."[86] Sheen argued that the community is a needed absolute: "The human heart must have an absolute."

The young people in these totalitarian countries were dissatisfied with the husks of a secularized culture; they wanted an absolute that would command conviction, the hardy wine of sacrifice, a truth for souls and a fire for hearts, and an altar for oblations, and they found it in a religion which is anti-religion. Their answer to a civilization that had forgotten the Christian religion was to be anti-Christian. . . . Deny man the right to make a pilgrimage to the shrine of a saint, and in fifty years he will be making pilgrimages to a tank factory. Deny man a God Incarnate, and in a few generations he will adore the emperor as the incarnation of a sun god.[87]

Vann insisted that the Roman Catholic tradition avoided both extremes of fascist tribalism and atomistic individualism; it sanctioned communities like family, church, and nation without deifying any of them. Issue 9 of *The Sword of the Spirit*, entitled "Nazis or Neighbours?," stressed the point that true community is more than the government-mandated cooperation one finds in all totalitarian states. "Love of neighbor" cannot be achieved in states that glorify some limited portion of humanity, like the state (Italy), the race (Germany), or the proletariat (Russia). One must love the entire human race, without subdivision. Furthermore, you cannot love your neighbor if you are not made in the image of God but of the state.[88]

Temple spoke for many when he asserted that the only remedy for fascism is true religion; the only remedy for Hitler is Jesus Christ. Hitler's "leadership principle" is perfectly sound psychologically. "If we are to build up a community characterised by goodwill, it must be a community which has found as its leader someone who is Himself the incarnation of Goodwill. Leaders like Hitler know how to win a whole-hearted response by appeal to what is best and worst in human nature in service to the same cause, but Christ will appeal only to our best nature."[89]

Few doubted that Nazism would eventually fall. Landau predicted, "The Brown Paradise and with it its creator will disintegrate into nothingness. They will remain no more than the dark memory of a nightmare: a nightmare filled with more suffering, more corpses, and more injustice than the world has ever known before. And yet not a reality. Merely a nightmare."[90]

Davies always kept things in the proper providential context. God is doing with fascism exactly what He did with the Cross—diverting man's evil to the support of His eternal kingdom. Do not miss the point: It is our *sin* God is using, not our righteousness. If you can attain to this insight you will never hate the enemy, for he too is God's instrument. "The God who could turn the evil of the Cross into the means of man's redemption will not be at a loss in dealing with the sin of Hitlerism."[91]

NOTES

1. *The Hope of a New World* (London: SCM Press, 1940), 27.

2. *The Theology of Politics* (London: Oxford University Press, 1941), 22. The Italians themselves showed concern over the radical nature of Nazism, especially its anti-Christian leanings. In December 1942, an issue of *Gararchia*, a monthly review founded by Mussolini, carried an article entitled "Religious Life in the New Europe" by Francesco Orestano. In very careful, high-sounding language, the author rendered an Italian rebuke to the strange direction that Nazism had taken spiritually. See *Spiritual Issues of the War* 169 (28 January 1943): 4.

3. *We Have Seen Evil: A Background to War* (London: Faber & Faber, 1941), 162.

4. *Diplomacy and God* (London: Longmans, Green, 1941), 43, 151.

5. See Rudolf Olden, *Is Germany a Hopeless Case?* Tr. Edwyn Bevan (London: Allen & Unwin, 1940), 10. Olden cited a young female political science graduate as saying, "Exterminate them!"

6. T. E. Jessop, *The Treaty of Versailles: Was It Just?* (London: Nelson, 1942), 53; Phyllis Bottome, *Our New Order or Hitler's?* (Harmondsworth, England: Penguin, 1943), 86. Temple received a pamphlet which said, "No decent person can nowadays believe that the majority of the German people are still human beings" (*William Temple Papers* 51: 135).

7. Paton, *The Church and the New Order* (London: SCM Press, 1941), 93; Davies, *Secular Illusion or Christian Realism?* (London: Eyre & Spottiswoode), 119; Landau, *We Have Seen Evil*, 66; Belloc, *The Catholic and the War* (London: Burnes and Oates, 1940), 31; Zimmern, *Spiritual Values and World Affairs* (Oxford: Clarendon, 1939), 95.

8. Davies, *The Two Humanities: An Attempt at a Christian Interpretation of History in the Light of War* (London: Clarke, 1940), 126; Temple, *Citizen and Churchman* (London: Eyre & Spottiswoode, 1941), 10; Zimmern, *Spiritual Values*, 20; Dunning, *Settlement with Germany* (London: SCM Press, 1943), 89. See also John Hadham, *God in a World at War* (Harmondsworth, England: Penguin, 1944), 50.

9. *Our War Aims* (London: Secker & Warburg, 1939), 84.

10. *Ministry of Morale: Home Front Morale and the Ministry of Information in World War II* (London: Allen & Unwin, 1979), 159.

11. *The Everlasting Man* (Garden City, N.Y.: Doubleday, 1926), 140.

12. *Europe's Catastrophe and the Christian Faith* (London: Nisbet, 1940), 12.

13. *Faith for Living* (London: Secker & Warburg, 1941, 36.

14. *Faith in Dark Ages* (London: SCM Press, 1944), 24.

15. *The Religious Prospect* (London: Muller, 1939), 122.

16. *A Sword Is Sharpened* (London: Marshall, Moran, & Scott, 1941), 145, 147.

17. The clergy made good use of some of the books written on Nazism in the 1930s, such as Nathaniel Micklem, *National Socialism and the Roman Catholic Church* (London: Oxford University Press, 1939), *Theology of Politics*, and *Europe's Own Book* (London: Morrison & Gibb, 1944); Henry P. van Dusen, *What Is the Church Doing?*; and Mario Bendiscioli, *Nazism versus Christianity*, tr. Gerald Griffin (London: Skeffington, 1939) and *The New Racial Paganism*, tr. George Smith (London: Burns, Oates, & Washbourne, 1939).

18. Quoted in van Dusen, *What Is the Church Doing?*, 25; and Fulton J. Sheen, *Philosophies at War* (London: Blanford, 1945), 123. The translations are slightly different in these two accounts. For a good translation of some of Rosenberg's major works, see *Alfred Rosenberg: Selected Writings*, ed. R. A. Pois (London: Cape, 1970).

19. Quoted in Micklem, *National Socialism*, 185.

20. *Religious News Bulletin* 20 (9 March 1940): 2.

21. *Theology of Politics*, 33; *National Socialism*, 175.

22. Micklem, *Theology of Politics*, xii.

23. Micklem, *National Socialism*, 193.

24. Micklem, *Europe's Own Book*, 42; *Spiritual Issues of the War* 97 (13 April 1940): 1.

25. *Spiritual Issues of the War* 110 (11 December 1941): 1–2.

26. *The Ten Commandments in the 20th Century* (Westminster: SPCK, 1941), 36.

27. Sidney M. Berry, *The Great Issue and Other War-Time Studies* (London: Independent Press, 1941), 9; Barry, *Faith in Dark Ages*, 29; Leo, *Give Christ a Chance* (London: Drakers, 1941), 7; Hadham, *God in a World at War*, 52; Paton, *The Church and the New Order*, 32.

28. See Bendiscioli, *The New Racial Paganism*, 2–4; Micklem, *National Socialism*, 19–21. For the same view of Christianity, see the essay by Martin Bormann written in 1944, reprinted in George L. Mosse, *Nazi Culture: Intellectual, Cultural and Social Life in the Third Reich* (New York: Schocken, 1981), 244–247. Hitler attempted to recall all copies of this essay when it first appeared but was unsuccessful.

29. *The Religious Prospect*, 68, 106–107.

30. "Our Propaganda to Germany—The Spiritual Note," *Spiritual Issues of the War* 88 (10 July 1941): 3.

31. *The New Racial Paganism*, 68–69, 72; see also Alec R. Vidler, *God's Judgment on Europe* (London: Longmans, Green, 1940), 73.

32. *Our War Aims*, 112.

33. *Settlement with Germany*, 41.

34. Cited in *Spiritual Issues of the War* 63 (16 January 1941): 3.

35. *Intellectual Liberty and Totalitarian Claims* (Oxford: Clarendon, 1942), 12–13. This book was a publicaton of the Romanes Lecture, delivered in Rhodes House, 12 June 1942.

36. *As Man to Man: Broadcast Talks to the Forces* (London: Mowbray, 1940), 46.

37. These remarks were broadcast to the United States in the summer of 1940 in a series entitled, "The Spiritual Issues of the War." See *Weekly Bulletin on the Spiritual Issues of the War* 45 (5 September 1940): 3.

38. See A. J. Hoover, *Friedrich Nietzsche: His Life and Thought* (New York: Praeger, 1994), 121–123.

39. *Philosophies at War*, 41, 120.

40. Dorothy L. Sayers, *Begin Here: A War-Time Essay* (London: Gollancz, 1940), 90–91; John Armitage, *To Christian England* (London: Longmans, Green, 1942), 82; Temple, *Hope of a New World*, 76.

41. Belloc, *The Catholic and the War*, 27; Matthews, *Moral Issues of the War* (London: Eyre & Spottiswoode, 1942), 19; Henson, *The Good Fight* (London: Nisbet, 1940), 21; Mumford, *Men Must Act* (London: Secker & Warburg, 1939), 40.

42. Davidson, *A Sword is Sharpened*, 50–51; *Spiritual Issues of the War* 79 (8 May 1941): 2. See also 103 (23 October 1941): 4, where an article from *Der Schwarze Korps* (25 September 1941) refers to "the everlasting bloodstream, which must not be betrayed" as the magic guide for ethical conduct.

43. Walter C. Langer, *The Mind of Adolf Hitler: The Secret Wartime Report* (New York: Basic Books, 1972), 190.

44. *The Bible Speaks to Our Day* (London: SCM Press, 1941), 13–14.

45. *Theology of Politics*, 4.

46. Ibid., 59–60; see also *Europe's Own Book*, 33–34.

47. *Personal Religion and the Future of Europe* (London: SCM Press, 1941), 42, 50–51.

48. Mumford, *Faith for Living*, 138; Sheen, *Philosophies at War*, 107; Davidson, *A Sword Is Sharpened*, 93.

49. Mumford, *Men Must Act*, 198; Demant, *Religious Prospect*, 95; Niebuhr, *Europe's Catastrophe*, 18–19; Vidler, *God's Judgment on Europe*, 73.

50. *Two Humanities*, 44.

51. *The Menace to Faith* (London: Oxford University Press, 1940), 11. See also Rom Landau, *Hitler's Paradise* (London: Faber & Faber, 1941), 41; Bendiscioli, *New Racial Paganism*, 6.

52. See Barth's article, "The Protestant Churches in Europe," *Foreign Affairs* 21:2 (January 1943): 262–263.

53. Carpenter, *Faith in Time of War* (London: Eyre & Spottiswoode, 1940), 44; Sayers, *Begin Here*, 38, 116, 119.

54. *Thinking Aloud in Wartime: An Attempt to See the Present Situation in the Light of the Christian Faith* (London: Hodder & Stoughton, 1939), 105.

55. Davies, *Two Humanities*, 28; Inge, *A Pacifist in Trouble* (London: Putnam, 1939), 41; Rabbi Lehrmann is quoted in *Spiritual Issues of the War* 71 (13 March 1941): 4.

56. William W. Simpson, *Jews and Christians To-day: A Study in Jewish and Christian Relationship* (London: Epworth, 1940), 11–12.

57. Matthews, *Foundations of Peace* (London: Eyre & Spottiswoode, 1942), 85; Vann, *Religion and World Order* (Westminster, England: Dacre, 1945), 6; Dunning, *Settlement with Germany*, 46–47; Temple, *Citizen and Churchman*, 92; Green, *Forty Short Prayers for War-Time Based on Passages from the Holy Scriptures* (London: Hodder & Stoughton, 1943), 25.

58. *Lang Papers* 320: 50–53.

59. *Idea of a Christian Society* (New York: Harcourt Brace, 1940), 54.

60. Rosenberg's remarks are noted by Bendiscioli in *New Racial Paganism*, 4, and in *Nazism versus Christianity*, 81. Also see Micklem, *National Socialism*, 19; Landau, *We Have Seen Evil*, 74; Demant, *Religious Prospect*, 104.

61. Foreword to "Germany's National Religion," *Friends of Europe* 13, a series of small booklets studying the pagan theology of the Third Reich. Volume 50 was entitled, "Getting Rid of Jesus Christ," an examination of the strange theology of Matilde Ludendorff. Several Roman Catholic scholars looked at Rosenberg's *Myth* in Volume 27, "Rosenberg's Positive Christianity."

62. *Begin Here*, 140–141.

63. Matthews, *Foundations of Peace*, 52; Hadham, *God in a World at War*, 42, 73.

64. Dunning, *Settlement with Germany*, 32, 78.

65. *Jews after the War*, reprinted from *The Nation* (21 February 1942), (New York: American Palestine Committee, 1942), 6–8.

66. For good studies of totalitarianism see Hanna Arendt, *The Origins of Totalitarianism*, 2d ed. (London: Allen & Unwin, 1957); William Ebenstein, *Totalitarianism* (New York: American Jewish Committee, 1962); Norman Cohn, *The Pursuit of the Millenium* (London: Temple Smith, 1957).

67. *Spiritual Issues of the War* 103 (23 October 1941): 1.

68. Temple, *Citizen and Churchman*, 5, 73; Demant, *Religious Prospect*, 38; Macnutt, *Four Freedoms: Atlantic and Christian* (Leicester, England: Thornley, 1943), 32.

69. Temple, *Christianity as an Interpretation of History* (London: Longmans, Green, 1944), 12.

70. Micklem, *National Socialism*, 231; Paton, *The Church and the New Order*, 156. See also the *Sword of the Spirit* entries, "Nazism and the Family" and "Catholics under the Swastika," preserved in *Lang Papers* 84: 350–352.

71. Sayers, *Begin Here*, 121; Micklem, *Theology of Politics*, 35.

72. Stewart, *Personal Religion and the Future of Europe* (London: SCM Press, 1941), 73; Vann, *Morality and War* (London: Burns, Oates, & Washbourne), 68; Kirk, *The Menace to Faith*, 5.

73. Carpenter, *Faith in Time of War*, 61; Kirk, *Menace to Faith*, 12.

74. Matthews, *Foundations of Peace*, 22–23; Murry, *Christocracy*, 64; Davies, *Two Humanities*, 127.

75. *Lang Papers* 77: 125, clause 4; 88: 327–329, 341; *William Temple Papers* 58: 391–398.

76. Butterfield, *Christianity and History* (London: Bell, 1949), 104; Vidler, *God's Judgment on Europe*, 19.

77. Davidson, *A Sword Is Sharpened*, 104; Matthews, *Foundations of Peace*, 33; Davies, *Two Humanities*, 149.

78. Thomas Moloney, *Westminster, Whitehall and the Vatican: The Role of Cardinal Hinsley, 1935–43* (Burnbridge Well, Kent, England: Burns & Oates, 1985), 58–60.

79. Ibid., 59.

80. Hinsley, *Sword of the Spirit*, BBC Home Service, Sunday, 10 December 1939: 6–7.

81. Moloney, *Westminster, Whitehall*, 134.

82. Eric Waldram Kemp, *Life and Letters of Kenneth Escot Kirk, Bishop of Oxford, 1937–1954* (London: Hodder & Stoughton, 1959), 83.

83. *Sword of the Spirit*, BBC Home Service, Sunday, 10 December 1939: 3–4.

84. Moloney, *Westminster, Whitehall*, 142, 147, 172, 178.

85. *Settlement with Germany*, 84.

86. *Real Life Is Meeting* (London: Sheldon Press, 1942), 17.

87. Sheen, *Philosophies at War*, 106.

88. Vann, *Morality and War*, 15. "Nazis or Neighbours" is preserved in *Lang Papers* 84: 358.

89. "The Religious Quality of Great Political Questions," in *Our New Order or Hitler's?* ed. Phyllis Bottome, 21–22; *The Hope of a New World*, 112–113.

90. *Hitler's Paradise*, 62.

91. *Two Humanities*, 20. The philosopher C.E.M. Joad wrote a critique of Nazism very similar to that analyzed in this chapter. See "Sketch of the Nazi Tradition," Ch. 6 of C.E.M. Joad, *What Is at Stake and Why Not Say So?* (London: Gollancz, 1940), 69–91.

CHAPTER 5

The Decline and Fall of Liberal Humanism

Defending a just war requires hard thinking. If your side is right and the other wrong, there must be some criterion by which to judge. This must be a moral universe where truth and right are somehow grounded in the substance of eternal reality. If truth exists, then doctrines, dogmas, and ideas are important. If ideas are important, then it is supremely puerile to say, "It doesn't matter what you believe." Ideas have consequences. Fulton J. Sheen quipped, "It makes a war of difference what you believe." Richard Brook, bishop of St. Edmundsbury and Ipswich, said, "In the light of what has happened in Nazi Germany no thinking person will ever again say that it does not matter what a man believes."[1] Just a few days before Pearl Harbor, Lewis Mumford wrote to Frederic Osborn,

If this war has done nothing else, it has shaken all our complacencies. It has disclosed the weak points in our daily routine, and it has made us conscious of weaknesses that might have been fatal to us, if we had not been challenged by an outside power. The fact that each nation has shown the same blindness and has made the same mistakes, makes it plain that our common scheme of life was somewhat at fault. It may still be necessary for us in America to suffer some terrible reverse, like that you met at Dunkirk, before we face the real facts on the world situation and throw ourselves into the conflict with all our might and main. The one thing that I dread, to speak frankly, is a peace participated in by an unawakened and unchastened U.S.[2]

The crisis of fascism and World War II caused many British intellectuals and clerics to rethink their philosophical, theological, and historical positions. They tended to agree with Mumford that there was something amiss in "our common scheme of life." The general theme was the defeat of humanism and the recovery of religion; the stone the builders rejected turned out to be the chief cornerstone (Ps. 118:22). Those who had been "soft on humanism" discovered their error, and those who had always been "hard" rejoiced in the historical confirmation of their position. Many concluded that they had been poor observers of the drift of Western thought all along; their Christian culture was changing under their noses, and they did not notice it. Gerald Vann wrote, "The change from a predominately Christian to a predominantly pagan structure of society has been a slow process; and its slowness tends to make us overlook the fact that it is radical."[3]

MISTAKES OF LIBERAL HUMANISM

Humanism had a strong tendency toward naturalism or materialism. Its universe had only one story—the lower one; anything beyond the physical or empirical world was suspect. The first thing recovered from the fall of humanism, therefore, was God Himself, or the idea of the holy, the sense of religion, or the notion of the spiritual or supernatural. This meant a defeat for materialism, positivism, and scientism—the worldview that says all is matter, science alone produces truth, and science cannot study immaterial things, so they do not exist. This empirical prejudice is not difficult to refute. One of the most obvious phenomena in history is "human purpose," but, as Dorothy L. Sayers noted, science can no more investigate purpose than a microscope can investigate color. Lewis Mumford charged that this empirical bias is why science tends to neglect fields like aesthetics, ethics, and religion. Humanists treated such "subjective" areas of experience as if they would eventually drop out of existence, "mere vestiges of the race's childhood." Sheen thought it significant that before the war, Germany was the most scientific nation in the world. By making science an ultimate we have "deprived ourselves of a criterion by which to judge our cause from theirs." William Ralph Inge contested the old saw that science deals with facts in abstraction from values by noting that "science is wholly devoted to the service of Truth which is one of the ultimate values." Douglas Stewart pointed to the second law of thermodynamics as undermining any belief in salvation through science: "Science cannot promise the race on this planet anything except eventual annihilation, so that if hope in a perfect historical order be pushed far enough it must change into despair as it envisages the onset of eternal night and death throughout the Universe." A. Price Hughes did not mince words when describing the arrogant humanists:

There are stupid people within our communities, arrogating to themselves the intellectual leadership of the world, who have neither faith in God nor hope for man. They boast of their unbelief, as though it were a cause of virtue and secret of strength. . . . No man can lead others to fine things in virtue of his doubts. . . . Many would-be leaders have no faith to offer and no hope to inspire. They think that faith in God is a silly, sentimental survival of an unscientific age. It is time we told plain truths to these materialistic philosophers. They are full of their own emptiness, and they invite us to share in their poverty.[4]

On the night of 14 November 1940, the German Luftwaffe sent 439 airplanes against the city of Coventry. Over 500 tons of high explosive bombs, 50 land mines, and 30,000 incendiaries were dropped, decimating the heart of the city. The city's beautiful cathedral was practically annihilated. A materialist would argue that if the body is gone, everything is gone. But on the Sunday after the bombing the Holy Communion was celebrated in the Provost's drawing room in order that the cathedral tradition of worship might not be broken. Afterward, members of the congregation gathered in the ruins of the building and joined in prayers, as the clock in the tower still standing struck eleven o'clock, the hour of morning worship. Provost R. T. Howard said the appropriate words: "They may have destroyed our Cathedral but they have not destroyed the spirit it represents. When the war is over we will build another where the spirit will dwell."[5]

Materialism, positivism, and scientism usually exist in the same philosophical matrix as "rationalism," which could be defined as the worship of the human intellect. Rationalism is not the same as a proper emphasis on reason, which the Christian faith has always honored. In Sheen's words, "Rationalism . . . glorifies human reason by detaching it from the eternal reason of God." The rationalist thus cuts himself off from God and sings the hymn of Swinburne, "Glory to man in the highest! For man is the master of things." He repeats the old Greek fallacy and says that "knowledge is virtue." But the truth is otherwise; knowledge does not automatically produce ethical behavior. "The essential error in all modern interpretations of human nature," said Reinhold Niebuhr, "is to regard man's reason as essentially good and to think of it as a force which gradually extricates him out of the limitations of nature, and the parochialism and prejudice of time and place and sets him 'upon a rock' of the eternal and unchangeable truth."[6]

Like scientism, rationalism has a bias against certain realities, which means that modern intellectuals work themselves into a strange state of stupidity. George Glasgow noted that the "pure intellectual is nearly always wrong in his judgment of future probability, no matter how deeply fortified his judgment may be by knowledge of worldly facts. There are tramps who read no books, whose interpretations of what is at present taking place rings truer than that of learned peoples, as those who talk to tramps discover for themselves." Mumford maintained that the instincts of simple people in the present crisis had been sounder than the instincts of intellectuals: "My neighbors are not subtle enough to be as stupid as some of my more sophisticated friends. They still know enough to draw their hands away from a hot fire."[7]

Liberal rationalists are incapable of understanding the irrational in history. Leo gave a fine example in Sir Norman Angell's book, *The Great Illusion*, an indictment of war that came out in 1910 and went into a second edition in 1933. Angell attempted to refute the belief that war and conquest brought a nation great economic advantage and insured its living space and access to markets, trade, and raw materials. In the end, war is not cost-effective—it is financially foolish. But nations go to war anyway, for honor, glory, excitement, and other motives besides profit.

Mumford used the illustration of slavery. Reason could not talk the southerners out of their slaves—it finally took force. Lincoln trying to persuade slaveowners reminds one of Chamberlain trying to appease the fascist dictators. Those who say slavery would have gradually died out for economic reasons have a poor understanding of human nature; have they never seen someone hold onto something in spite of monetary loss? Liberals always think that evil is to be combated only with intellectual tools like persuasion. If they refuse to use anything beyond persuasion, they resemble the doctor who refused to operate on his patient with a knife to save him, because the diet he proposed did not work.[8]

Matthews remembered how the shallow intellectuals ridiculed love of country and displayed a "snobbish antipatriotism" during the 1930s. When the war came, however, all that snobbery mysteriously vanished. "Though we could not define very clearly what we meant, we knew that we loved the country with a love which is beyond reason. It is, in fact, deeper than any conscious reason. It grows out of the collective unconscious and is the outcome of the experience of many generations." Ideas which are also forces are the ones that "crystallize the deep and largely unconscious tendencies of the instinctive nature."[9]

Britain was fortunate to have a leader during the war who was more than a pure rationalistic intellectual. Winston Churchill, with all his faults, did have an integrated personality—a persona balanced between reason, will, and emotion. His behavior disturbed the cool Lord Halifax, who thought him very much like Hitler—romantic, intuitive, blustering, theatrical, and given to hyperbole. Yet Halifax's recent biographer, Andrew Roberts, says that Churchill's instincts proved correct in 1940. In seeking for a truce with Hitler after the fall of France, Halifax "attempted to bring logic and reason to a problem long since devoid of either. A truce would only have led to another conflagration, probably within the decade and with a Germany in possession of radar, rockets and possibly even nuclear weaponry."[10]

Scientific, humanistic rationalists usually stress education as the key to progress in civilization. Implant the growing mind with right ideas, and the future will be bright. If knowledge is virtue, then education will produce virtuous behavior. D. R. Davies jeered this optimism; writing during the Blitz he said, "We are experiencing not only a black-out of our towns, cities and villages, but also a black-out of a whole faith and philosophy and civilization. . . . The dream of Humanism has turned into the nightmare of Nazism." Stewart said that no amount of rational education would help us understand the big problem of the time: evil. The bad will is the problem and all the conferences in the world will not eradicate it. How comical that the school was liberated from the Church at the behest of the rationalists and then promptly enslaved by the state, that great guardian of truth and objectivity! The Nazis and the Communists had proved how unobjective the state can be in the classroom. An age that worshiped "enlightenment" has seen its greatest thinkers driven into exile by a half-educated fanatic preaching an irrational racism.[11]

J. H. Oldham questioned one of the most sacred cows of humanistic education: freedom of speech. Good liberals have been taught that all views should be aired because "the truth will out" in the long run—who are we to claim that our version of things is the only valid one? Views, like individuals, should have "equal rights." The success of Goebbel's propaganda machine in Germany would cause one to wonder if the truth will always out. Oldham issued this serious caveat: "When the basis of society is threatened, it is not possible to treat all views as having equal rights. A decision becomes necessary. Society is forced to make clear to itself its purposes and aims. It must consciously choose the values by which its life will be governed; and it must deliberately set itself to instil in the rising generation belief in these values and to encourage conduct that accords with them. . . . Education needs a unifying conception to direct it; without an integrating purpose it cannot achieve its ends."[12]

Humanism foolishly flirts with a flux ontology, the notion that everything is constantly changing. Hilaire Belloc called this view "great rubbish" and threw the magisterial Roman Catholic tradition of Thomism squarely against it. Following Hegel, he noted, such half-wits say God is not, but he is becoming—in such a mad scheme absolute right and wrong disappear. Only we Catholics, he asserted, "possess a system of philosophy which corresponds exactly to the known facts of human life, and explains that life and informs it." And why do Catholics enjoy this advantage? Because "we attach particular and sacred value to truth, that is, to reality as it is discovered by the human reason which we regard as the great gift of God to Man: the gift whereby Man resembles his Creator."[13]

A flux ontology arises out of the theory of evolution, or, more accurately, out of a "total" theory of evolution, whereby change and becoming are posited as the essence of Being. Now it is impossible to define a constantly changing entity; so, as Demant noted, this scheme is a species of irrationalism. Furthermore, it denies the doctrine of the Fall and says that perfection of being is something to be realized within the cosmic process of becoming itself. A significant fact must be carefully noted here: *Both liberalism and totalitarianism accepted this flux ontology*. Liberal humanists are just as wedded to total evolution as the fascists; both accept the biological interpretation of reality, but the fascists are far more consistent and radical in their interpretation. As Demant says, fascism is "a more vigorous embodiment of the ideal of Becoming."

Liberals made a big mistake when they denied absolutes and swallowed whole the doctrine of evolutionary becoming. The doctrine they wanted to defend—personal dignity and freedom—was defeated by the more deliberate and thorough incarnations of becoming. If the temporal is the only dimension, then the individual loses value against the society and state. Put simply, survival of the fittest drove out the liberal principle of equality. Liberals stupidly regarded any theory of becoming as an ally. As it turned out, a hard interpretation of evolution destroyed the cardinal liberal principles.[14]

Stewart also gave some salutary warnings about the simplistic use of the theory of evolution. Fascism has shown how dangerous it is to apply evolution to history, because there is a moral problem in history but not in biology. "No theory worked out in the animal world, however much light it may and does shed upon the origins and physical characteristics of man, can tell us anything about man's moral life." Since man's moral and intellectual nature marks him off from the rest of creation, it is a profound fallacy to apply to history, without great alteration, laws and principles which appear adequate in other sciences.[15]

The liberal utopian view of progress falls when humanism falls. Clergymen like Davies marveled that some thinkers were still unrepentant after the storm of fascism had swept through the Western philosophical house. In their shallow thinking they were still looking for a "brave new world" after the war—a world of universal enlightenment, love, leisure, prosperity, and peace. They must have been asleep since 1933. Stewart said, "The last thing the nineteenth century Liberal Idealist could have envisaged would be the actual history of the twentieth century." Niebuhr tried to show that even though genuine progress comes in science, technology, and culture, such progress never guarantees a final victory of good over evil, cosmos over anarchy, or justice over injustice. Every advance creates a more complicated realm of order, which is subject to quicker dislocation than simpler forms of life. Each new level of order is more precarious and tentative than the previous level. The Biblical conception of history as "moving toward the revelation of both Christ and anti-Christ" is a better description of the historical process than "the simple Utopian dreams of our contemporary culture."[16]

When liberal humanism falls, original sin makes a comeback. Nathaniel Micklem observed correctly that "no doctrine proclaimed by the Church is so unpopular as original sin; people greatly resent being told that they are all miserable sinners." Martyn Lloyd-Jones said it is no wonder that Christianity is ridiculed by moderns: "If the Christian doctrine of sin is right and true then the very basis of the modern doctrine of man is entirely destroyed." The enormity of the volte-face is evident when you hear the Anglican Davies praising Calvin! "Calvin is much more adequate to our situation than Condorcet or Rousseau. Our world is underlining the great word of the Bible about man—that he is accursed by some abysmal, radical, inaccessible powerlessness."[17]

Lloyd-Jones uttered the argument found in hundreds of sermons and on millions of lips: *"After Adolf Hitler, can you ever again doubt that evil ex-*

ists?" Mumford claimed that "the sinful men and women in the pages of Tolstoy, Zola, or Proust seem virtually angels alongside the sub-men than Nazism has fashioned." Inge said that liberalism made a big mistake when it got rid of evil and the devil, even though it was a humiliation for the philosophers; recent events were clearly an outbreak of "real Satanism."[18]

Liberal humanists make light of sin and evil. They say sin is just the legacy of evolution. We must "work out the tiger" in us; every day in every way we are getting better and better. But this cannot explain human behavior; there is nothing comparable in animal instincts to evil and irrationality in humanity. There is no sin in the animal kingdom; sin enters the world with reason and consciousness. Liberals had ignored the difference of man. History has a way of rubbing man's nose into the obvious that he has ignored. To think that graham flour, good food, vitamins, straight teeth, or adequate housing would finally solve man's problem of sin is ludicrous. You can give him all these and the poor creature still sins! When a supremely evil man like Hitler comes along, the liberal has no capacity to interpret him; he just calls him "mentally immature." Both the Greeks and the Hebrews had a myth of the primal rebellion, but they interpreted it in different ways. The Greeks viewed Prometheus as a hero for stealing fire from Zeus and bringing it down to man, but the Hebrews saw a great tragedy when Adam and Eve disobeyed the clear command of God. In a sense, then, the humanists follow the Greeks, and the Christians follow the Hebrews.[19]

The history of humanism showed the folly of separating ethics and theology. Humanists blithely assumed that the law of love and other Christian ethical principles would survive the demise of the historical Christian faith. They jettisoned the Bible, Christ, and God and shifted to a materialistic naturalism they then expected nothing to change ethically, not realizing they had destroyed the foundation of moral philosophy. The French philosopher Voltaire once removed his hat as a large religious procession passed by. His friend expostulated in amazement, but Voltaire said, "We salute but we do not speak." That is, religion becomes the viewpoint of the mere bystander, the spectator who questions and discusses but never takes a real stand for anything. The adjective "Christian" comes to mean "civilized" in a vague, harmless sense—something that a "gentleman" would follow, a sad watering down of its original meaning.

Stewart put his finger squarely on the problem. Why do people think Christian altruism is self-evident and needs no proof? "It is because for centuries England has been steeped in the Christian tradition." When Christian ideas become a habit, then later generations conclude that they got them by reason, not revelation. We say we want the Christian ethic without the Christian faith, but there is no such independent, self-evident morality. Stewart took this story from Plato's *Republic*: the crew of a certain ship decided that the pilot was mad because he kept looking at the stars so much, whereas everyone knows that ships sail on water. The crew did not realize that for navigation you must have a fixed point beyond the relativities of wind and wave, a point that will guide your true course.[20]

Churchmen and Christian thinkers insisted, therefore, that the famous "values" of Christianity are dependent on Christian theology. You cannot have the fruit of Christian altruism without the root of Christian theology. Demant insisted that "failure awaits all forms of religion which confine themselves to the level of ethics . . . without power released by dogmatic assurance moral aims become debilitating fantasies." Rosalind Murray said that in the pagan civilization we have developed, there is no "quality control. Human opinion is acknowledged as final and there is no other law to test it." Stewart agreed: "The great Christian heritage is being squandered by millions of obscure individuals who live on derived traditions, and have in themselves no root of faith." Lloyd-Jones insisted that "religion must precede morality if morality itself is to survive." Sayers said we have changed the Scriptural order of the commandments—love God and love your neighbor—to simply love your neighbor. But the second commandment depends on the first, and "without the first, it is a delusion and a snare."[21]

In sum, there can be no brotherhood of man without the fatherhood of God. Christian love is not self-evident; it depends on the Christian faith.

LIBERAL HUMANISM AND PACIFISM

Prime Minister Chamberlain, like the good liberal he was, worked very hard in the years of 1938 and 1939 to keep the peace in Europe. His hopes led him to employ the policy of appeasement with the German dictator. It is always good to remember that "appeasement" was not a pejorative term when the policy first started. Chamberlain honestly felt that he could reason with Hitler. When he came home from the Munich Conference with an agreement in hand, people hailed him as the savior of peace and linked his name with that of Jesus Christ. But when Hitler broke his promise the next year and seized the rump of Czechoslovakia, the scales began to fall from their eyes. Finally, when Germany attacked Poland and unleashed the war, Chamberlain said, "It is evil things we are fighting." Why did it take this decent man so long to see that Hitler was evil? Many people asked the same question of themselves: "Why did it take *me* so long?"

Most Christians answered this question by pointing to the *Zeitgeist*, the spirit of the times between the wars. Liberal humanism with its misguided optimism blinded the eyes of millions of Britons during the 1920s and 1930s. Alec R. Vidler says that liberalism had its zenith in the nineteenth century. It got a blow in 1914 from which it never recovered, yet it enjoyed a sort of Indian summer from 1919 to 1939. Expiring systems of thought often shout the loudest. Davies said, "The brief and troubled peace of 1918 to 1939 is a grim and lurid commentary on the Liberal doctrine of progress." E. G. Rupp noted that many people were born in the war years of 1914 to 1918 who had been taught as a matter of gospel that war was done with, that world disarmament would soon be accomplished, that narrow nationalism would be swallowed up in a broad internationalism, and that the League of Nations would be the focus and frame of the whole wonderful arrangement. During that time, wrote Micklem, the Church of England made the mistake of pinning all its hopes on the League of Nations. When the League went down, the Church lost a great deal of its political influence.[22]

During this Indian summer of liberalism, pacifism was taken for granted by millions of people; it needed no proof, it was self-evident. People looked to the League as if it possessed some kind of strange magical power to end war forever. The history section of Arthur Mee's *Children's Encyclopaedia* (1925) was called "The March of Man from the Age of Barbarism to the League of Nations." Britons forgot that the League Covenant, far from abolishing war, laid down clear rules on how a war would be waged against an aggressor nation. John Hadham looked back over this strange period and said, "We neither trusted God nor kept our powder dry." Alfred Zimmern related that at the 1937 Oxford Conference on the Church, in the Commission on International Relations, a backbench member said, "Give me a clear ringing message that I can take back to my congregation—a message that will make them feel that world peace is on the way!"[23] We note the typical liberal attitude: everything is possible, because evil will yield to the efforts of good will and moral determination.

Zimmern, Montague Burton Professor of International Relations, Oxford, blamed Christian ministers for weakening the British national will in the contest with the dictators. He spoke kindly of true Quakers, but distinguished them sharply from pseudo-Quakers or wartime Quakers—pacifists who "claimed to have arrived at the Quaker position, but without the aid of the inner light." They were "a very mixed company, the flotsam and jetsam of the period of intellectual confusion and spiritual disintegration through which we are passing." They have "beguiled British public opinion and, by so doing, have brought shame upon our country and let loose a flood of suffering and evil upon the world."[24]

T. E. Jessop marveled at the effect that pacifism produced at such a critical juncture of world history: "The conviction that Britain would not, in any circumstances, face the prospect of war, has been one of the most powerful factors in international politics in the last ten years or so; it determined the attitude of France as much as that of Germany." He marveled also at how anyone could call this stance Christian: "It is incredible to me that a spirit that has shown itself so inept in the presence of obvious evil on an obviously large scale can fairly claim to be called Christian."[25]

Jessop wrote a book in 1942 entitled *The Treaty of Versailles: Was It Just?* to prove that the treaty of 1919 was not totally to blame for World War II, as many people thought. The Allies had made a lot of mistakes, true, but none bad enough to justify fascist aggression. German propaganda had been so effective that most Britons have come to take it for granted that the Allied treatment of Germany was "simply monstrous." Hitler skillfully exploited this guilt feeling in the 1930s. To judge the treaty by a standard of perfection is not idealism "but a mixture of stupidity and inhumanity."

Germans complained that the blockade, which did not end until 12 July 1919, killed many of their people, but this is hard to confirm since an influenza epidemic swept over Europe at the same time. Any fool could see the military justification of the blockade, reasoned Jessop, since Britain was obliged to retain any advantage she had to secure the peace. What most people do not realize is that Germany never really "surrendered"—they signed an armistice, which had to be renewed several times before the final treaty signing.

Germans complained that the treaty left two million Germans outside the Reich. This is a classic case of special pleading. The treaty liberated about thirty million minorities, leaving Europe with less than 1 percent of its peoples unfree, a smaller percentage than ever before. Moreover, in each treaty ending the war, the new states were required to give a formal pledge to respect the rights of minorities.

Jessop admitted that article 231, the infamous "war guilt clause," was tactless, done obviously to satisfy the jingo contingent. Actually the foolish clause was unnecessary, since the idea of reparations was already in the armistice. The demand for war crimes trials for the kaiser and other military leaders was also impractical. Not even the Weimar government could possibly be expected to turn over men like William II, Hindenburg, and Ludendorff.

Germans tried to appear innocent and persecuted, but the record shows that they were very tricky in the negotiations leading to the armistice of 11 November 1918. They offered to accept an armistice and work for a settlement based on the Fourteen Points of Woodrow Wilson, knowing that Britain and France could not oppose the move since they desperately needed the support of the United States. Thus the deal made it look as if the Germans had a moral right to be treated in accordance with the Fourteen Points, which had the effect of making the later treaty look like a breach of trust. The whole episode was "the last masterstroke of the dying Imperial Government." The Germans maneuvered the Allies into making promises they could not possibly keep and then fully exploited the putative breach of contract.

Jessop concluded that British public opinion on Versailles was not built on knowledge but induced by German propaganda. "The case of the Allies has been entirely submerged under the widely propagandized case of Germany, whose skill has consisted in convincing a public without an intellectual, and therefore with an imperfectly moral, conscience that only the German case deserves to be heard."[26]

Jessop predicted that when the history of the last few years comes to be written,

It will be noted that nearly all the imagination, skill, sacrificial effort, and boldness have been on the side of evil, while the good folk and the decent nations, relying too exclusively on their goodness and decency, lapsed into increasing futility. Men possessed by the crudest lust for power threw every ounce of their strength and brains into the pursuit of their ambition, while far better men did little more than shrink from accumulating horrors, hug their comfort, and say their prayers. The splendid efficiency of evil, the pathetic impotence of goodness—that has been the tragic contrast of our day.[27]

One is reminded of the prophetic lines of William Butler Yeats in his poem, "The Second Coming":

> The best lack all conviction, while the worst
> Are full of passionate intensity.

MODERNISM AND NAZI EXEGESIS

Humanism worms its way into all facets of life and thought. When it gets into theology it produces a special view of Scripture that theologians usually called liberalism or modernism. Modernists came in many sizes and shades but they usually had a weak view of revelation; the Bible was viewed not as a clear message from God but merely as a record of the religious experiences of the Jews. Thus the authority of Scripture was severely damaged; one could "pick and choose" from an incredible variety of ideas and principles in the Bible to customize his own personal theology. Religion became very pragmatic. One is reminded of Goethe's methodology: "With all the manifold facets of my being, one way of thinking is not sufficient for me; as a poet and artist I am a polytheist, but a pantheist as a student of Nature, and either belief I hold with equal determination. And if I need a divinity for my personal being, my moral existence—well, this need too is promptly cared for."[28]

When the Nazis took over Germany, they employed a crafty exegesis of the Bible to foster their own pagan religion. It was clear that they wanted to eventually eliminate Christianity from the Third Reich, but they fell into two schools on tactics: the radicals and the gradualists. The radicals said attack Christianity immediately and root it out quickly. The gradualists warned that Christianity was too deeply entrenched to eradicate immediately, especially in wartime when the loyalty of all citizens is needed. Better to change it slowly by blending it with German nationalism. Goebbels and his propaganda machine could accomplish that easily. One could see the two schools fighting it out on the German radio: The Christmas celebrations of 1940 and 1941 had no mention of Christ or Christianity, but in 1942, when the Reich was in trouble, they returned to the traditional yuletide program.[29] The Soviet Union also was compelled by the war to allow greater freedom for the Russian Orthodox Church, at least for the duration of the conflict. Stalin and his war planners concluded that the Russian people would not fight for Communism but they would fight for "Mother Russia"—a concept deeply embedded in traditional Russian religion.

The British followed developments in Germany as best they could in order to plot the Nazi attempt to "coordinate" Christianity and Hitlerism. For example, when the Germans produced a current translation of Christ's Sermon on the Mount, certain passages had a new rendering. "Blessed are the peacemakers" was changed to "Happy are they who keep peace with their fellow countrymen"—a clear perversion of the universalism in the context. The new translation cut out all references to Moses, the prophets, and anything Hebrew. Christ's injunctions against anger were limited to those who "abuse and persecute their fellow countrymen" and "thereby destroy the national fellowship."[30] In 1940 a new hymn book appeared for German Christians in which all Old Testament and Jewish names were removed. All references to Jerusalem or Zion were omitted. One could no longer shout "Hallelujah!" since that translated "Praise Ye Yahweh!"[31]

When it came to the Savior, Jesus Christ, the Nazi abuse of Scripture was especially repugnant. In the face of clear facts, Nazi theologians had the temerity to assert that Christ was not a Jew but an Aryan! The notorious Jew-baiter, Julius Streicher, maintained that there was no contradiction between National Socialism and Christianity. He pictured Jesus as a warrior, an unknown simple man like the Führer, who arose from the common people and called the masses to fight against Judaism. If you should protest that this picture of Jesus contradicted the four canonical gospels, you would be quickly reminded that higher criticism had long since destroyed the historicity of the early Christian sources. Micklem put the point well: "It is really possible that Herr Streicher genuinely supposes himself to represent true Christianity in distinction from the spurious variety offered by the Christian church; for, if Jesus Christ were not, and did not, that which the Gospels and the Church catholic have always said that He was and did, then perhaps Herr Streicher's reconstruction is as good as another man's. This is the nemesis of theological 'Liberalism.'"[32]

Mario Bendiscioli charged that Nazi theologians were merely carrying out what they had learned from their German university professors like Adolf Harnack, who twenty years earlier had declared it "unreasonable" for Christians to retain the Old Testament as a sacred book. Vidler said that the "German Christians" were precisely those Christians "whose theology had been so emptied of its traditional content by liberalism that it could without any sense of embarrassment accommodate the pagan theology of Nazism. They have rediscovered not the God who is Judge, but the God who is German." T. S. Eliot called the new German National Religion a "nationalistic unitarianism."[33]

The Vatican consistently contradicted the Nazi separation of Old and New Testaments. In 1941 Vatican Radio broadcasted a message into France which proclaimed, "The Church has always maintained that the New Testament grows organically out of the Old. Old and New Testament form together one supreme structure, elements of which cannot be wilfully removed without endangering the whole building."[34]

In the United States, Bishop Sheen predicted that American soldiers would see the light about Jesus on the battlefields and exclaim like Mary, "They have taken away my Lord and I don't know where they have laid him" (John 20:13).

"They will begin to realize that the intelligentsia robbed them of their greatest possession—faith. . . . And when they come marching home there will be a judgment on those who told them they had no soul; they will live like new men and they will give a rebirth of America under God."[35]

Christ laid down the rule that "by their fruits you will know them" (Matt. 7:16). The fruit of modernistic hermeneutics could be clearly seen in the tortured interpretations the Nazis made of the Bible. The Nazi distortions opened the eyes of many people, making them repudiate modernistic hermeneutics and dedicate themselves anew to the traditional respect for Scripture.

A CASE HISTORY: D. R. DAVIES

Some thinkers embody intellectual changes; their lives are like an ideological seismograph. One of the most loveable, intelligent, energetic, stimulating, and outspoken clerics in all England was D. R. Davies. His checkered career beautifully illustrated the thesis of the decline and fall of liberal humanism. Born in the Welsh mining village of Glamorgan, he grew up in poverty, but his strong-willed mother and crippled father kept alive the family's Christianity as well as a love for music and ideas. Davies matured without a personal experience of God but with a capacity for intense involvement in an ideal—the kind of person Lenin and Hitler loved to recruit. He was a miner, a tramp, a Unitarian theological student, a Congregational minister, and a popular Socialist speaker who identified himself completely with the miner's cause in the 1920s. In 1929 he resigned his ministry because he had pressed his beliefs to their logical conclusion—the separation of the Church and state.

In the early 1930s Davies became attracted to Marxist Socialism and worked in the Socialist League. His devotion to the secular utopia, however, was somewhat ambivalent. He read Niebuhr's *Reflections on the End of an Era*, and it shook his "humanist, self-sufficient hope of inevitable progress." Niebuhr also shook his Marxism; he said the American theologian was a divine who obviously knew his Marx and knew that Marxism badly underestimated original sin. The Russian Purge trials (1934–1938) disturbed his faith in the Soviet Union; he referred to "the satanic guilt of Stalin."[36]

A trip to Spain during the Civil War finally broke his back. It was like "shaking hands with death." At the same time his second marriage was plunging toward failure. "On my journey to Spain I possessed a dying faith. On my return I brought back a corpse. Within a few months, despair had made my life an insupportable burden." The war in Spain was presented by some as a civil war in defense of Christianity, but Temple rightly observed, "This is rubbish." The Spanish Civil War with its promiscuous bloodletting demonstrated to Davies the futility of all human striving:

I went to Spain a politician merely. I returned a theologian. Let the reader not mistake my meaning. In saying that I became a theologian, I do not lay claim to theological learning or scholarship. In that sense I never have been nor ever shall be a theologian.

What I mean is that the realization of an inner, personal need, beyond the power of social action to satisfy, displaced politics as the *supreme* issue in human existence. I might define theology as the science which deals with the fundamental personal need of the human being in all its variety of expression. . . . Social development and historic progress ceased to be the supreme end and value. Now it began to appear as an element in the drama of the personal soul.[37]

With his marriage and his socialist faith in shambles, Davies decided to commit suicide. He jumped into the sea, but then suddenly realized the enormity of what he was doing. In this crisis he found God, for the first time, and he also found himself. He decided to return to the only spiritual home he could imagine for himself, the Church of England. He was ordained by Archbishop William Temple in 1942 and spent many happy years until his death in 1958, preaching, writing, and performing pastoral duties. After the attempted suicide, he came to the conclusion that despair was a necessary element in the Christian experience. He compared himself with Paul, Augustine, Francis, and Kierkegaard: "I had but repeated the classic Christian discovery of all ages." After his wrenching conversion he felt resentful at modernism for "its vulgarization of the revolutionary new birth into a mere natural, psychological process. A generation which has been poisoned by this ghastly heresy finds it very, very difficult to realize the necessity of a revolutionary second birth for every human soul, and especially for themselves."[38]

After his conversion Davies reread Niebuhr's *Reflections* and then "devoured" all of his books. "I can never be sufficiently grateful to Reinhold Niebuhr," he wrote, "for what his books did for me. He fitted together the elements of my last ten years' experience. The more of him that I read the more clearly I came to see, not only the meaning of my own experience, but the meaning of European politics and indeed of European history."[39] From Niebuhr he went to the Bible and "drenched" himself in Scripture. It spoke to him as never before; he was clearly "open" to its message for the first time in his life. Commentaries are good but no commentary can beat sharing the same experience as the writer, for example, St. Paul in Romans 7. For the first time in his life he felt a great need to worship.

In all his books, Davies stressed original sin and the futility of human striving. He made effective use of Arnold Toynbee's massive *Study of History* in arguing the thesis that all human civilizations are just man's puny attempts to live without God. God made man free and loves man so much that He will not interfere with these efforts to construct godless cultures. He will let the human race play this farce out to the end. Toynbee showed that in three thousand years of human history, man has created twenty-one civilizations and then destroyed them all. The same will happen to Nazi Germany, Soviet Russia, and possibly to Great Britain. We must return to Augustine's *City of God* and learn to live our personal Christian lives within the Church and not worry too much about politics. "If existence is itself dust and ashes, what do Fascism, Communism, Socialism, New Orders, matter?"[40]

UNDERSTANDING CHURCH HISTORY

Historians can sometimes be caught saying that "every generation must rewrite history for itself." There is a very good reason for this: Your interpretation of the past changes with your experiences. A change in your political, philosophical, or theological perspective will cause a change in your estimation of certain episodes in history. If you convert from Christianity to Islam, this will obviously alter your estimation of both Mohammed and Christ. Many British clerics and intellectuals found that the decline and fall of humanism had altered their views on European history and the history of Christianity. As they looked back on the failed experiment of humanism, they reflected on that earlier experiment of the Middle Ages when the Roman Catholic Church tried to build a totalitarian Christian culture.

For the purposes of this discussion, we may say that the history of the Christian Church falls into three general periods:

1. *The early Church*. The Roman Empire was the only state form, and Christians were persecuted off and on but nevertheless grew in numbers, confident that they were "in the world but not of the world."

2. *From Constantine to the Reformation*. The Church becomes legal and gradually unfolds the great experiment of controlling the state, which brings it into conflict with kaisers and kings.

3. *The modern era, from the Reformation to the present*. The Church splits and new relations are worked out with nation-states. Some states absorb the church, and some develop free churches in a free state, while politics and economics become autonomous.

Temple, Vidler, Davies, and Sayers devoted considerable time to stage 2, the great medieval experiment. When the Roman Empire fell because of the barbarian invasions, the Church inherited the civilizing mission of Rome, placed on top of what God had already given her, the redemptive mission of Christ. Most Christians, even Roman Catholics, will now admit that this was a fatal and contradictory combination of missions. The Church became deeper and deeper immersed into politics, where Lord Acton's law rules with grim results. The strong popes of the High Middle Ages, Gregory VII and Innocent III, defended papal prerogatives by asserting the primacy of the spiritual over the material. But then they turned around and used material force—they excommunicated Kaisers, burned heretics, and put kingdoms under the interdict.

The strong political popes thus compromised the spiritual character of the Church when they won a political victory. Yet this hazard was built into the process; if Christendom was to be a political unity, it must have a center possessing political strength. Christians make the sad discovery that popes, too, are human—all too human. They are not perfect moral creatures, and they rarely make good political administrators. As Davies said, "Popes may exercise power in the name of Christ, but they create Hell just the same." The whole system destroyed all respect for the office of the papacy. After a few centuries, the Holy Father came to be viewed by other rulers as a petty, corrupt Italian politician who used his spiritual role to magnify his political power, which rested on nothing political. Papal claims reached their apogee in Boniface VIII, who crossed swords with the powerful French king, Philip IV, around 1300, which may be taken as the year the great medieval experiment ended. For the next two centuries, medieval Europe and the ideal of unity decayed. By the 1500s the Reformation had begun—the "Western Schism"—and the papacy was forced to redefine its role to Europe. At the Council of Trent (1545–1563), the papacy essentially retreated from its universalist political claims but started regaining its spiritual authority. Nevertheless, papal arrogance had driven northern Europe into rebellion and the Church would never again become the center of universal political–religious authority.[41]

What should one say about the great medieval experiment? It was a noble attempt—but we cannot go back to it. Probably it needed to be tried at least once, because it did embody a central truth: Christianity by its very nature must be totalitarian—it must claim to control the whole of life. Thus, for any civilization to aim at achieving the title "Christian" is a splendid idea. Vidler said that it was "the most magnificent attempt—indeed the only large scale attempt—that has yet been made to achieve a civilisation that could properly be called Christian, i.e. in the sense that the Christian values were acknowledged as supreme and as the final court of appeal in the secular as well as in the sacred order."[42]

Then what went wrong? Vidler said the nearer such an experiment approaches the ideal, the greater is the danger of corruption from within. Ecclesiastical rulers imagine they are administering the very kingdom of God and become victims of a terrible pride. When they sin they can rationalize it as easily as a fascist dictator. Temple said that it was natural for the Church, as repository and trustee of the divine revelation, to attempt to control the state. It was a laudable enterprise, "but it rested on a false expectation of success within history and was so led to adopt measures which betrayed the very nature of the Church." In a sense, it was based on the same fallacy as humanistic modernism: "History is not leading us to any form of perfected civilisation which, once established, will abide. It is a process of preparing the way for something outside history altogether—the perfected Kingdom of God."[43]

So both papalism and humanism stand convicted at the bar of history. They have both been tried and found wanting. The conclusion from both experiments is clear: The kingdom of God will arrive not in history but beyond history. Sin has corrupted and will continue to corrupt every civilization that man can build in time.

At this point someone is bound to ask, "How, then, can you ask us to fight for the Allied cause? If sin corrupts all human endeavors, does it not corrupt the Allied cause?" The answer brings us back to the argument of the beard. There are degrees of sin and righteousness in different civilizations. The degree of difference between the Allies and the Axis was very great—great enough to justify a war leading to unconditional surrender. We will never attain perfect justice in time, but we must continue to fight for it. If we do not fight, we betray the eternal ideal that lies outside of time and informs all our moral insights.

This leads us logically to Chapter 6, as the British clergy explains the war for Christian civilization.

NOTES

1. Sheen, *Philosophies at War* (London: Blanford, 1945), 23; Brook cited in *Spiritual Issues of the War* 105: (6 November 1941): 4.

2. Michael R. Hughes, ed., *Letters of Lewis Mumford and Frederick J. Osborn: A Transatlantic Dialogue 1938–70* (Bath, England: Adams & Dart, 1971), 20.

3. *Morality and War* (London: Burns, Oates, & Washbourne, 1939), 8.

4. Dorothy L. Sayers, *Begin Here: A War-Time Essay* (London: Gollancz, 1940), 53; Mumford, *Faith for Living* (London: Secker & Warburg, 1941), 53; Sheen, *Philosophies at War*, 38–40; Inge, *Fall of Idols* (London: Putnam, 1940), 257; Stewart, *Personal Religion and the Future of Europe* (London: SCM Press, 1941), 115; Hughes, *A Warrior on Wings: Tribute, Comfort and Challenge* (London: Epworth, 1942), 25; see also V. A. Demant, *The Religious Prospect* (London: Muller, 1939), 12; Vann, *Morality and War*, 23; J. H. Oldham, *Real Life Is Meeting* (London: Sheldon Press, 1942), 49; Peter Green, *The Moral Condition of Great Britain To-day* (London: Mowbray, 1943), 5.

5. *Weekly Bulletin on The Spiritual Issues of the War* 56 (21 November 1940), 1.

6. Sheen, *Philosophies at War*, 26; Niebuhr, *Europe's Catastrophe and the Christian Faith* (London: Nisbet, 1940), 19.

7. Glasgow, *Diplomacy and God* (London: Longmans, Green, 1941), 179; Mumford, *Faith for Living*, 84–85.

8. Leo, *Give Christ a Chance* (London: Drakers, 1941), 16; Mumford, *Faith for Living*, 71–74.

9. Matthews, *Foundations for Peace* (London: Eyre & Spottiswoode, 1942), 42–43.

10. "The Holy Fox": A Biography of Lord Halifax (London: Weidenfeld & Nicolson, 1991), 220–226.

11. Davies, *The Two Humanities: An Attempt at a Christian Interpretation of History in the Light of War* (London: Clarke, 1940), 27; Stewart, *Personal Religion*, 69, 73.

12. *Real Life Is Meeting*, 62.

13. *The Catholic and the War* (London: Burns & Oates, 1940), 6.

14. *Religious Prospect*, 57, 73, 76–83.

15. *Personal Religion*, 36.

16. Davies, *Two Humanities*, 37; Stewart, *Personal Religion*, 34; Niebuhr, *Europe's Catastrophe*, 38–39.

17. Micklem, *Europe's Own Book* (London: Morrison & Gibb, 1944), 13; Lloyd-Jones, *Plight of Man and the Power of God* (London: Hodder & Stoughton, 1942), 43; Davies, *The Church and the Peace* (London: Nisbet, 1940), 8.

18. Lloyd-Jones, *Why Does God Allow War? A General Justification of the Wars of God* (London: Hodder & Stoughton, 1939), 97; Mumford, *Faith for Living*, 9; Inge, *Fall of Idols*, 278.

19. See Rosalind Murray, *The Good Pagan's Failure* (London: Hollis & Carter, 1943), 60–61; Sheen, *Philosophies at War*, 60; Davies, *The Church and the Peace*, 16.

20. *Personal Religion*, 57–58.

21. Demant, *Religious Prospect*, 124; Murray, *Good Pagan's Failure*, 138; Stewart, *Personal Religion*, 21; Lloyd-Jones, *Plight of Man*, 29; Sayers, *Why Work? An Address Delivered at Eastbourne, April 23, 1942* (London: Metheun, 1942), 19.

22. Vidler, *God's Judgment on Europe* (London: Longmans, Green, 1940), 17; Davies, *Two Humanities*, 15; Rupp, *Is This a Christian Country?* (London: Sheldon Press, 1941), 60; Micklem, *The Theology of Politics* (London: Oxford University Press, 1941), xiv.

23. Alfred Zimmern, *Spiritual Values and World Affairs* (Oxford: Clarendon, 1939), 7; Hadham, *God in a World at War* (Harmondsworth, England: Penguin, 1941), 45.

24. *Spiritual Values*, 117–118.

25. *Has the Christian Way Failed?* (London: Epworth, 1941), 11–12.

26. *The Treaty of Versailles: Was It Just?* (London: Nelson, 1942), v, 12, 14, 30, 36, 41, 63.

27. *Has the Christian Way Failed?*, 17.

28. Letter to Jacobi, 6 January 1813, cited in Erich Heller, *The Disinherited Mind: Essays in Modern German Literature and Thought* (New York: Farrar, Straus, & Cudahy, 1952), 51.

29. See W. E. Sangster, *Ten Statesmen and Jesus Christ: A Christian Commentary on Our War Aims* (London: Hodder & Stoughton, 1941), 147–150.

30. L. Mueller-Weidemann, "The Germanization of the New Testament," *Friends of Europe* 64: 6–7.

31. *Home Press Bulletin* 22 (30 March 1940): 2.

32. *National Socialism and the Roman Catholic Church* (London: Oxford University Press, 1939), 226.

33. Bendiscioli, *The New Racial Paganism*, tr. George Smith (London: Burns, Oates, & Washbourne, 1939), 52; Vidler, *God's Judgment*, 64; Eliot, *Idea of a Christian Society* (New York: Harcourt Brace, 1940), 73.

34. Reported and translated in *Spiritual Issues of the War* 63 (16 January 1941): 4. For similar pronouncements in the 1930s, see Bendiscioli, *New Racial Paganism*, 71–72.

35. *Philosophies at War*, 46–47.

36. *In Search of Myself: The Autobiography of D. R. Davies* (London: Geoffrey Bles, 1961), 167–168.

37. Ibid., 180.

38. Ibid., 190–192.

39. Ibid., 193.

40. Ibid., 182. For Davies's use of Toynbee, see *Divine Judgment in Human History* (London: Sheldon Press, 1941), 44, and *Secular Illusion or Christian Realism?* (London: Eyre & Spottiswoode, 1942), 72.

41. See William Temple, *Citizen and Churchman* (London: Eyre & Spottiswoode, 1941), 13–19; Vidler, *God's Judgment*, 58–59; Davies, *Secular Illusion*, xiv; Sayers, *Begin Here*, 35–45.

42. Vidler, *God's Judgment*, 57.

43. Ibid., 58; Temple, *Citizen and Churchman*, 8.

CHAPTER 6

The War for Christian Civilization

Nietzsche's prophet, Zarathustra, encouraged his students to love war for its own sake, not for any "cause" that was involved. "You say it is the good cause that hallows even war? I say to you: It is the good war that hallows any cause. War and courage have accomplished more great things than love of the neighbor."[1] Nietzsche's attitude was unusual, however, because when most intellectuals praise war they usually point to its creative results. John Ruskin maintained that "all the pure and noble arts of peace are founded in war; no great culture ever arose on earth, but among a nation of soldiers."[2]

In two world wars the British clergy has defended the profession of the soldier but warned against the praise of warfare for its own sake. Gandhi asked what difference it made to the dead if the destruction was done in the name of totalitarianism or democracy. Hemingway wrote that in modern war you die like a dog for no good reason. Britons usually believed that if you fell in war you died for a good reason—for your country, for your children, and for future generations. In World War II they very often said that the struggle was for Western civilization or Christian civilization.

Of course, you always have the cynics who debunk any idealistic interpretation of the war. Rom Landau encountered an individual who told him, "My dear man, we are fighting this war for exactly the same reasons as we did in the last war—to preserve our Empire, to keep the European balance of power, and to save ourselves." He introduced the theory of moral equivalence: "There is just as much idealism on the German side as there is on ours—probably very little, but all that stuff about Christian civilization and the rest is eye-wash; of course the newspapers talk a lot about it, and a damn good thing they do—but that's all."[3] S. J. Marriott, canon of Westminster, quoted a letter from the *Tribune* that rejected the Christian justification:

Every Sunday and several times a week the B.B.C. tells the world that we are fighting for Christianity. Who says so? Certainly not the people who are doing the fighting. Are the Russians fighting for Christianity? Are the Jews fighting for Christianity? Are our own men fighting for Christianity? The boys in the Commando and parachute regiments—did they volunteer for the job because they were devout Christians? The boys who flew to bomb Augsburg in daylight, knowing that they would never come back—were they inspired by the vague miasma which is called the Christian way of life [*sic*]. Like hell.[4]

Archbishop Temple got very irritated whenever anyone said the war was for the Church or for Christianity. To use force for Christ would be a betrayal of the Gospel; Christianity exists only when it is freely accepted. Better to die for Christ than to kill for Him. But this limitation did not apply to a Christian civilization. "We are fighting to preserve a civilisation that has never, of course, been completely Christian, but has been very deeply influenced by the Christian view of life; and we are fighting to keep open the possibility of a still more truly Christian civilization in the future." The kingdom of God could not be advanced by war, but fighting could prevent the Christian civilization from being destroyed. Temple admitted that most people fighting in the war would not appreciate this nuanced formulation of the Allied objective, so for them we say we are fighting for justice, freedom, and truth.[5] (This reminds us of Churchill's maxim that in wartime, truth is so precious, she must be accompanied by a bodyguard of lies.)

John Hadham labored to make it clear that they were not fighting for the Churches. "If we are fighting on the side of God, we are not fighting for the organised Churches, with their outworn creeds and services, their financial anomalies, their vested interests." God is helping us by war to bring a new world into being and whether we cooperate with Him or not, nothing can bring back that tired world of 1939.[6]

T. S. Eliot confessed that the Munich crisis of 1938 had awakened him to the problem of defending a system against the new ferocity of the barbarian Nazis. Hitler's victory at Munich caused him to feel humiliated; it was not so much a criticism of the government "but a doubt of the validity of a civilisation." How could we match conviction with conviction? What ideas would counter Hitler's ideas? "Was our society, which had always been so assured of its superiority and rectitude, so confident of its unexamined premises, assembled around anything more permanent than a congeries of banks, insurance companies and industries, and had it any beliefs more essential than a belief in compound interest and the maintenance of dividends?"[7]

THE DEFENSE OF THE WAR:
SIMPLISTIC AND CRITICAL

Some clergymen presented the war in rather simplistic terms, with no casuistry to confuse the simple people. They agreed with Gerald Vann, who insisted that the only war the Christian could fight was one for "the defense of absolutes."[8] This stringent criterion turned some into pacifists. But, if you opt for war, you are obligated to make something absolute in your war aims.

Perhaps the finest example of the simplistic approach was Arthur Winnington Ingram, who finally retired from being bishop of London in July 1939, but unfortunately did not retire his naive clerical nationalism. As Alan Wilkinson observed, "He had learned nothing from the scandal which his war-time utterances had given to the inter-war generation."[9] In 1940 the bishop wrote a book entitled *A Second Day of God*, which harked back to *A Day of God*, first published in 1914. He cited Wordsworth's "Happy Warrior" and quoted Sir Edmund Ironside: "It is a great thing to be born for such a day as this." St. Paul provided the rationale for the conflict: "Who is weak and we are not weak?" (2 Cor. 11:29)—that is, England was once again fighting for the small nations, just as in the Great War. Old England has "guarded the gate of the House of Liberty" in two world wars, and "this is exactly what we are doing now, and, mind you, with God's help, shall do successfully." This is the greatest day that Great Britain has had for a thousand years—all alone guarding the House of Liberty! The grand thing for us civilians is that we are all in the battle line together: "Bombs have no respect for Bishops or anyone else; we are all in the battle together, and it is a great day for us all." Compared to the Battle of Britain, Agincourt, Crecy, and Waterloo were mere skirmishes. "On the result of this battle depends the future of the world for perhaps a thousand years. . . . God grant that we may not fail Him on this 'Second Great Day of God' as He wraps the colours of His regiment round us, and bids us fight for the right to the death!"[10]

Donald Davidson brought the entire history of modern England into God's providential plan. Writing after the Battle of Britain was won, he bade his compatriots to look back with pride:

We have only to think of what God has done for our country in times past. Whenever, as a nation we have cried out to God for deliverance, He has never failed to hear us. He delivered us when the whole might of Spain, the most powerful empire in the world, was concentrated against us. He delivered us when Napoleon was waiting with his invading forces, all ready to launch the attack that was to bring us to our knees. He delivered us in the last war, even though our enemy brought us to the very verge of starvation, and victory was almost within his grasp. . . . Our Army was delivered out of the jaws of death, and thanks to the miracle of Dunkirk, what might have proved a crushing disaster, was converted into one of the most glorious exploits in history. . . . London still stands, while the wreckage of the German squadrons strews the countryside.[11]

Bishop Hensley Henson told his flock this was no common war, but a war in defense of "ultimate things" like justice, mercy, freedom, and law, which are the constituents of morality, and the essentials of human duty. "Few, if any, wars in Christendom have been undertaken with so much reluctance, with so clear a perception of the terrific sacrifices which it would entail on the belligerent powers or with so clear a sense of moral obligation as that which the Allies are now waging with Hitlerite Germany." F. R. Barry quoted Lord Balfour's observation that "a living God takes sides" and concluded, "We cannot believe that it is His will that the world should be overrun by the power of evil. His 'name,' His honour seems to be at stake." Matthews said, "Who lives if England dies? This renowned and valiant people has, we believe, a place in the world which can be filled by no other: it shall not die."[12]

A more critical, nuanced defense of the war stressed the shortcomings of the Allies as well as the Axis, but maintained that God was nevertheless using the Allies to crush the Axis. "You needn't mention the obvious, that the Allies have self-interest at work," said William Temple, because "it is not wrong for a man to act justly on occasions when it is to his interest to do so; on the contrary, it is still his duty." In the mysterious providence of God, said D. R. Davies, self-interest is often a contributor to social progress. We are "mean instruments" in the hands of God, so "let us not, as a nation, glory in our righteous innocence; for we have none. Before God and History we are guilty. Rather may we be humbled by the knowledge that our national interests have, for the hour, been absorbed by God's providence for the world."[13]

Landau told his readers that "the evil represented by Germany is really terrifying in its depth and magnitude. . . . Never before," he affirmed, "have we been confronted with an issue that was so universal, that went so radically to the roots of our very being." He saw Western European civilization as "an ideal rooted in the eternal verities of the human spirit," while fascism was merely a belief "manufactured by propaganda and inculcated into people by the mesmerizing force of repetition." He came close to identifying the West with the kingdom of God:

The entire evolution of the western world points to a growing ascendency of the Christian principles. . . . This is not a war of any individual empire for its own survival. In its fullest meaning it touches the very roots of universal principles and ideals which are far from having reached their harvesting stage. What is happening today is a crisis of those ideals. . . . So, if I were a German, I could not help admitting that I was fighting on the losing side and that nothing could stop the victory of the enemy. . . . From our point of view a clear vision and recognition of spiritual realities conveys, not merely hope, but certainty.[14]

The eminent Catholic historian, Christopher Dawson, lent the weight of his pen to the Allied cause. While admitting that England was far from perfect, he said it would be a grave error to ignore what is "sound and living in our national tradition." England has not lost her soul; she is a nation with a Christian inheritance that every Englishman has a right to share and a duty to defend. The Christian cause in the war is also the common cause of all who are defending our civilization against "mass despotism and the idolatry of power, which has resulted in a new paganism that is destructive of all moral and intellectual values."[15]

By 1943 George Bell was so concerned with the possible collapse of European civilization that he delivered a speech called "The Threat to Civilization" to the Upper House of the Convocation of Canterbury. The house passed the following resolution unanimously: "That this House calls attention to the increasing danger of a collapse of European civilisation, due to the prolongation of the sufferings caused by the Nazi regime to millions in the occupied and invaded country, and presses upon the British public the necessity of a deeper sense of the urgency of the situation, and of far stronger insistence on the spiritual factors involved, as well as the need of greater austerity and readiness for sacrifice."

Bell explained that in his judgment the British people were not fully aroused to the urgency of the situation. His recent trip to Sweden convinced him that "the structure and culture of Europe are doomed unless we in this country in particular are made to wake up." Hitler was the arch-destroyer: "He has indeed dynamic force, but his force is for killing and not for making alive. Wherever he goes he brings death. . . . Wherever the Nazi rules he sows the seeds of hatred." He described the systematic deportation of the Jews, the forced importation of foreign workers, and the murder of over 500,000 hostages by the Gestapo. "Europe . . . is now being destroyed economically as well as in civilisation and culture." However, the most important thing was that the Nazis had a faith—a diabolical faith—that inspired them in their destructive work. He warned that Britain would not be able to defeat the Nazi faith unless it had a faith "far greater than any we have hitherto revealed as a nation" and "a far greater reliance on the highest spiritual forces." Our limp faith, he said, was shown in the fact that the output of beer had not at all been reduced during the war! Compared with Russia, Britain's conditions were "approaching luxury."[16]

ROLE OF THE BRITISH EMPIRE IN GOD'S PLAN

Those who defended the war usually believed that the English people and the British Empire had a special role to play in God's historical plans. To understand this properly we must recall the many provisos established thus far: (1) all human beings sin, both as individuals and as collectives, (2) no person or group ever acts from a purely selfless motive, (3) sometimes we must choose the lesser of two evils, (4) individuals and groups often differ greatly in their degree of good and evil, (5) to achieve a victory for love you may need to seek justice, (6) sinless perfection is not required for one to judge or act, else judgment and action would cease, and (7) the kingdom of God will be approximated but never fully achieved in history.

Given these premises, the defender can defuse one of the major arguments against Great Britain—that the war was just an imperialistic war. One could grant that charge, but argue that God could indeed be using the British Empire to bring about something good, because there was a significant difference in the degree of imperialism. In both World Wars I and II, the Germans compared Britain to a retired burglar, who, now that he had his plunder, preached law and order to the rest of the world and called in the police when someone else tried to imitate his former crimes. In both wars churchmen replied that the British Empire was not a typical empire—that it had no single guiding will—that it grew slowly, haphazardly, and pragmatically, changing by response to specific needs and precise historical circumstances. It was a curious mixture of force, vision, fraud, realism, and idealism.[17]

The enemy reasoned in this fashion: Britain has an empire, therefore she must be imperialistic. The war is between the British Empire and the German Reich. Everyone knows that "Reich" means "empire"; ergo this is simply an empire against an empire—an imperialistic war. The logic sounds simple, but the conclusion was very wrong. In contrast to Hitler's empire, the British Empire approximated a genuine community. Matthews said it would be fairer if we used some other terms like "commonwealth" or "the British family of nations." The British Empire is no artificial construction like the French Empire that fell in 1763; it had grown without conscious planning. "It has the enormous power and vitality of that which is produced by the instinctive forces of a race. It can therefore command the loyalty of millions of simple people who feel deeply but reason little." Perhaps, Matthews asserted, the final destiny of the commonwealth is to die in order that something greater might live. In that case, true lovers of Britain would will its death, for nothing is worthy to live unless it is ready to die for some noble end.[18]

Two Americans stepped forward to defend the British Empire. Lewis Mumford charged that those "who cannot see any difference between the sins of the British Empire and the sins of Nazi Germany are incapable of making elementary distinctions." Reinhold Niebuhr conceded that no system is perfectly Christian; but, it must be obvious that any social structure in which power has been made responsible, and in which anarchy has been overcome by methods of mutual accommodation, is preferable to either anarchy or tyranny. "If it is not possible to express a moral preference to the justice achieved in democratic societies, in comparison with tyrannical societies, no historical preference has any meaning."[19]

Dorothy L. Sayers compared Britain to St. Paul, who admitted that he was "least of all the apostles," yet did not abdicate his apostolic office and "labored more abundantly than them all" (1 Cor.15:9). It is doubtful if she meant to imply that Britain was "least" of all the nations, but rather that Britain, while accomplishing great things, should exhibit the same humble attitude. Despite her faults, she must fight this war because Nazi Germany had committed the sin against the Holy Ghost—deliberate nihilism.[20]

Alfred Zimmern argued that it would be morally wrong for Britain to abdicate any of her powers at the present time. The argument for abandonment of her position would be valid only "if world conditions were in fact such as to enable us to renounce our traditional responsibilities without risk of disaster for the world as a whole." The choice is not between power and no power but between different kinds of power: "An abdication of Great Britain of her share of world-power could, as the world now is, only lead to an increase of arbitrary and irresponsible power wielded by one or more dictators." As Niebuhr reasoned, the balance of power is surely inferior to love, but given the sinfulness of man, it is a basic condition for justice.[21]

In 1943 the government ordered that the nation should celebrate on 26 September the third anniversary of the great victory over the German Luftwaffe. On this "Battle of Britain Sunday," Archbishop Temple recalled that in 1940 an American friend had suggested to him that the British evacuate to Canada! Everyone back then had written Britain off, but we were not thinking that way at all, he said, which compels us three years later to ask the question, "Why should God preserve us?" Temple's answer had the usual balance between confidence and humility:

We may not suppose that He has some special favour for us above all other members of His great family. Our knowledge of ourselves is enough to assure us that it is not because we are conspicuous above all others in moral desert. But we may and must believe that He Who has led our fathers in ways so strange and has preserved our land in a manner so marvelous, has a purpose for us to serve in the preparation of His perfect Kingdom. In the tradition of our nation and Empire we are entrusted with a treasure to be used for the welfare of mankind. That we still enjoy it is due to God's preservation of us from the enemy whose triumph would have destroyed it. . . . Thanks be to God Who preserved us from destruction; to Him for evermore be pledged the service of our lives.[22]

Because the values of British Christian civilization and those of the United States were similar, it became obvious that the United States should thus be aligned with the British Commonwealth in the war against fascism. Churchill certainly wanted this alignment, as did Roosevelt, and many clerics agreed. As early as 21 June 1940, Archbishop Lang received an urgent letter from William Paton, Secretary of the International Missionary Council, pleading with him to get the king and queen to make a special personal appeal to the United States. This had been suggested to him by the American theologian, Henry van Dusen. Lang replied that this was not practical inasmuch as it would make it seem as if Britain was in the "last ditch."[23]

The next year William Paton published his book, *The Church and the New Order*, a few months before Pearl Harbor. He foresaw the coming world alliance between the United States and Britain. No other nation with any power outside the Commonwealth cherished liberal ideas except the United States. These two represented Western civilization, the key idea of which is that the state is not supreme, but under transcendent law, a view which was a fruit of Christianity. The traditions and inherited spirit of these two should make them less likely to become tyrannical than any other powers in the world. There is an "absolute difference of value" between democracy and fascism. "We lay down, therefore, as the only practical possibility open to those who, in our given historical situation, desire to see an order of international freedom in the world, such a coincidence of fundamental judgment and policy between the United States and the British Commonwealth as may enable those two great powers to use their immense resources for common ends."[24]

Even farther back, in 1939, Zimmern had observed that the United States and the British Commonwealth between them controlled over 75 percent of the mineral resources of the globe, had 60 percent of the manufacturing power of the globe, and had control of all oceans except the northern Pacific, thus insuring near mastery of world transportation. In the mysterious providence of God, the civilization with the right philosophy had also acquired the power to defend it.[25]

Millions rejoiced, therefore, when Churchill and Roosevelt met and signed the Atlantic Charter (August 1941), making public certain common principles in British–American foreign policy. Assuring the world that their countries sought no aggrandizement, these leaders pledged their support for basic rules of international morality—that territorial changes be made only with the expressed wishes of the people concerned, that people be given the right to choose their form of government, that nations have free access to trade and raw materials, that nations cooperate in improving economic conditions, that peace be established that will allow men to live their lives in freedom from fear and want, that all men may travel the high seas and oceans without hindrance, and that all nations abandon the use of force and take steps to disarm. The contrast with fascism was glaring. Archbishop Lang exulted, "The whole world is now able to see the difference between the kind of 'new order' which the British Commonwealth and its Allies and the Government of the United States desire and that which Hitler would impose by force and oppression."[26]

It is curious to note that other religions besides Christianity interpreted the war in an apocalyptic mode. In India, Nolini Kanta Gupta wrote an analysis of the war entitled, *The World War: Its Inner Bearings*. Every so often, Gupta explained, a demon arises in history called the *Asura*, whom the Divine Mother must slay. Since this war involves such a creature, it is different from previous conflicts: "It is not a war of one country with another, or one group of Imperialists with another, nor is it merely the fierce endeavour of a particular race or nation for world-domination: it is something more than all that. This war has a deeper, a more solemn, almost a grim significance." The "New Order" proposed by Japan and Germany is strong, powerful, fierce, ruthless, cruel, and regimented; it seeks to pull man down from the level he has attained to the lower level of animals.

The *Asura* is the arrest of all evolution; it means a reversal for man. The *Asura* is a fixed type of being—he does not change. His is a hardened mold—a settled immutable form—which is essentially egocentric, "violent and concentrated self-will." The Nazi differs from other kinds of oppressors: "One is an instance of the weakness of man, of his flesh being frail; the other illustrates the might of the Asura, his very spirit is unwilling. One is undivine; the other antidivine, positively hostile." People who cannot discern this difference are colorblind. Hence, those who have stood against the *Asura* have "sided with the gods and received the support and benediction of the Divine."[27]

CHRISTIANITY AND WESTERN VALUES

In a war for Christian civilization, one must be convinced that the culture for which young men are asked to die embodies Christian principles and values. The feeling was widespread among the British clergy and religious people that the most important social, cultural, and political principles of Western civilization came from the Christian faith and were grounded in that faith. Nathaniel Micklem insisted that "our political philosophy, explicitly or implicitly, rests upon our theology. All political problems are at bottom theological." Morale, said Sidney Berry, cannot be sustained by trivial and ephemeral things like an addition to our rations or a touch of added brightness to our entertainments. "To keep the spirit of triumph indomitable through the warring tests of the months and years demands from us all a deep faith that the things for which we strive are of eternal value, and that to lose them would be to lose everything."[28]

The most fundamental notion in this precious mosaic of Western ideas was that of *individuality*. The Hebrew–Christian view of man stresses the ultimacy and value of individuality, in contrast to the religions of the Far East, where the indivisible, all-encompassing cosmic spirit is the primary fact and the fleeting expressions of individuality have no permanence or value. For Eastern monism the individual is a problem, but for the Christian, individuality is not only fully real but also good in principle. The Biblical doctrine of creation gives sanctity to particulars; they are not lost in abstractions or drowned in categories. As John Henry Newman said, religion has to do with the real and the real is always particular. Micklem asserted, "The only centers of activity, of feeling, of function, of purpose which we know are individual selves." Groups or collectives such as states, churches, and nations are not subsistent metaphysical entities but only relations between persons.[29]

Next comes the idea of the value or dignity of the individual person. It is one thing to say that reality is particular, but how do you prove that some particulars are more valuable than others? You use the doctrine of the image of God. God made one particular creature special. He loves this creature, who is of His image, in a very special way. Alan Richardson argued that we respect the individual "because God cares for it. . . . When every other reason for respecting the personalities of others has broken down, this will always endure; when every motive of self-interest, national interest, or class interest has disappeared, the Christian commandment of love will still remain. On this foundation alone can a 'true humanism' be established and a world-community be built, which will transcend the 'natural' limitations of nationality, class or political creed."

The political implications of individualism are clear: Man is particular and valuable in himself. He has rights against the state. The state cannot just treat man as a means for its own ends. In Demant's terms, "Man is a person sui juris, an absolute in his own way, relative only to God. He is a man before he is a citizen, he has rights before he has uses, he is free to determine himself before he can be treated as a producer." Temple adapted an expression from Jesus: "The State was made for men and women, not men and women for the State."[30]

The Western notion of human equality lies implicit in this doctrine of individualism. The American Declaration of Independence says, "We hold these truths to be self-evident, that all men are created equal, that they are endowed by their Creator with certain unalienable Rights." The French Declaration of the Rights of Man and Citizen begins with the assertion, "Men are born and remain free and equal in rights. Social distinctions may be based only on considerations of the common good." All this ultimately can be traced back to the Christian gospel: "There is neither Jew nor Greek, there is neither slave nor free, there is neither male nor female; for you are all one in Christ Jesus" (Gal. 3:27). Given enough time, this principle will level most hierarchies; it will destroy nationalism, racism, elitism, sexism and any other "-ism" that seeks to inject a value differential between individual human beings.

Temple explained how the principle of equality got into the English coronation service. When the king is crowned, all people present render homage to him while he is seated on his throne. But then the order of Holy Communion occurs right after that, conducted in exactly the same manner as in any village church. The king drops to his knees, like any peasant, to receive the holy sacrament. In the great things—things of God—king and pauper are on the same level.[31]

It seemed obvious to all clergymen that Western liberalism could never survive in a system of secular humanism, but could be sustained only by a belief in "the Eternal Beyond," as Demant expressed it. "Only in a religion which makes personality sacred will Liberalism be able to keep living." J. H. Oldham said the war was "for the status and dignity of man, for the freedom of the human person, for the possibility of human community. . . . To assert this truth about man as man is the definite obligation of Christians and an essential part of the witness of the Church."[32]

But this same valuable, individual person must be free! Lord Acton was often cited: "Liberty is the central theme of all history." St. Paul said, "Where the spirit of the Lord is, there is freedom" (2 Cor. 3:17). Man is above all else a spiritual being, and the essence of spirit is freedom. Spirit is the realm where you cannot use force; if you try, it always backfires on you. Frederick B. Macnutt said, "Both freedom of speech and freedom of worship are necessary to enable the Christian to bear his witness and fulfill his fellowship with God and man in Jesus Christ." Western people talk a lot about freedom. People from other parts of the world think this must be an Occidental eccentricity. But as T. G. Dunning asserts,

Freedom is not a democratic oddity, but something inevitable and fundamental to the life and destiny of man. God predestined man to be conformed to His likeness and so had to give to man some measure of His own responsibility and freedom. Spiritual ends must be freely chosen. We need not deny that for certain ends, a group of robots might be more efficient than a community of free and responsible beings. But those ends could not be human and spiritual. . . . We believe that the love of freedom is not a British trait, but a God-implanted instinct, and that in the end what really opposes Nazi slavery–morality is not British imperialism, but the very nature of man.[33]

Why do men die for freedom? asked Wickham Steed. If they have food and drink, why do they fight and die for something so abstract as liberty? The materialistic interpretation of history cannot explain man's mysterious love of freedom. Davies quoted Dostoevsky in saying that freedom is the deepest thing in man; he must have "individual volition at all costs." Matthews argued that the suppression of free thought and free speech is the slowing down of the advance of science and all moral and intellectual activity. "Without freedom of the spirit man stagnates and putrifies. . . . The liberty of the individual . . . is the most precious ideal of western civilisation. If that perishes the soul of the West is dead."[34]

Demant reasoned that a democratic system of government is a logical development of the spiritual view of man. Liberty is man's conscious participation in power; that is, by making free, rational decisions he asserts himself, his circle of being, against the otherwise unfree, determined nature in which he lives. Free choices display human power, hence authority is innate in man's rational, moral nature. When several humans get together and discover their common nature, they reason that each should have a part in the decision making that rules the group; thus you have a democracy. But this liberalism is rooted in a definite cosmology, and one that makes the individual person special—a thesis denied by fascism, which sacrifices individual goals for social cohesion.[35]

Foremost among the freedoms of a free society, said John Middleton Murry, is the "liberty of prophesying"; that is, the freedom to preach the gospel. Thus the Christian Church is the archetype of all those voluntary associations in the state that form the most solid safeguard against the development of totalitarianism. By a strange turn of events, this freedom of religion and religious speech came to England by way of the Protestant cults. Murry bade us remember that it was against the censorship of the Anglican Press that Milton wrote his famous plea for the "liberty of unlicensed printing." Micklem noted that "our

religious liberties were won for us first and foremost by those who were prepared to shed their blood for what they called 'the Crown Rights of the Re-
deemer.'" Temple pointed out that Calvinists and Jesuits, who had no belief in
liberty as a principle, became its champions in practice "because they set a
limit to the omnicompetence of the State in the rights of all men to worship
God according to their consciences." E. G. Rupp said that "without William
Tyndale and his English New Testament, and apart from Thomas Cranmer and
the English Liturgy, there could have been no John Milton and his *Areopagitica.*
And without these men and their friends our national ideal of freedom would
have been a maimed, limping, fettered thing."[36]

The freedoms enjoyed in Western nations can thus be traced back to Christianity. Micklem said you cannot really trace democracy back to Athens, because that society was based on slavery and disfranchised women: "Not till
the triumph of the Christian conception of the value of the individual life is
the way prepared for a free society of free men." Apart from man's duty to
God, he concluded, "there is no ultimate philosophical basis for his rights; nor
can we fail to see in the world today that, where the religious outlook is lost or
neglected, the rights are likewise overruled." Barry agreed: "There is no security or guarantee for the Rights of Man or the claims of personality apart from
that valuation of man's life in the light of God and immortality which is the
gift of the Christian religion." Matthews insisted that apart from Christian
philosophy, "the ideas of the value of persons as such, and the equality of all
rational beings, on which democracy is founded, cannot persist, for in every
other philosophy these ideas must appear as pleasing fictions." Phyllis Bottome
stated that Britons were fighting for something which was intelligible only
"on the basis of faith in God and an understanding of men and women as
children of God destined for eternal fellowship with him." Bishop Sheen concluded that "never before has the cause of democracy been so coincident with
Christianity."[37]

Stressing individual freedom, however, can go too far. It can lead to an
uncritical, unbiblical, antigovernment libertarianism that verges on anarchy.
Temple warned that a liberty based on mere selfhood can tear a democracy
apart, unless the "selves" are enlightened and taught to curb their desires. The
state cannot possibly meet all the desires of all sinful men. Liberty rooted in
the consciousness of divine sonship provides a much more stable government.
Your first duty is to God and this may require you to defy some earthly leaders, but it would never cause you to rebel against society itself, because society is a principle of union. The state is not an alien power; it is the organ of the
community and exists to serve the community. Any individual who asserts his
will against the law is displaying egocentricity, which is his essential sin. In a
well-ordered state, every crime is also a sin. "The State which punishes crimi-
nals, thereby checking criminal tendencies and enlisting the self-regarding
motives in support of justice, is helping men and women to be true to their real
nature as God created it."[38]

Temple explained that the true value of democracy is often missed by its advocates. Loose talk about the voice of the people being the voice of God (*vox populi, vox Dei*) is nonsense. The defense of democracy is not that the majority is always right, because they are often wrong. It is usually true, however, that the majority will not be as wrong as some of the minorities, and stability is what government is usually about. But the real defense of democracy connects good government to the spiritual nature of man and the need for human fellowship. By calling upon people to exercise responsible judgment on the matters facing the nation,

you develop their personal qualities. You make them feel that they belong to one another in this corporate society, and so you tend to deepen and intensify personal fellowship. You are leading people forward from the relationship of the herd to that of real fellowship by the mere process of calling upon them to take their share in the government of the groups of which they are members. That is the real value of the thing, its educational effect upon the citizens, and through that, of course, you get a more alert, a more disciplined intelligence in the citizens—less liable to be swayed by mass hysteria and the like—less likely to be victims of propaganda, one of the subtle perils of democracy at all times—and through that once more you will get, in the long run, a wider and better government because it is government by wiser and better citizens.[39]

Most clerics would have agreed with the dictum of the great French philosopher, Baron de Montestquieu (1689–1755), who said that virtue is necessary for a republic to survive, while a monarchy must have honor and a despotism fear (*Spirit of Laws*, III, 9). Douglas Stewart noted that the modern state must become more powerful, as secularism increases, because the decline of religion makes the individual more unruly. State control must remedy the failure of self-control. "Let any generation spend its youth without religion and it will spend its age under a tyrant." The men of modern Europe may have decided to dispense with the Christian faith but "if so let them be under no illusions as to the results of such a decision. Secular freedom is always hovering on the brink of tyranny. Freedom imposes a moral strain which is intolerable without the dynamic of religion."[40]

The Bible played a crucial role in the development of Western civilization. Micklem wrote a book in 1944 entitled *Europe's Own Book*, a tribute to the place of the Bible in British history. He contrasted Britain with Germany where Nazis blamed the Bible for deflecting the German nation from the natural development of its own inherent genius. Micklem noted wryly that though many Britons rejected the Biblical view of the universe and never read the Bible, none would ever suggest that the Bible represented an unfortunate interlude in the nation's history or that "the fair destiny of our people depends upon our going back to the ideas held by our forefathers before Christianity reached our shores." He predicted that "we shall have no true and lasting peace unless once again the Bible is recognized as 'Europe's own book.'"[41]

In November 1941, the British and Foreign Bible Society published a report entitled "The Book of Freedom," which stressed the connection between the free dissemination of the Scriptures and the growth of political and social freedom. The report said, "This is an hour of destiny and the outcome of the present war may determine the future of mankind for centuries. It is a struggle . . . between the forces that stand for Christian freedom and the powers that lead to the darkness of pagan servitude. Among the influences that make for the liberty of the human spirit the Bible towers supreme."[42]

King George VI sent out a special edition of the New Testament to all British soldiers with this benediction: "To all serving in my Forces by sea, land, or in the air, and indeed, to all my people engaged in the defence of the Realm, I commend the reading of this book. For centuries the Bible has been a wholesome and strengthening influence in our national life, and it behooves us in these momentous days to turn with renewed faith to this Divine source of comfort and inspiration."[43]

Lord Halifax became a traveling evangelist for this "Gospel of Western civilization." When he stepped down as Foreign Secretary in December 1940, Churchill named him as the ambassador to the United States, a post in which he rendered great service to the Allied cause. During 1941, when Britain stood alone, he used every opportunity possible to urge the American people to support Britain and enter the war against the Axis. He always appealed to the common spiritual ties that bound the two nations together. For example, in a speech given to the New York Pilgrims on 25 March 1941, he referred to the principles that were essential to life, such as the absolute value of every human soul, the moral principle of respect for personality and conscience, and the social principle of individual liberty. These principles came from Christianity and other great religions. "They have drawn vitality from the best of human thought throughout the centuries. For us they are expressed and protected by democracy, and that is why we value it." He said we only delude ourselves if we think that "the civilization we share with you could survive a Nazi victory."[44]

Prayers were said to God all over the world for the preservation of Britain and Western civilization. Rupp encouraged people to pray and cited examples from English history to prove the power of prayer: "The living present is different because Oliver Cromwell halted his men, bareheaded in the morning mist, and sang with them the 117th Psalm before the pursuit at Dunbar, and because the Duke of Marlborough occupied part of the Eve of Blenheim in prayer, receiving the sacrament, and because Drake and Nelson knelt in their cabins before Cadiz and Trafalgar."[45]

The belief in the power of mass and collective prayer found a focus in the "Big Ben Minute." At nine o'clock each evening, the BBC would broadcast around the world the chimes of Big Ben striking the hour as a prelude to the nine-o'clock news. A campaign started in May 1940 to use this time as a special "silent minute" in which citizens could all pray at the same "minute" for

Britain and the war. The custom caught on and soon spread around the world, to the United States and the Dominions, and even to Europe in the POW camps. In Malta British soldiers would often end their letters, "Give my love to Ben." W. Tudor Pole explained the mysterious attraction of the silent minute: "This power operates through the working of a natural law, one that is always available for our use. When we join together in keeping the Silent Minute at 9 o'clock each evening, this law is brought into action and can become a source of strength and inspiration for ourselves, the nation as a whole and for freedom-loving peoples in every land." Alexis Carrel said that "when we pray we link ourselves with the inexhaustible motive power that spins the Universe."[46]

The silent minute was so successful that many people asked the BBC to highlight the time period and recognize the special status it had achieved in the eyes of religious people. The BBC refused, noting that in their opinion it was just a time signal and if anyone wished to make it a moment of reverence, that was their business. Major-General L. L. Hoare, Chairman of the Big Ben Council, wrote Temple asking him to approach the Prime Minister to pressure the BBC into identifying the minute as more than just a time signal. He pointed out that the war was approaching its supreme crisis, and people needed this concerted, united, spiritual effort. Temple made one attempt, but the BBC would not change its policy.[47]

There was one fly in this ointment, and it was a big one—Russia. When the Soviet Union joined the war against the Axis, a feeling of unease rippled through the British community—unease composed of both gratitude and fear. Churchill illustrated the mixed feelings with his remark that if Hitler were to invade hell, he could probably find a few kind words to say about the devil in the House of Commons. Russia's entry into the war made Britain's moral case against Germany sound hypocritical. Murry said that Russia was as great a sinner as Germany in the cardinal matter of unlimited brutality against the individual person in the name of the deified state. Thus, "in so far as Britain is defending herself against Germany, she is defending Christianity, but in so far as she is actively aiding Russia, she is aiding paganism."[48] Those trained in Niebuhrian dialectics would probably shrug and quote Walt Whitman:

> *Do I contradict myself?*
> *Very well then . . . . I contradict myself;*
> *I am large . . . . I contain multitudes.*

THE ECUMENICAL WINDFALL

At his enthronement in April 1942, the new archbishop, William Temple, pointed to an encouraging unity among Christians that had been developing during the last few years: "God has been building up a Christian fellowship which now extends into almost every nation, and binds citizens of them all together in true unity and mutual love. It is the great new fact of our time."[49]

Although it is easy to exaggerate the unifying effect that fascism and the war had on the European churches, there is some evidence to suggest that Temple's conviction was not just wishful thinking.

First, there was the German Church conflict, which had caused Catholics and Protestants to rediscover some common ground.[50] Dunning rejoiced that several world bodies had already in the 1930s warned the German Evangelical Church of its fatal compromise with the Nazi government—groups like The Universal Council of Life and Work, The Swiss Church Federation, The American Federal Council of the Churches of Christ, the Baptist World Alliance, and the Ecumenical Conference at Oxford on Church, Community, and State. In September 1937, Niebuhr called for "churchmen of all parts of the world to manifest their sympathy for their brethren in Germany, who are seeking to uphold the freedom of the Church and to resist the pagan tendencies of a totalitarian political movement."[51]

Once they were faced with bona fide paganism, German Catholics and Protestants discovered that their differences did not matter as much as they thought. They found that both confessions were still basically Christian, and that the Reformation was a family squabble, not a war between two different religions. Protestants discovered that Catholics believed Christ was the center of worship, the Bible should be read, and Scriptural revelation needed no supplement from *Mein Kampf*. Catholics found that Lutherans became their best allies in the domain of religious policy, in the defense of the legal position of the creeds, in the defense of the denominational schools, in the right of the Church to educate its own, and in the fight against irreligious propaganda from the state.[52]

British Christians showed deep concern over the Church situation in Germany during the 1930s and throughout the war. Temple dramatized the solidarity between German and British Christians by delivering a special sermon on the birthday of Pastor Martin Niemoeller on 14 January 1943, to the German Lutheran Church, Montpelier Place, London. He praised Niemoeller as one "whose name is become a symbol of Christian fidelity in resistance to oppression." He said he wished to "express among you here the feelings of reverence which English Christians share with you for the German man who has come to stand in our minds so conspicuously for Christian integrity amidst the spiritual corruption of Nazi Germany. With him we honour the other leaders of the Christian Church in Germany, both Catholic and Evangelical, who have stood boldly for the rights of the Christian people and of the Church itself." Then the archbishop changed his tone and said that duty compelled him to point out the limitations of the German Christian witness: There had been no protest against such crimes as the attempt to exterminate the Poles or the massacre of the Jews. What is at stake in this war, he reminded them, was not just the survival of an ecclesiastical institution, but also "the capacity of the Christian fellowship to give fearless testimony to Christian truth."[53]

Christians all over the world loved to quote the testimony of Albert Einstein on the internal German situation. He praised the Christian Church for being the only institution that really resisted the Nazi takeover of German culture:

Being a lover of freedom, when the revolution came to Germany, I looked to the universities to defend it, knowing that they had always boasted of their devotion to the cause of truth; but no, the universities were immediately silenced. Then I looked to the great editors of the newspapers whose flaming editorials in days gone by had proclaimed their love of freedom, but they, like the universities, were silenced in a few short weeks. Then I looked to the individual writers who as literary guides of Germany had written much and often concerning the place of freedom in modern life; but they too were mute. Only the Churches stood squarely across the path of Hitler's campaign for suppressing truth. I never had any special interest in the Church before, but now I feel a great affection and admiration because the Church alone has had the courage and persistence to stand for intellectual truth and moral freedom. I am forced thus to confess that what I once despised I now praise unreservedly.[54]

Further evidence of growing ecumenicity could be found in the new spirit of cooperation among British churches during the war. During the blitz churches began to help each other by sharing each other's homes and church buildings and helping each other to clear up the rubble. Clergymen even swapped pulpits and conducted combined communion services. Rupp quipped that "a few months of air raids have done more than many conferences seemed likely to achieve."[55]

The Ministry of Information seized every opportunity to highlight such unity meetings through its weekly bulletin, *Spiritual Issues of the War*. For example, it reported one meeting on Good Friday in April 1941, where all the churches joined together in unified witness in a London suburb. The procession first assembled at an Anglican church, led by ministers of all the churches in their robes, accompanied by their choirs and crucifixes, with a Salvation Army band supplying the music! The main service was held in a Methodist church, conducted by representatives of the Presbyterians, Methodists, and Quakers, while the address was given by an Anglican. The meeting house was crowded to capacity. One vicar testified that the groups had been meeting like this for some time, a situation required by the enemy bombing raids.[56]

After changing names several times, *Spiritual Issues* reached issue 250 on 17 August 1944, and the editors took a moment to exult in the success of their weekly bulletin. As soon as a bulletin is printed in Great Britain, they explained, a copy goes by airmail to America and is distributed to some ten thousand leading churchmen in the United States. Considerable extracts are translated into Swedish and cabled to Sweden. For Far Eastern Christians, an abridged version is produced in Chungking on rice paper. Portions of some bulletins are broadcast into Germany every Sunday. The editors concluded, "It is no exaggeration therefore to say that the ramifications of this unpretentious little paper have become almost world-wide."[57]

The arrival of the Americans in Britain offered another opportunity for the demonstration of ecumenicity. On New Year's Day, 1943, the Manchester Cathedral hosted an Anglo–American Friendship Service, in which contingents of both British and American armies and the RAF participated. Sermons were rendered by Guy Warman, bishop of Manchester, and C. J. Wright, president of the local Free Church Federal Council. Later in the year, Rev. W. B.

Pugh, chairman of the General Protestant Commission on U.S. Army and Navy Chaplains, told the *The New York Post* (31 August) he would "like to impress upon the people of America the fact that the Churches of the British Isles have opened their doors to all our troops. The rectors and ministers have gone to our chaplains and officers and told them the Churches were theirs to use while they were in Britain. . . . It is a demonstration of Church unity without parallel."[58]

Temple worked with Rev. William Paton, Free Church ecumenical leader, in drawing up a document called "The Christian Basis for the Reconstruction." They sent this paper to several key figures in the Allied community, such as the American Presbyterian, John Foster Dulles, who had served as legal counsel to the U.S. delegation at the Versailles Peace Conference and helped prepare the United Nations charter. Dulles responded in a telegram dated 30 July 1943: "Please express to signatories our commissions deep appreciation their statement its lofty spirit and sound substance greatly impress us and I feel sure it marks significant forward step in achieving essential goal of unity of British and American Christians on common program for world order."[59]

The growing ecumenical sentiment in Britain was bolstered by the unusual regard for the person of Archbishop William Temple, whose broad Christian sentiments were just what was needed during the war. He was a respected intellectual leader for the entire nation, something rarely achieved by English archbishops. He was probably too humble to realize how much influence he wielded, and so William Paton tried to explain it to him in a letter dated 20 January 1943:

My dear William, I have had it on my mind to write and say one thing to you which is bourne in on me as I wander up and down the country. I wonder if you realise the extent to which your leadership is accepted by the Free Churches and (I might also say, 'even') by the Church of Scotland. I find on all hands that, whatever may be the case among the bankers and the army colonels, there is an enormously widespread acceptance of your general lead and that Nonconformists in England do in fact accept you as the spokesman of the whole Church in a way which is quite new in our experience. When I was in Scotland in December I was interested to find the same thing there and it has attracted the attention of some of the Scottish church officials. I think you are probably too humble a person to believe this easily but I think it is right to tell you of this widespread feeling, for it is a new thing in this country and very valuable and precious.[60]

Paton's opinion of Temple was shared by H. H. Rowley, professor of Semitic Languages at the University College of North Wales, who mentioned in a public address that Temple would be a good man to send as a British delegate to the peace conference. Such a gesture would be "a public recognition of the fact that religion is not unrelated to our need," and it would be a practical move "since the present Archbishop is one who so uniquely represents British Christendom, not merely his own Church but all the Churches—to a degree few can ever have attained." Temple responded in the negative: "I believe ecclesiastics ought to be very much on the fringe and not in the center when it comes to practical political decisions." Rowley was persistent; he asked Temple to reconsider. He informed him that he held a "unique position in the estimate of the country, different from that of your predecessors." He could "represent the non-Anglican Churches to-day in a way in which no individual from within any of those Churches could." Temple also had "qualities of statesmanship rare in this age." The peace conference needed a strong Christian voice in its counsels. "There is no reason for men of principle to leave its drafting to men who have none. It is important that within the Conference there should be men who are vitally committed to Christian principles, and who test all by those principles . . . it is of utmost importance that the Treaty should be as nearly Christian as is practically possible. Your appointment as a delegate would be a recognition of that importance."[61]

There were limits, of course, to all this ecumenicity. A Unitarian minister asked Temple if his group could join in evangelism with the orthodox Christians and the archbishop responded with a brief explanation of the doctrine of the Incarnation. "Personally I find this distinction so vital," he said, "that I could not actively co-operate with Unitarians in anything resembling evangelism . . . for preaching the Gospel I have to recognise that there is a difference between us at a vital point." A certain Lord Samuel asked Temple to get the churches to become associated with a World Congress of Faiths. The archbishop reminded him that Christianity is "a profoundly intolerant religion, not of course in the sense that it justifies persecution . . . but in the sense of drawing a very sharp line between those who attempt to follow its way and those who only regard this as one among a number of good ways."[62]

Temple died on 26 October 1944, after serving as archbishop for only two-and-a-half years. No archbishop of Canterbury or York had ever published so much. More than seventy items under his name are listed in the British Museum catalogue. He was a philosopher, a theologian, a social teacher, an educational reformer, an ecumenical leader, a husband and father, and primate of all England. Niebuhr's eulogy was appropriate: "The man, the hour and the office stood in a creative relation to each other in a way we are not likely to see again in this generation."[63]

The difficulties of cooperation between Anglicans and Catholics were seen in an episode involving a movement called "The Sword of the Spirit" or simply "The Sword." It was inaugurated by His Eminence Cardinal Hinsley in August 1940 to deal with issues raised by the fearful isolation of England— the need for national unity and for the defense of principles like human liberty and natural law for which the British Commonwealth was fighting. The cardinal made no bones about the controlling theology: The principles they were defending found "their fullest development and justification" in Catholic teaching. The group said membership was "open to all who accept the aims of the Movement, and their full cooperation will be welcomed in the common cause of Truth and Justice." But it had two levels of membership: "ordinary membership," which was open to all Catholics who accepted the aims of the movement, and "associate membership" which gave one the right to receive literature and notice of activities but withheld the right to vote.

The purpose of the movement was to unite men in prayer, study, and action to restore an order of justice and peace, to combat the totalitarian systems that undermine human society and Christian civilization, to spread the knowledge of the principles of social and international order and of the Christian inheritance, and to ensure that the postwar settlement would be a just one, incorporating the Five Peace Points of Pope Pius XII. The group would achieve these ends by the organization of public meetings, lectures, conferences and retreats, private discussion groups, the production of literature, and in the general coordination and direction of Christian influences in national and international life.[64]

George Bell was anxious for Anglican–Catholic cooperation under the auspices of The Sword, but he found Lang, as usual, very cautious. When Bell asked Lang to initiate cooperative procedures, Lang complained, "I have some reason to suspect that those who at present are very busy in putting the Roman Church in the country forward as the only really active agency on the Christian side of patriotism are making the most of this Sword of the Spirit and comparing it with the apparent inactivity of the Church of England." Temple, who was at York at the time, wrote Lang, complaining that the movement in Lancashire was inviting everyone to join, claiming it was "a united Christian movement for forming a united Christian front against paganism. If Anglicans hold back they are at once represented as not caring about resistance to paganism and the Sword of the Spirit remains a pure Roman Catholic Society." Bell was unable to convince his primate, and Hinsley was unable to convince his bench of bishops.[65]

The really sticky problem was that joint meetings meant joint prayers and services. Cardinal Hinsley consulted Canons Smith and Mohoney on this and received a considered and detailed opinion: No compromise was to be allowed. The Holy See decreed that non-Catholics could be admitted to full membership of The Sword only if they excluded all public religious activity, Catholic as well as Protestant, from the movement. And so, in Moloney's description, "the crisis of the movement was reached in an extraordinary paradox: the crusading, essentially religious inspiration of the 'Sword's' progress was to be shed by all its participants who would then find their common cause in a vague, ethical sub-masonic friendly society from which all vital bonding characteristics, notably prayer and worship, would be excluded."[66]

The last chapter of this sad story was the "wing" phase, where various denominational wings of the organization would meet and pray, but always separately, never together. Christopher Dawson, who had emerged as the lay spokesman for the group, was very disappointed, remarking that the movement was degenerating into "a sort of Better Britain movement which could be done better under purely secular auspices." Bell went to see Hinsley in October 1941, and after a long conversation, they both agreed that full cooperation in the movement could not be achieved; they had reached the limits of intercommunication allowed by their churches. The bishop of London, Dr. Fisher, described the vision of Hinsley and Bell as "a measure of joint action such as had not happened in this country since the Reformation."[67]

The original Sword movement lost much of its impetus after the death of Cardinal Hinsley in 1943, but happily, the principle of cooperation had been broached and would bear fruit in coming years. After the war, a joint delegation of British churchmen, including Roman Catholics, visited the British Zone in Germany in October 1946 and produced a report entitled, *The Task of the Churches in Germany*. In 1947 a joint delegation of British churchwomen made a similar visit and published a report, *What We Saw in Germany*. Such joint missions would have been unthinkable before the war.[68]

CONCLUSION

World War II was widely portrayed as a struggle to defend Western or Christian civilization—the culture that had been formed under a thousand years of influence by the Biblical faith and the Christian Church. It was the thousand-year pagan Reich against the thousand-year Christian Europe. There should be no wonder, they said, that the makers of the total state should see in the Christian Church their greatest enemy. There, said Demant, "totalitarianism meets the flaming sword that guards the tree of life." The fascist dictators recognized the Church, said Sayers, "as the ultimate source of opposition to the establishment of any absolute temporal value or of any absolute temporal authority."[69]

What did the future hold? Georges Bernanon put the problem in three short sentences: "Christianity has been the making of Europe. Christianity is dead. Therefore Europe must die too. Unless—."[70] One may finish that sentence in many ways. Most British churchmen would finish it in the spirit of T. S. Eliot: "unless Europe returns to the faith that gave it spiritual unity in the first place."

NOTES

1. *Thus Spake Zarathustra* (I, 10), in *The Portable Nietzsche*, ed. Walter Kaufmann (New York: Penguin, 1959), 159.

2. *The Crown of the Wild Olive* (New York: John Wiley & Sons, 1876), 116.

3. *We Have Seen Evil: A Background to War* (London: Faber & Faber, 1941), 120.

4. Cited in William Temple, *Towards a Christian Order* (London: Eyre & Spottiswoode, 1942), 12.

5. Ibid., 8.

6. *God in a World at War* (Harmondsworth, England: Penguin, 1941), 40.

7. *The Idea of a Christian Society* (New York: Harcourt Brace, 1940), 65.

8. *Morality and War* (London: Burns, Oates, & Washbourne, 1939), 24.

9. *Dissent or Conform? War, Peace, and the English Churches 1900–1945* (London: SCM Press, 1986), 246.

10. *A Second Day of God* (London: Longmans, Green, 1940), x–xi, 7–10; see *A Day of God: Being Five Addresses on the Subject of the Present War* (London: Wells, 1914).

11. *A Sword Is Sharpened* (London: Marshall, Moran, & Scott, 1941), 128.

12. Henson, *The Good Fight* (London: Nisbet, 1940), 23, 43; Barry, *Faith in Dark Ages* (London: SCM Press, 1940), 56; Matthews, *Our War for Freedom: A Broadcast on the Day of National Prayer, October 8, 1939* (n.d., n.p.), 5. See also the pastoral letter from the Commission of the General Assembly of the Church of Scotland, signed by the Right Reverend Professor Archibald Main, Moderator: "To-day the fundamental moral ideals that make life worth living are imperilled in Europe, and we are fighting to defend them." *Home Bulletin on Spiritual Issues of the War* 7 (18 November 1939), 3.

13. Temple, *A Conditional Justification of War* (London: Hodder & Stoughton, 1940), 21; Davies, *The Two Humanities: An Attempt at a Christian Interpretation of History in the Light of War* (London: Clarke, 1940), 21.

14. *We Have Seen Evil*, 144, 149, 246.

15. See "The Mission of England" in *Sword of the Spirit* and the article in *The Dublin Review* (July 1940), both preserved in *Lang Papers* 84: 357, 388.

16. *Threat to Civilization: A Speech Delivered on October 15ᵗʰ 1943, in the Upper House of the Convocation of Canterbury* (Westminster, England: Press and Publications Board of the Church Assembly, 1943), 2–4.

17. For World War I, see Hoover, *God, Germany, and Britain in the Great War: A Study in Clerical Nationalism* (New York: Praeger, 1989), 67–69.

18. *The Foundations of Peace* (London: Eyre & Spottiswoode, 1942), 49–50.

19. Mumford, *Faith for Living* (London: Secker & Warburg, 1941), 77; Niebuhr, *Europe's Catastrophe and the Christian Faith* (London: Nisbet, 1940), 40.

20. *Begin Here: A War-Time Essay* (London: Gollancz, 1940), 90.

21. Zimmern, *Spiritual Values and World Affairs* (Oxford: Clarendon, 1939), 107, 110; Niebuhr, *Europe's Catastrophe*, 38.

22. Cited in *Spiritual Issues of the War* 204 (30 September 1943): 2.

23. *Lang Papers* 88: 303–304.

24. *The Church and the New Order* (London: SCM Press, 1941), 92, 102.

25. *Spiritual Values*, 101.

26. Lang's remarks appeared in the *Times* (19 August 1941). The Scottish Moderator, the spokesman for the free churches, declared that "the Roosevelt–Churchill statement is the most notable event since the declaration of war." Both are reported in *Spiritual Issues of the War* 95 (28 August 1941): 2. The publishers of Fulton J. Sheen's book informed the reader that "this work appears exactly as it was published in America. No revision or alteration has been made for it was felt that what applies to one great English-speaking democracy also applies to the other with equal force." *Philosophies at War* (London: Blanford, 1945), 4.

27. *The World War: Its Inner Bearings* (Calcutta, India: Culture Publishers, 1942), 3, 6, 8, 10.

28. Micklem, *The Theology of Politics* (London: Oxford University Press, 1941), x; Berry, *The Great Issue and Other War-Time Studies* (London: Independent Press, 1944), 66.

29. V. A. Demant, *Religious Prospect* (London: Muller, 1939), 49–50; Micklem, *Theology of Politics*, 43.

30. Richardson, *The Message of the Bible in War-Time* (London: SCM Press, 1940), 53. Demant, *Religious Prospect*, 50–51; Temple, *Citizen and Churchman* (London: Eyre & Spottiswoode, 1941), 27.

31. *Citizen and Churchman*, 22.

32. Demant, *Religious Prospect*, 42; Oldham, *Real Life Is Meeting* (London: Sheldon Press, 1942), 64–65; Sayers, *Begin Here*, 31–32.

33. Macnutt, *Four Freedoms: Atlantic and Christian* (Leicester, England: Thornley, 1943), 10; Dunning, *Settlement with Germany* (London: SCM Press, 1943), 47–48.

34. Steed, *Our War Aims* (London: Secker & Warburg, 1939), 179; Davies, *Two Humanities*, 39; Matthews, *The Moral Issues of the War* (London: Eyre & Spottiswoode, 1942), 21.

35. *Religious Prospect*, 35–38.

36. Murry, *Christocracy* (London: Dakers, 1942), 91, 94; Temple, *Thoughts in War-Time* (London: Macmillan, 1940), 119; Micklem, *Theology of Politics*, 88; Rupp, *Is This a Christian Country?* (London: Sheldon, 1941), 12.

37. Micklem, *Theology of Politics*, 13, 69; Barry, *Faith in Dark Ages*, 24; Matthews, *Foundations of Peace*, 19; Bottome, *Our New Order or Hitler's?* (Harmondsworth, England: Penguin, 1943), 19; Sheen, *Philosophies at War*, 112.

38. *Citizen and Churchman*, 29–30; Temple, *Thoughts in War-Time*, 119.

39. A. E. Baker, *William Temple and His Message: Selections from His Writings* (Harmondsworth, England: Penguin, 1946), 218–219.

40. *Personal Religion and the Future of Europe* (London: SCM Press, 1941), 80–81.

41. *Europe's Own Book* (London: Morrison & Gibb, 1944), 7–8.

42. Cited in *Spiritual Issues of the War* 105 (6 November 1941), 1.

43. A copy of the inscription is listed in *Lang Papers* 88: 257.

44. Cited in *Spiritual Issues of the War* 74 (3 April 1941): 3.

45. *Is This a Christian Country?*, 6.

46. W. Tudor Pole, *A Lighthouse Set on an Island Rock: Being the Substance of an Address Given at the Oddfellows Hall, Worthing, Sunday, September 13th, 1942* (London: Big Ben Council, 1942), 6. Carrel quoted in *William Temple Papers* 57: 21.

47. See *William Temple Papers* 57: 19, 25, 27, 31. Chief Rabbi J. H. Hertz composed a pamphlet from the Jews on the silent minute, asserting Jewish solidarity with "co-religionists" on the need for this kind of silence.

48. *Christocracy*, 57.

49. Cited in Hugh Martin, *Christian Counter-Attack: Europe's Churches against Nazism* (New York: Scribners, 1944), 17. For a very detailed account of the ecumenical movement, see Ruth Rouse and Stephen Charles Neill, eds., *A History of the Ecumenical Movement 1517–1948* (London: SPCK, 1967).

50. For accounts of the German Church's struggle, see E. C. Helmreich, *The German Churches under Hitler: Background, Struggle, and Epilogue* (Detroit: Wayne State University Press, 1979); E. H. Hanton, *Christians against Hitler* (London: SCM Press, 1952); Klaus Scholder, *A Requiem for Hitler and Other New Perspectives on the German Church Struggle* (London: SCM Press, 1989); R. P. Ericksen, *Theologians under Hitler: Gerhard Kittel, Paul Althaus, and Emanuel Hirsch* (New Haven, Conn.: Yale University Press, 1985); A. C. Cochrane, *The Church's Confession under Hitler* (Philadelphia: Westminster Press, 1963); T. N. Thomas, *Women against Hitler: Christian Resistance in the Third Reich* (Westport, Conn.: Praeger, 1994). Two con-

temporary accounts by leading theologians are Paul Tillich, *The German Church in Conflict* (New York: Federal Council of Churches, 1934) and Karl Barth, *The German Church Conflict* (London: Lutterworth, 1965).

51. Dunning, *Settlement with Germany*, 88; Niebuhr's remarks are in the foreword to "The Protestant Opposition Movement in Germany," in *Friends of Europe* 55: 4. Britons noted with satisfaction the startup of a new journal from America, edited by Niebuhr and Henry van Dusen, and called *Christianity and Crisis*, intended to be an ecumenical journal focusing on world events that had a bearing on the life of the Church.

52. See Mario Bendiscioli, *Nazism versus Christianity*, tr. Gerald Griffin (London: Skeffington, 1939), 130–132; *The New Racial Paganism*, tr. George Smith (London: Burns, Oates, & Washbourne, 1939), 62.

53. The rough draft of this sermon is preserved in *William Temple Papers* 58: 358–363. It has many changes and corrections written in pen over the typed manuscript, indicating that the archbishop may have struggled with the wording of this sensitive address. The sermon was broadcast over the radio. For a few excerpts, see *Spiritual Issues of the War* 168 (21 January 1943): 2–3.

54. This testimony occurs in many sources but this quotation is taken from Henry van Dusen, *What Is the Church Doing?* (London: SCM Press, 1941), 39.

55. *Is This a Christian Country?*, 36.

56. *Spiritual Issues of the War* 76 (17 April 1941): 1.

57. Ibid., 250 (17 August 1944): 2–3.

58. Ibid., 166 (7 January 1943): 1–2; 202 (16 September 1943): 4.

59. *William Temple Papers* 57: 357.

60. Temple, *Some Lambeth Letters*, ed. F. S. Temple (London: Oxford University Press, 1962), 56–57.

61. *William Temple Papers* 51: 143–146.

62. Temple, *Some Lambeth Letters*, 20, 41.

63. Quoted in David L. Edwards, *Leaders of the Church of England, 1828–1944* (London: Oxford University Press, 1971), 328.

64. See *Constitution of the Sword of the Spirit* (London: Richard Madley, n.d.), 1–2.

65. *Lang Papers* 84: 285, 321.

66. *Westminster, Whitehall, and the Vatican: The Role of Cardinal Hensley, 1935–43* (Burnbridge Wells, Kent, England: Burns & Oates, 1985), 200.

67. Ibid., 200–203. Ian McLaine points out that the Religious Division of the Ministry of Information gave a great deal of assistance to the *Sword of the Spirit*, a fact which they were anxious to conceal. The Church, furthermore, did not prove too cooperative with the MOI in its declarations about the war. *Ministry of Morale: Home Front Morale and the Ministry of Information in World War II* (London: Allen & Unwin, 1979), 151–152. For a summary of Anglican–Catholic cooperation during the war see O. T. Tomkins, "The Roman Catholic Church and the Ecumenical Movement, 1910–1948," in *History of the Ecumenical Movement 1517–1948* (Geneva: World Council of Churches, 1953), 688–689.

68. See Ronald C. D. Jasper, *George Bell: Bishop of Chichester* (London: Oxford University Press, 1967), 254.

69. Demant, *Religious Prospect*, 53; Sayers, *Begin Here*, 78.

70. Quoted by Douglas Stewart, *Personal Religion and the Future of Europe* (London: SCM Press, 1941), 125.

CHAPTER 7

1945: A New Order?

"In war there is no substitute for victory," said the American Caesar, General Douglas MacArthur. Few things are more discouraging to mankind than fighting a long war and then losing the peace. The Allies were determined that this unparalleled struggle called World War II would not peter out into a shameful negotiated peace, leaving the fascists in control of Germany and Italy. They demanded an "unconditional surrender" from the European Axis powers, and they got it.

On 24 April 1945, American and Russian forces met at Torgau on the Elbe River. Three days later, Italian partisans captured and executed Mussolini in Milan. German forces in Italy surrendered 2 May; and on the same day, Berlin fell to the Russians. Two days before, Hitler and his wife, Eva Braun, had committed suicide in the Berlin Bunker, leaving the government under the control of Grand Admiral Karl Doenitz. Early on the morning of 7 May, General Alfred Jodl of the German high command entered Allied headquarters in a red school building at Reims, France, and signed the terms of unconditional surrender on behalf of what was left of the German government. After five years, eight months, and seven days, the great war in Europe was over. The thousand-year Nazi Reich had lasted a little over twelve years!

The Allies designated 8 May as V-E (Victory in Europe) Day. The churches of Great Britain filled with grateful people, believers and unbelievers alike.

Winston Churchill led both houses of Parliament across the street to Westminster Abbey for a special thanksgiving service. Across town at St. Paul's Cathedral, Dean Matthews, who had watched over his sanctuary the entire war, observed that the "scenes in the Cathedral and around it defy description. Surely never have so many worshipers been in St. Paul's before. From early morning until late in the evening services followed one another, each attended by a reverent concourse. It is estimated that no fewer than 35,000 persons were present at services on that day, besides many other thousands who spent some moments in private devotion."[1]

The following Sunday, 13 May, was declared a day of "National Thanksgiving for Victory in Europe." The king and queen and the entire government joined in the services at St. Paul's. The famous Choir School had just returned from exile in Truro, Cornwall, and everything seemed back to normal. "When we heard the full choir," said Matthews, "with the voices of the singing boys rising like a fountain into the Dome, we knew that the tradition of St. Paul's as well as its structure had been preserved. Our faith had been justified."[2]

By the spring of 1945, the Allies had uncovered most of the German concentration camps, and the full horror of Nazi brutality was slowly beginning to dawn on the world. Dr. Fisher, now archbishop of London, used this as a final Q.E.D. for the war: "We have been wrestling with the power of darkness itself, with a spiritual horror. We always knew it; the stark evidence of the concentration camps has shocked us into a fresh knowledge of how dark and dreadful it was. We have seen unclean things in the human heart and that has sobered us." In a thanksgiving sermon he adapted the words of Lincoln's second inaugural address (4 March 1865) to the occasion:

Grant, O merciful God, that with malice toward none, with charity to all, with firmness in the right as thou givest us to see the right, we may strive to finish the task which thou hast appointed us; to bind up the nation's wounds; to care for him who shall have borne the battle, and for his widow and his orphan; to do all which may achieve and cherish a just and lasting peace among ourselves and with all the nations through Jesus Christ our Lord. Amen.[3]

The Allies had defeated the Axis, discredited fascism, and saved Christian civilization. What now? Shouldn't people just go back to "business as usual" and keep on doing whatever they ordinarily do in Western civilization? Many churchmen said no. On the contrary, they contended, the end of the war gives us a grand opportunity to clean up our own house. But why should our house need cleaning?

THE NEED FOR REFORM

One of the strangest results of World War II was the strong feeling among the British people that they were obliged to reform their own civilization even after they had defended it for six years against its mortal enemies. What was the source of this feeling?

First, there was a deep conviction that such a terrible, destructive war somehow signaled a major break with the past—even the past you have defended. During the blitz, as the defenders of St. Paul's watched the city of London burning around them, one of them said, "It is like the end of the world." A coworker replied, "It is the end of *a* world!"[4] Britain would obviously have to rebuild much of the nation's infrastructure and thus, by a typical quirk of divine providence, God was giving the nation an opportunity to build better than before. If you scoff at this notion, are you not suggesting that the previous Britain was perfect and needed no improvement?

Rom Landau took seriously the thesis that the war was a struggle for Christian civilization; hence he pressed on to the inevitable conclusion about the postwar period: Even the winners must make some drastic changes. "If we really are fighting for the decencies of a civilisation inseparable from religious beliefs," he maintained, "then the successful outcome of this war must be an intensification of that civilisation." In other words, if we truly believe in our own propaganda, then the war's end will be merely the beginning of a great new chapter in European history. If God grants the victory, we must become even more conformed to the principles we defended.

This war more than any other national issue in the past has become a test case for our beliefs and our civilisation. What for many years has been latent in our lives has finally been brought to a head and reached its crisis. No longer can there be room for any quibbling about the issue. The war is the lens through which our shortcomings are seen with terrifying clarity. . . . If we think of this war as the culmination of a spiritual conflict, the like of which has never shaken Europe before, we must admit that spiritually we are only just beginning to proceed in the right direction.[5]

After defending the principle of individualism against fascist totalitarianism, many churchmen and religious people reexamined and redefined it in a better context—a Christian context stressing love and fellowship. As Matthews noted, "The Christian principle that we are members one of another is sound economics, and its scope is not limited by national frontiers." In fact, argued Sampson Micklewright, it was the "bad individualism" of the Western world under capitalism that led to fascism and communism, with their inordinate stress on community. Christopher Dawson insisted that the choice was not between individualism and collectivism, because the Christian principle of fellowship by definition meant some kind of collectivism. The choice was between a mechanistic collectivism like fascism or communism and a true spiritual collectivism like the Christian Church.[6]

If one may use the word "social" as the opposite of "individual," then "socialism" can easily become a synonym for community, love, caring, and fellowship. Any student of the Bible knows that God dislikes the bad form of individualism; we must be our brother's keeper (Gen. 4:9). In the good sense of the term, then, all Christians should be socialists. Phyllis Bottome cited the hyperbolic exclamation of Alfred Adler: "If there is a baby in China with a headache, we are responsible." Canon S. J. Marriott said, "Everything points to a great socialization in the life of man."[7]

Capitalism came under direct attack in the name of Christian morality. John Drewett, in a book on the Ten Commandments, deplored the fact that many Christian utterances attacked fascism and Communism but left the impression that capitalism was perfectly compatible with Christian faith. "The almost incredible maldistribution of wealth in capitalist society strikes at the root of all true morality." The rugged individualist extolled in capitalistic hagiography is a clear case of bad individualism in action. Capitalism is thus a subtle form of idolatry. "The self-made man is unaware of his Creator; he thought that the world and his soul were his own." Drewett argued cogently for the communal ownership of raw materials:

Apart from the fact that raw materials are God's gift to mankind, the other powerful argument in favour of public ownership is that the vast increase in wealth in the past 200 years has been due to the inventive genius and labour of the whole community. This new wealth is therefore the property of the community, and those who appropriate it for themselves are in fact breaking the moral law. It is a measure of the falseness of our values that, far from being thought of as thieves, such people are the recipients of honours and are held up as patterns to be followed by those who would get on in the world.[8]

Capitalism is usually defended as a logical corollary of democracy, but Nathaniel Micklem disputed the idea that capitalism was compatible with classical liberalism. Any system that gives tremendous economic power to a few unrepresentative, unelected individuals gives them unwarranted control over the destinies of millions of people. Is this not a form of tyranny? Would we tolerate this condition in the political sphere? Why then do we tolerate it in the economic sphere? "If in the present war we are fighting for freedom, then in the minds of the majority in this country we are fighting against our own past as well as against the enemy."[9]

John Hadham hoped the future would bring a broader view of God's concern for all of human life. It is a deeply rooted Christian fallacy, he insisted, that God is interested only in men's souls, not their bodies. God is interested in men's total lives, "in their health and education, their capacity to enjoy beauty, to understand truth, to practise goodness, in the development of their whole personalities." Christians should share this same holistic concern for the entire personal life.[10]

Lewis Mumford considered the development of capitalism in modern history as an aspect of same "de-moralization" of society that culminated in fascism. He complained that we have created great engines of power but have eroded all moral systems to control them. The Church was corrupted by capitalism as early as Gregory VII, who, fearful of losing some monetary support, chided St. Francis for his sermons against wealth and luxury. Proof that capitalism rotted the hearts of its adherents could be seen in the fact that businessmen in the Allied nations sold things to the fascists, knowing they would be used for unlawful conquest. Such "poltroons" resembled those "chicken-hearted American business men," who cowered before gangsters in the protection racket.[11]

It seemed to many, therefore, that Socialism was an idea whose time had come. Individualism and capitalism seemed condemned by some of the same logic that refuted fascism and Nazism. Adam Smith's free-market system justified greed and destroyed human fellowship. The current economic system made "a man's relation with his fellows . . . subordinate to the blind play of economic forces."[12] If our Christian civilization wished to become even more Christian, something would have to be done about traditional capitalism.

Already by 1940 war aims and domestic reform had been joined together in a proposal called the "Ten Peace Points." The first five points had been suggested by Pope Pius XII on Christmas Eve, 1939, as the basis for a postwar peace. The Holy Father called for equality of rights to life, the independence of all nations, general disarmament, an international institution to guarantee and revise the peace settlement, and adequate attention to the demands of nations, populations, and racial minorities. The British clergy added five more principles, which it called "standards by which economic situations and proposals may be tested."

1. Extreme inequality in wealth and possessions should be abolished.
2. Every child, regardless of race or class, should have equal opportunities of education, suitable for the development of his peculiar capacities.
3. The family as a social unit must be safeguarded.
4. The sense of a Divine vocation must be restored to a man's daily work.
5. The resources of the earth should be used as God's gifts to the whole human race, and used with due consideration for the needs of the present and future generations.[13]

These principles were known as the Five Economic Standards of the Oxford Conference of 1937. The same five principles were issued after the Malvern Conference in 1941, a meeting of Anglican churchmen that included twenty bishops and nearly two hundred other members of the Church, both men and women. Dorothy Sayers attended Malvern and offered her special insights on economics, later to appear in the book *Why Work?* Sir Richard Ackland enlivened the conference with a rousing plea for the abolition of large-scale private ownership. One of those attending, John Armitage, testified that after the conference, "many of us felt, perhaps with certainty for the first time, that we were not alone in our struggle for a world which would, in some small measure, reflect our Christian faith."[14] By adding domestic reforms to international policies the clergy hoped to insure that the end of the war would bring about a comprehensive set of changes. Churchill, ever mindful of the rash promises given at the end of World War I, was very reluctant to promise anything definite to the war-weary British.

WILLIAM TEMPLE'S CONTRIBUTION TO REFORM

Probably no archbishop in English history has had the common folk more in his thoughts and in his heart than William Temple.[15] His concern for the working class was a matter of record: He was a member of the Labour Party from 1918 to 1925 and president of the Workers' Educational Association from 1908 to 1924. At one point in his career he was seriously considering the possibility of becoming a missionary in India, but Archbishop Davidson stepped in and said, "He is the only man in the Church at home who can act as liaison between the working man and the Church, and he simply cannot be spared."[16] These were prophetic words!

Temple saw a connection between war and capitalism. You may argue that the fascists controlled their economies to the detriment of the individual entrepreneur, but that does not address the real problem. Fascism and capitalism are both expressions of the will to power and power always corrupts and never wants to be under social control. The predominance of the profit motive is itself a source of war; our whole economic system has a tendency to war. Though most businessmen do not really want war, they nevertheless "desire what tends to destroy peace, and thus the working of the system has an inherent tendency towards international rivalry, jealousy and conflict."[17]

Controlling capitalism, therefore, could perhaps be defended on the same grounds as controlling crime or anything else that disturbs social order. Maybe we should put "cut-throat competition" in the same category as the literal cutting of throats. If capitalism creates disorder, the regulation of it is clearly the state's business, which will be the end of laissez-faire. "It can reasonably be claimed that the evil conditions in factories immediately after the Industrial Revolution were acute forms of disorder, and that Lord Shaftesbury's Factory Acts were passed for the establishment and maintenance of reasonable order in that sphere."[18]

Temple believed in the right to property, up to a point. He concurred with St. Thomas Aquinas, that property is necessary for human life, but he insisted that the right of property is a form of stewardship rather than of ultimate ownership. He pointed to the Jubilee Year of the Law of Moses (Lev. 25:8–24) as a good, humane custom whereby land must revert to its original owner every fifty years. Thus the purchase of land in perpetuity was forbidden: "The land belongs to God and is granted by Him to His people for their use. Now it is the Common Law of England at this moment that all the land of England belongs to the King as representing the whole community and the divinely constituted authority within it. And so-called landowners hold the use of the land but not absolute dominion over it. They can therefore be restrained for a use or development on the land which might be profitable to them but detrimental to the public interest."[19]

All these ideas and arguments came together in Temple's most famous book, *Christianity and the Social Order*, which represented the climax of his life's thought on social questions. By the time of his death, he was fully ensconced in the ranks of the great Christian Socialists such as Frederick Maurice, John Ludlow, Charles Kingsley, Thomas Hughes, Scott Holland, and Charles Gore. The book was originally published by Penguin, and quickly sold over 130,000 copies. It moved to Pelican in 1961 and has been reprinted ever since. For the writing of this small, highly compressed and effective book, Temple sought out the advice of economists John Maynard Keynes and R. H. Tawney. Keynes, who supplied the rationale for Roosevelt's New Deal, is widely considered the most important economist of the twentieth century. For years Tawney had championed the medieval concept that economics, unlike physics and chemistry, is a branch of ethics and ethics a branch of theology. Temple agreed and often praised the medieval policies of the just price and the prohibition of usury.

The goal of a Christian social order is *"the fullest possible development of individual personality in the widest possible fellowship* (italics added)." Temple suggested some fundamental changes in British society that could move the nation toward these most worthy goals: universal education up to age eighteen; decent housing; workers' voice in the control of enterprises; sufficient leisure, including a five-day work week and an annual holiday with pay; and the guarantee of freedom of worship, speech, assembly, and association. All this would require the heavy hand of the state to implement, but Temple seemed strangely unconcerned with the details—where the devil often lies. He offered the incredible suggestion that what Christianity could do was "to lift the parties to a level of thought and feeling at which the problem disappears."[20]

Temple probably recalled the disastrous coal strike of 1926, when a group of bishops attempted to bring the government, the coal owners, and the miners together in an effort to settle the dispute. Prime Minister Stanley Baldwin was so miffed at this "intrusion" by the clergy that he inquired how the bishops would like it if he referred a proposed revision of the Nicene Creed to the Iron and Steel Federation! The archbishop preferred for the Church to be the conscience of the nation and to work behind the scenes. He preferred to be like John Wesley, who had no intention of bringing the Church into politics, but nevertheless, by his preaching and revivalism, eventually brought about the abolition of the slave trade and slavery.

Temple's views brought him into line with the thinking of Lord William Beveridge (1879–1963), whose influential book, *Social Insurance and Allied Services* (1942), became known as the popular "Beveridge Report." Ever since his *Unemployment: A Problem of Industry* (1909), Beveridge had argued that unemployment was largely a matter of industrial organization, not an iron law of classical economics. Later he came under the influence of Keynesian economics and set forth a revised account in *Full Employment in a Free Society* (1944), a study which was used after the war in working out the new British welfare system.

Beveridge had a simple argument for full employment: If we did it in war, we can do it in peace. All we need is the same determination. Many people agreed with this ideology. Micklem insisted that there was nothing utopian about a planned economy: "It is only necessary that we carry over into peace the spirit that now animates us in war." "What a poor advertisement for a system," said Ackland, "that it can only employ the whole of its resources for purposes of destruction in time of war."[21]

The reply to this simplistic argument is obvious: War is a unique situation which can seldom be duplicated in peacetime. In war the very existence of the nation is at stake, but in peacetime people must be motivated by less alarming challenges. Citizens are simply not prepared to sacrifice themselves for a peacetime aim in the same way as they are for a wartime aim. Soldiers transcend the economic motive, it is true, but that is simply because they are trained to die for their country (and they face a firing squad if they desert). Are we certain that we want to use the same methods just to combat unemployment in peacetime? To treat every social problem as if it were a war requiring military methods reminds one of the fascist dictators.[22]

A planned economy frightens the conservatives because it requires regimentation, and thus it poses a threat to traditional individual freedoms. Guy M. Kendersley, a stockbroker and former member of Parliament, asked Temple not to give any support to the Beveridge Report because it involved the "greatest of all political issues—the liberty of the citizen and the dangers inherent in the claims of the omni-competent State." Every encroachment on individual liberty by the state, he said, "should be regarded by Christians with suspicion." Temple answered by affirming that "there are certain Christian principles alongside of liberty—notably fellowship—which find peculiarly vivid expression in the Beveridge Plan." Since the British people have a special knack for working out in practice the correlation of principles that seem to be logically opposed to each other, he felt that they might be able to show the world "what is not so much a middle path between communism and individualism as a genuine expression of the sound principles lying behind each." At any rate, the Primate of all England took the clear position that a certain level of economic security must have precedence over liberty: "I believe myself that the Beveridge plan at any rate can be so administered as to increase actual liberty, for it seems to me that the primary necessity for effective liberty is security as regards the basic consumer goods; a liberty in which one of the alternatives theoretically open is existence below the level of civilised life is not a real liberty. I believe that by a deliberate ordering of the economic basis of life we can greatly increase personal freedom."[23]

One of Temple's critics charged that he had changed the wording of the Great Commandment from "love thy neighbor" to "love thy poor neighbour and hate thy rich neighbour."[24] In books, speeches, and radio addresses, Temple had indeed suggested that a profits-limitation clause should be included in a company's original articles of association. Persons who invest money in an industry should not have an everlasting claim on its profits; we should let an investor double his profits and then stop there. He recommended that the interest receivable on a loan should be limited to a sum equal to the principle. He seemed delighted to have found an old Hindu law that contained the same regulation. His stand placed him with several great civilizations—Hebrew, Greek, Christian, Muslim, and Indian—in his suspicions of usury.[25]

All this did not make the archbishop a Socialist or a Communist, but when you are performing the Hegelian tightrope act, you are misunderstood by both right and left wings. In a speech to Americans in Manchester, Temple let slip the remark that he saw no incompatibility between Christianity and "economic communism." However, in certain media reports of the speech the word "economic" was omitted, making it sound as if he were endorsing communism as Christian. Temple explained that "there is a communism which is flatly unChristian because it makes no allowance for . . . individual freedom of mind and spirit. Christianity insists on two complimentary principles: personal freedom and fellowship."[26]

Some industrialists agreed with Temple. C. J. Bartlett, managing director of Vauxhall Motors Ltd., wrote that the need for profits-limitation was the general feeling of a large number of people in the automobile industry: "A good number of us, at any rate, believe that until we have grappled with this problem there will be no lasting industrial peace."[27]

The surprising Labour Party victory of July 1945 indicated that a good portion of the British people were thinking along the same lines as Temple and the Socialists. By May 1945, all parties in the wartime coalition wanted an early election. Churchill wanted the coalition to continue at least until the defeat of Japan, but the Labour Party forced the election. As the architect of the recent victory over fascism, Churchill seemed unbeatable; the vote showed that people honored him as the war leader, not as the leader who would bring about the changes they wanted *after* the war. The Labour victory reduced the Conservatives to 213 seats in a Parliament of 640.

It was said at the time, and has been repeated since, that the Labour Party owed its victory to Temple more than to any other man.[28] The sweeping reforms put into place from 1945 to 1950 seemed to be a clear beginning in the building of a Christian social system. If we now look back with less enthusiasm, we must never forget the idealism that launched it. We must always remember that many Britons of 1945 felt a deep obligation, after six years of war, to bring their economic system into line with the principles they had preached while defending the war. The Church of England has had a bad conscience for two centuries over its failure to play a worthy role in the Industrial Revolution, but many people felt that the Church had finally caught up with the times in the period from 1945 to 1950.

Temple, like most welfare statists, talked as if the state had a bottomless purse—it was a great horn of plenty that would never be exhausted. Money did not matter and deficits did not matter, as his mentor Keynes argued. The archbishop talked as if every social problem must have an answer—the mark of a utopian dilettante. When a theologian and churchman pontificates, as he did in *Christianity and Social Order*, and then confesses in a postscript that he is just an amateur, this is irresponsible. The truth is, he *was* an amateur in sociology and economics, but a world-recognized professional in his true fields—philosophy and theology. Yet thousands of clergymen and religious people, then and now, took him to be an expert in sociology and economics. The criticism of Carmichael and Goodwin is just: "William Temple had every reason to know that the influence of his personal views and wishes was tremendous, that it was enhanced by his exalted positions in the Church, and that his disciples would assume that he was speaking with a proper sense of responsibility if not actually *ex cathedra*."[29]

In Temple's defense, one may note that a crucial "spiritual imperative" was often ignored by media reports of his speeches. For example, in March 1943, he made a speech at Leicester where he discussed his economic policies, but he ended the speech with a long passage that stressed the religious dimension. All these economic suggestions will be futile, he predicted, unless the hearts were right; and thus evangelism and conversion were vital to the success of all his practical projects. The Press Association supplied this speech to every newspaper in Britain but cut off the religious part. Hence the reader missed the spiritual imperative and took the speech as "nothing but a judgment expressed on certain political expediencies."[30] Already in his *Hope of a New World*, Temple had said that knowledge is not enough; what we need most is not guidance but redemption. If there is to be a Christian civilisation, "we need not only citizens who have the right picture of society, but also enough citizens who have found the redeeming power that is in Christ."[31]

VOICES OF CONCERN

Many of the people in this study stressed the same spiritual imperative and, because of it, were a bit suspicious of any new order that might be coming after the war. When you see atheists like H. G. Wells calling for a completely secular education in the "New World Order," said E. G. Rupp, it is time to make clear that we are fighting godlessness wherever it appears. Thus a new order "which is democratic and secular is no more tolerable than the systems of the Communists or Fascists."[32]

Frederick B. Macnutt insisted that no plan for social reordering, democratic or totalitarian, is safe from being wrecked "by the sinfulness of man untouched by the redeeming grace of God." Martyn Lloyd-Jones argued that "religion must precede morality if morality itself is to survive. . . . Any attempt to organise society without that basis is doomed to failure even as it always has been in the past." Gerald Vann warned that if you try to "build a purely human world, without reference to divine law," you will "sink to sub-humanity." William Paton felt that no plan of political federation or economic reorganization would work by itself: "There must be, to put it at its lowest, a willingness to work it, and there will be no such willingness unless there are common convictions, common standards, and some underlying unity of spirit."[33]

Leslie Weatherhead noted that "men's hearts are never changed by battle," and "war has no power of itself even to begin a new age or a new order, it only provides the opportunity." How often have we heard people say that, given goodwill, any problem on Earth could be solved? It is easy to say, but who gives this goodwill "except the Spirit of Him who came to bring peace and goodwill to men"? What the world needs is that mysterious bond of fellowship that Christ created between two natural enemies, Simon the Zealot and Matthew the Publican. No mere secular moral code could have accomplished that. Weatherhead said he was often drawn to some proposals of Socialism, but "so many of my Socialist friends are so bitter and hostile to all who think differently from them, their creed has led to such a soulless materialism in some places where it has been tried, that I find it quite impossible to see a new world born from Socialism."[34]

L. P. Jacks, who had lived through World War I and its aftermath, was filled with loathing as the end of World War II approached: "Alas, the old vocabulary has come to life again: the same stock phrases, the same catchwords, the same pious platitudes, the same airy projects." He warned that utopia, a perfect society, required a perfect people to operate it: "The people I meet are mostly good people, many of them, thank God, far better than I, and yet, like me, not good *enough* for living the great life and doing the great deeds an ideal system would require of us all. . . . I am very sure, my friends, that if you and I were suddenly launched into an ideal world, we should be unable to play the part, we should make a terrible mess of that world, and soon wreck it."[35]

Dorothy L. Sayers warned Christians to keep the proper order in the Great Commandments: Love God first, then your neighbor. The second commandment depends on the first. Without the first, "the second is a delusion and a snare." The humanist makes man the measure of all things and puts neighbor above God. We should beware of all new orders based on mere neighbor-love: "To suppose that any human problem can be disposed of out of hand by the solemn invocation of some minor deity such as 'social credit' or 'the land for the people' or even 'abracadabra' is to believe in magic." We must put economics in its place, Sayers said, as a necessary condition of human existence but not the sole or even the sufficient condition.[36]

D. R. Davies sounded the loudest warnings of all. He said the Church "imperils both the world and her own witness whenever she is unduly influenced by secular urgency." Every new order is just man's latest attempt to live independently of God—an effort he has been making since his expulsion from the garden. "Unregenerate society nurses the illusion that the next experiment—European Federation, Socialism, or what not—will succeed. *The Church knows it will fail*. But man must find that out himself. He will not believe it otherwise (italics added)." Concern for the poor as a mass is not the same as the Biblical "love of the brethren. . . . Agitate for the poor, by all means, but don't deceive yourself that by doing just that, you are being Christian. Christian love lies in another realm entirely." A great many Socialists are tormented by the doubt over "whether the achievement of Socialism is possible without the destruction of the political and cultural heritage of Europe." Europe's greatest need is for "a generation of men and women who believe in Heaven, in an order of reality transcending time [because] a minority of men with this realisation in the roots of their being have in them the power to launch civilisation on a new career."[37]

Hence, World War II ended like World War I, with one part of the clergy working for a new order and another part suspicious of all social engineering. Both groups would have agreed with this dictum: There can be no brotherhood of man without the fatherhood of God. One would have to say, moreover, that the optimists of 1945 were much more subdued than those of 1919. They had hopes for the future, but they were not misled by any silly theory of "inevitable progress" like those of the 1920s and 1930s. After 1945 the British people seldom displayed a blind faith in the United Nations or their own social engineering. It will probably be a long time before such naive, liberal optimism afflicts them again. When it does, we sincerely hope they will drag out their history books and read once more about that "nightmare decade" of the 1930s and the terrible war that followed.

NOTES

1. Matthews, *St. Paul's Cathedral in War-Time, 1939–45* (n.p.: Hutchinson, 1946), 67.

2. Ibid.

3. *Spiritual Issues of the War* 287 (10 May 1945): 4; *Fisher Papers* 272: 139.

4. *St. Paul's Cathedral in War-Time*, 35.

5. *We Have Seen Evil: A Background to War* (London: Faber & Faber, 1941), 177–178, 200.

6. Matthews, *Foundations of Peace* (London: Eyre & Spottiswoode, 1942), 36; Micklewright, "The Brotherhood of Man," in *This War and Christian Ethics* (London: Blackwell, 1940), 107; Dawson, *Christianity and the New Age* (Manchester, N.H.: Sophia Institute Press, 1931), 100–101.

7. Bottome, *Our New Order or Hitler's?* (Harmondsworth, England: Penguin, 1943), 111; Marriott, *Towards a Christian Order*, ed. William Temple (London: Eyre & Spottiswoode, 1942), 12.

8. *The Ten Commandments in the 20th Century* (Westminster, England: SPCK, 1941), 30–31, 59.

9. *The Theology of Politics* (London: Oxford University Press, 1941), 101.

10. *God in a World at War* (Harmondsworth, England: Penguin, 1941), 30.

11. *Faith for Living* (London: Secker & Warburg, 1941), 114–115, 117.

12. This is from the summary of the work of the Economic Section of the World Conference of the Christian Church in Oxford, 1937, presented in *Social Justice and Economic Reconstruction: A Statement by the Commission of the Churches for International Friendship and Social Responsibility* (n.p., n.d.), 6. The preface was written by William Temple, who was chairman of the commission.

13. The Ten Peace Points first appeared in the *Times*, 21 December 1940. The letter was signed by Archbishops Lang and Temple, Cardinal Hinsley, and Walter H. Armstrong, moderator of the Free Church Federal Council.

14. *To Christian England* (London: Longmans, Green, 1942), 89.

15. See the insightful study by Robert Craig, *Social Concern in the Thought of William Temple* (London: Gollancz, 1963).

16. *William Temple Papers* 47: 367.

17. Temple, *The Hope of a New World* (London: SCM Press, 1940), 17, 50.

18. Temple, *Citizen and Churchman* (London: Eyre & Spottiswoode, 1941), 30–31.

19. *The Hope of a New World*, 53.

20. *Christianity and the Social Order* (Harmondsworth, England: Penguin, 1942), 21.

21. See Beveridge, "Work for All after the War," in *Our New Order or Hitler's?*, ed. Phyllis Bottome, 53; Micklem, *Theology of Politics*, 107; Ackland, *Unser Kampf: Our Struggle* (Harmondsworth, England: Penguin, 1941), 63.

22. Nicholas Pronay shows how this naive argument got into films made by the Ministry of Information such as *Land of Promise*, which came out in 1945. See his essay, "*The Land of Promise*: The Projection of Peace Aims in Britain," in *Film and Radio Propaganda in World War II*, ed. K.R.M. Short (London: Croom Helm, 1983), 68.

23. Temple, *Some Lambeth Letters*, ed. F. S. Temple (London: Oxford University Press, 1962), 89–91.

24. See the letter from Rev. E. E. Skuse, *William Temple Papers* 47: 225. Skuse had accused Temple of "preaching socialism," which Temple said was "a thing I have never done and never would do!"

25. Letter to G. P. Dawnay, *William Temple Papers* 18: 37. Major General G. P. Dawnay was head of Dawnay, Day & Co., Ltd., London, and president of the Industrial Christian Fellowship, Westminster. He sent Temple a copy of his little booklet, *Some Thoughts on Usury*, and the two exchanged views on the subject.

26. See the special memo in *William Temple Papers* 46: 86. In a letter to a friend, Temple said it was rather curious that his Manchester speech should have led to so much discussion when the same point in two published books hardly attracted any attention at all (Ibid., 79).

27. *William Temple Papers* 46: 54. In a special memo following the Albert Hall speech on 26 September 1942, the letters show that most respondents were very favorable to Temple's reform suggestions. The memo was dated 19 October 1942, and came from the Lord Privy Seal, the office of Sir Stafford Cripps (Ibid., 47: 163–164).

28. The first time was by Hannen Swaffer in the *Daily Herald*. See John D. Carmichael and Harold S. Goodwin, *William Temple's Political Legacy* (London: Mowbray, 1965), vi.

29. Carmichael and Goodwin, *William Temple's Political Legacy*, 10.

30. Letter to E. E. Skuse, *William Temple Papers* 47: 209.

31. *The Hope of a New World*, 70–71.

32. *Is This a Christian Country?* (London: Sheldon Press, 1941), 36–37.

33. Macnutt, *Four Freedoms: Atlantic and Christian* (Leicester, England: Thornley, 1943), 18; Lloyd-Jones, *The Plight of Man and the Power of God* (London: Hodder & Stoughton, 1942), 30; Vann, *Religion and World Order* (Westminster, England: Daire, 1945), 9; Paton, *The Church and the New Order* (London: SCM Press, 1941), 48.

34. *The Church and the New Order*, 16; *Thinking Aloud in War-Time: An Attempt to See the Present Situation in the Light of the Christian Faith* (London: Hodder & Stoughton, 1941), 73–74; *This Is the Victory* (London: Hodder & Stoughton), 312.

35. *Confessions of an Octogenarian* (London: Allen & Unwin, 1942), 256, 259.

36. *Why Work? An Address Delivered at Eastbourne, April 23, 1942* (London: Metheun, 1942), 19; *Begin Here: A War-Time Essay* (London: Gollancz, 1940), 100.

37. *Divine Judgment in Human History* (London: Sheldon Press, 1941), 48; *The Church and the Peace* (London: Nisbet, 1940), 11, 24, 29; *Secular Illusion or Reality?* (London: Eyre & Spottiswoode, 1942), 118, 121.

CHAPTER 8

Reflections

War memorials are an interesting study. They reveal a lot about how people view their nation's military struggles. The British people erected thousands of memorials to the dead of World War I, but few separate memorials specifically to the dead of World War II. They often just added the dead of the second war on an existing or separate slate of a World War I memorial. "To those who erected the first war memorials," writes Alan Wilkinson, "the war was a unique and unrepeatable catastrophe; perhaps there would never be another war again. To us it looks rather more like the first war in a continuing world crisis."[1]

The clergy of World War I were content to view Germany as a Christian nation that had temporarily gone astray, but the churchmen of World War II saw her as a nation in the grip of a pagan totalitarianism—a regime that rejected Christianity, persecuted German Christians, and threatened the very existence of a religious civilization that had taken a thousand years to develop. The second war was justified as a struggle for the salvation of Christian civilization—a notion which has certain problems attached to it.

Was the war really for Christian civilization? That depends on whom you ask and on how you define the term "Christian civilization." You could define it in such a way that the answer is yes; but you could also define it in such a way that the answer is no. If Christian civilization is defined as one where every citizen is a Christian by definition, and where a non-Christian religion is illegal, then there has never been such a civilization, except perhaps in the High Middle Ages. Certainly World War II was not fought to preserve such a civilization, because it had long since ceased to exist. Our open, liberal societies are based on religious freedom. One can be a full citizen without being a member of any Christian church or religious community.

On the other hand, if Christian civilization is defined as one in which the broad, general culture and morality are based on the Hebrew–Christian faith, then the war in that sense was fought to preserve Christian civilization. It was fought to save *our* system, which, whether we like it or not, grew up under the strong influence of Christianity and at the time was still generally Christian. Temple always added that the war was fought to save *and extend* our Christian civilization; that is, we fought to preserve a kind of "launching pad" for an even better, more Christian, civilization.

One of the strongest claims made during the war was that Western liberalism, with its values of personal freedom, individual rights, and limited government, developed out of the Christian religion. To evaluate this claim thoroughly would get us into the tangled question of the geneology of ideas. It would be hard to find a historian who would not agree that Christianity made a significant contribution to the development of liberalism, but T. S. Eliot issued a salutary warning along this line: "To identify any particular form of government with Christianity is a dangerous error, for it confounds the permanent with the transitory, the absolute with the contingent."[2] It is also an error, one must add, because it suggests that only after Christianity had "evolved" for several centuries did it attain its "true" meaning in the mature fruit of Western European liberalism. Any such evolutionary paradigm placed on Church history would suggest that the complete Gospel was not preached in the early primitive stages of the church.

Christianity existed a long time before it produced the Magna Carta. Why did we not see free institutions developing before 1215? Why did free institutions not develop in the Orthodox East during the centuries under Christianity? Why did liberal institutions not develop in the lands under the Roman Catholic Church? Were these invalid forms of Christianity? Why did liberal ideas and institutions develop mostly in England and mostly in modern times? Was there something significant in England's geographical distance from Europe? It would appear that the freedoms Anglo–Saxons cherish owe more to Protestantism than to Catholicism and Orthodoxy, and, even closer to the truth, more to the Protestant left than to the magisterial mainstream. Liberalism owes more to Anabaptists and Calvinists than to Roman Catholics, Lutherans, and Anglicans. But it would be rather arrogant to say that the areas of Christendom that failed to produce political liberalism were somehow not truly Christian or were underdeveloped.

It is good for us to remember that the Gospel of Christ has spread and flourished for many centuries in nations that were not democratic or liberal; but it was nonetheless the Gospel. A churchman from World War II might argue at this point that it took a long time for certain ideals to sink in deeply enough to change European politics and culture to evolve toward the development of liberalism. If this point be accepted, then one could add this important consideration: *Since it took so long for it to develop, should we not be zealous to preserve it in its mature form?* This last point gives me some pause. I cherish these fragile free institutions; and they are fragile, as we saw from the sad history of the Weimar Republic. If it took a specific process to develop liberalism in the Christian West, we should perhaps consider it a plant of great value, worthy of our life's blood in defense.

We may have to leave aside the question of whether we can attach the adjective "Christian" to the civilization we decided to defend in World War II. I personally see no problem in calling it Christian in a general sense. But the real question is whether it was worth defending, whatever the adjective we may attach to it. The Christian would say that he defended it because it was Christian. The humanist would say he defended it because it was humane, civilized, or ethical. It was certainly worth defending when you consider the alternative—Nazi racism, with its ultimate corollary, the final solution of the "Jewish question." Those who uncovered the death camps and bulldozed the bodies in 1945 found it difficult to maintain any theory of the moral equivalency of civilizations. Our continuing analysis of National Socialism, the Holocaust, and Hitler's personality leaves no doubt in my mind that the British government and people did the right thing when they made that crucial decision to fight in 1939. After all the provisos, explanations, and apologies we must make about World War II, it would be tragic for us to lose sight of that fact.

NOTES

1. *The Church of England and the First World War* (London: SCM Press, 1978), 297.
2. *The Idea of a Christian Civilization* (New York: Harcourt Brace, 1940), 57.

Selected Bibliography

Ackland, Richard. *Unser Kampf: Our Struggle*. Harmondsworth, England: Penguin, 1941.

Armitage, John. *To Christian England*. London: Longmans, Green, 1942.

Baker, A. E. *William Temple and His Message: Selections from His Writings*. Harmondsworth, England: Penguin, 1946.

Ballard, Frank. F. *Does War Shake Faith?* London: Purnell and Sons, N.d.

Barclay, George. *The Bible Speaks to Our Day*. London: SCM Press, 1944.

Barry, F. R. *Faith in Dark Ages*. London: SCM Press, 1940.

Baynes, Norman H. *Intellectual Liberty and Totalitarian Claims*. Oxford: Clarendon Press, 1942.

Bell, George K. A. *The Threat to Civilization*. A Speech Delivered on October 15th, 1943, in the Upper House of the Convocation of Canterbury. Westminster, England: Press and Publications Board of the Church Assembly, 1944.

————. *God above the Nation: A Sermon Preached at St. Mary's, Oxford, before the University, Sunday, June 18, 1939*. Oxford: Blackwell, 1939.

Belloc, Hilaire. *The Catholic and the War*. London: Burns & Oates, 1940.

Bendiscioli, Mario. *Nazism versus Christianity*. Tr. Gerald Griffin. London: Skeffington, 1939.

————. *The New Racial Paganism*. Tr. George Smith. London: Burns, Oates, & Washbourne, 1939.

Berry, Sidney M. *The Great Issue and Other War-Time Studies*. London: Independent Press, 1944.

Bevan, Edwyn. *Christians in a World at War*. London: SCM Press, 1940.

Beveridge, William H. *The Pillars of Security and Other War-Time Essays and Addresses*. London: Allen & Unwin, 1943.

Bottome, Phyllis, ed. *Our New Order or Hitler's?* Harmondsworth, England: Penguin, 1943.

Briggs, Susan. *Keep Smiling Through: The Home Front 1939–45*. London: Cox & Wyman, 1975.

Brittain, Vera. *England's Hour*. New York: Macmillan, 1941.

Butterfield, Herbert. *Christianity and History*. London: Bell, 1949.

Calder, Angus. *The People's War: Britain 1939–1945*. New York: Pantheon Books, 1969.

Cammaerts, Emile. *The Peace That Was Left*. London: Cresset Press, 1945.

———. *Upon This Rock*. London: Cresset Press, 1942.

Cannadine, David. *The Speeches of Winston Churchill*. London: Penguin, 1990.

Carey, Walter. *As Man to Man: Broadcast Talks to the Forces*. London: Mowbray, 1940.

———. *A War-Time Faith for a Resolute People*. London: Nisbet, 1939.

———. *Thinking Straight about This War*. London: Mowbray, 1939.

Carmichael, John D., and Harold S. Goodwin. *William Temple's Political Legacy*. London: Mowbray, 1965.

Carpenter, S. C. *Faith in Time of War*. London: Eyre & Spottiswoode, 1940.

Causton, Bernard. *The Moral Blitz: War Propaganda and Christianity*. London: Secker & Warburg, 1941.

Christian Basis for the Post-War World: A Commentary on the Peace Points. London: SCM Press, 1942.

Clarke, Norman H. *Thine Is the Kingdom: A Book of Prayers for Use in Time of War*. London: Harrap, 1942.

Clay, N. L., ed. *This Half Century: 50 Poems from 1900 to 1949*. London: Heinemann, 1950.

Coates, J. R. *War—What Does the Bible Say?* London: Sheldon, 1940.

Cockin, F. A. *Religion and the Modern World: Six Broadcast Talks*. London: SCM Press, 1942.

———. *What Does "A" Do Next?* London: SCM Press, 1939.

Cohen, Israel. *Britain's Nameless Ally*. London: Allen, 1942.

Constitution of the Sword of the Spirit. London: Richard Madley, N.d.

Davidson, Donald. *A Sword Is Sharpened*. London: Marshall, Morgan & Scott, 1941.

Davies, D. R. *In Search of Myself: The Autobiography of D. R. Davies*. London: Geoffrey Bles, 1961.

———. *Secular Illusion or Christian Realism?* London: Eyre & Spottiswoode, 1942.

———. *Divine Judgment in Human History*. London: Sheldon Press, 1941.

———. *The Church and the Peace*. London: Nisbet, 1940.

———. *The Two Humanities: An Attempt at a Christian Interpretation of History in the Light of War*. London: Clarke, 1940.

Dawson, Christopher. *Christianity and the New Age*. Manchester, N.H.: Sophia Institute Press, 1931.

Demant, V. A. *The Religious Prospect*. London: Muller, 1939.

Devey, Bessie. *The Bells of Victory and Other Poems*. Ilfracombe, England: Stockwell, 1945.

Drewett, John. *The Ten Commandments in the 20th Century*. Westminster, England: SPCK, 1941.

Dunning, T. G. *Settlement with Germany*. London: SCM Press, 1943.

Edwards, David L. *Leaders of the Church of England, 1828–1944*. London: Oxford University Press, 1971.

Edwyn, Bevan. *Christians in a World at War*. London: SCM Press, 1940.

Eliot, T. S. *The Idea of a Christian Society*. New York: Harcourt Brace, 1940.

Eppstein, John. *Right against Might*. Oxford: Roman Catholic Social Club, 1940.

Fenn, Eric. *The Crisis and Democracy*. London: SCM Press, 1938.

Garlick, Phyllis L. *How Shall We Pray in War-Time?* London: SPCK, 1942.

Garnet, Clew. *Victory Vision*. Canterbury, England: Jennings, 1944.

———. *Our V Sign*. Canterbury, England: Jennings, 1942.

Glasgow, George. *Diplomacy and God*. London: Longmans, Green, 1941.

———. *Peace with Gangsters?* London: Cape, 1939.

Gollancz, Victor. *"Let My People Go": Some Practical Proposals for Dealing with Hitler's Massacre of the Jew and an Appeal to the British Public*. London: Gollancz, 1943.

Goudge, H. L. *The Case against Pacifism: A Sermon Preached before the University of Oxford, Sunday Morning, January 30, 1938*. London: Mowbray, 1938.

Green, Peter. *Forty Short Prayers for War-Time Based on Passages from the Holy Scriptures*. London: Hodder & Stoughton, 1943.

———. *The Moral Condition of Great Britain Today*. London: Mowbray, 1943.

Gupta, Nolini Kanta. *The World War: Its Inner Bearings*. Calcutta, India: Culture Publishers, 1942.

Hadham, John. *God and Human Progress*. London: Penguin, 1944.

———. *God in a World at War*. Harmondsworth, England: Penguin, 1941.

Haffenden, Alfred R. *99 Stanzas European*. London: Daniel, 1941.

Hedges, Sid G. *Christian Youth: The Alternative to Hitler Youth*. London: Camelot, 1943.

Henson, Hensley. *The Good Fight*. London: Nisbet, 1940.

Hinsley, H. E. *The Sword of the Spirit*. BBC Home Service, Sunday, 10 December 1939.

Hobhouse, Stephen. *Forty Years and an Epilogue: An Autobiography (1881–1951)*. London: Clarke, 1951.

Hughes, A. Price. *A Warrior on Wings: Tribute, Comfort and Challenge*. London: Epworth, 1942.

Hughes, Michael R., ed. *The Letters of Lewis Mumford and Frederick J. Osborn: A Transatlantic Dialogue 1938–70*. Bath, England: Adams & Dart, 1971.

Inge, William Ralph. *A Pacifist in Trouble*. London: Putnam, 1939.

Jacks, L. P. *The Confessions of an Octogenarian*. London: Allen & Unwin, 1942.

Jasper, Ronald C. D. *George Bell: Bishop of Chichester*. London: Oxford University Press, 1967.

Jessop, T. E. *The Treaty of Versailles: Was It Just?* London: Nelson, 1942.

———. *Has the Christian Way Failed?* London: Epworth, 1941.

Joad, C.E.M. *Adventures of the Young Soldier in Search of the Better World*. New York: ARCO, 1944.

———. *What Is at Stake and Why Not Say So?* London: Gollancz, 1940.

———. *Journey through the War Mind*. London: Faber & Faber, 1939.

———. *Why War?* London: Penguin, 1939.

Judd, Francis A. *A Call to Christendom in Reference to the War*. London: New Life Movement, 1941.

Kemp, Eric Waldram. *The Life and Letters of Kenneth Escott Kirk, Bishop of Oxford, 1937–1954*. London: Hodder & Stoughton, 1959.

Kent, Charles Weller. *Make Friends of the Wise*. Bath, England: Medip, 1941.

Kirk, K.E.K. *The Menace to Faith*. London: Oxford University Press, 1940.

Kirk, P.T.R. *Revolutionary Christianity: How Peace Can Be Saved*. London: Peace Book Company, 1939.

Knox, Ronald A., Gilbert Russell, Anthony Otter, and W. J. Hoble. *The World We're Fighting For*. London: SCM Press, 1941.

Landau, Rom. *Hitler's Paradise*. London: Faber & Faber, 1941.

———. *We Have Seen Evil: A Background to War*. London: Faber & Faber, 1941.

Lang, Cosmo Gordon. *Letters and Papers of Cosmo Gordon Lang, Archbishop of Canterbury, 1928–42*. Lambeth Palace Library.

Leo. *Give Christ a Chance*. London: Drakers, 1941.

Lloyd-Jones, Martyn. *The Plight of Man and the Power of God*. London: Hodder & Stoughton, 1942.

———. *Why Does God Allow War?: A General Justification of the Ways of God*. London: Hodder & Stoughton, 1939.

Lucas, W. W. *War and the Purposes of God: A Survey of Scripture Teaching*. London: Marshall, Morgan, & Scott, 1940.

Lyon, Hugh. *Challenge to Youth*. London: Christophers, 1940.

Macnutt, Frederick B. *Four Freedoms: Atlantic and Christian*. Leicester, England: Thornley, 1943.

Macpherson, Ian. *The Cross in War-Time*. London: Stockwell, 1941.

Martin, Hugh. *Christian Counter-Attack: Europe's Churches against Nazism*. New York: Scribners, 1944.

Matthews, W. R. *Saint Paul's Cathedral in War-Time, 1939–45*. N.p.: Hutchinson, 1946.

———. *The Foundations of Peace*. London: Eyre & Spottiswoode, 1942.

———. *The Moral Issues of the War*. London: Eyre & Spottiswoode, 1942.

———. *Our War for Freedom: A Broadcast on the Day of National Prayer, October 8, 1939*. N.p., N.d.

May, G. Lacey, ed. *War-Time Intercessions: Ten Forms of Prayer for Congregational or Private Use*. London: Skeffington, 1941.

McLaine, Ian. *Ministry of Morale: Home Front Morale and the Ministry of Information in World War II*. London: Allen & Unwin, 1979.

Micklem, Nathaniel. *Europe's Own Book*. London: Morrison & Gibb, 1944.

———. *The Theology of Law*. Oxford: Oxford University Press, 1943.

———. *The Theology of Politics*. London: Oxford University Press, 1941.

———. *National Socialism and the Roman Catholic Church*. London: Oxford University Press, 1939.

———. *May God Defend the Right!* London: Hodder & Stoughton, 1939.

———. *The Crisis and the Christian*. London: SCM Press, 1938.

Miller, Alexander. *Biblical Politics: Studies in Christian Social Doctrine*. London: SCM Press, 1943.

Moloney, Thomas. *Westminster, Whitehall and the Vatican: The Role of Cardinal Hinsley, 1935–43*. Tunbridge Wells, Kent, England: Burns & Oates, 1985.

Muir, Ramsay. *Civilization and Liberty*. London: Cape, 1940.

Mumford, Lewis. *Faith for Living*. London: Secker & Warburg, 1941.

———. *Men Must Act*. London: Secker & Warburg, 1939.

Murray, Rosalind. *The Good Pagan's Failure*. London: Hollis & Carter, 1943.

Murry, John Middleton. *Christocracy*. London: Drakers, 1942.

————. *Europe in Travail*. London: Sheldon, 1940.

Nazi Massacres of the Jews and Others: Some Practical Proposals for Immediate Rescue Made by the Archbishop of Canterbury and Lord Rochester in Speeches on March 23, 1943 in the House of Lords. London: Gollancz, 1943.

Niebuhr, Reinhold. *Jews after the War*. N.p.: Inter-University Jewish Federation, 1942.

————. *Europe's Catastrophe and the Christian Faith*. London: Nisbet, 1940.

————. *Why the Christian Church Is Not Pacifist*. London: SCM Press, 1940.

Olden, Rudolf. *Is Germany a Hopeless Case?* Tr. Edwyn Bevan. London: Allen & Unwin, 1940.

Oldham, J. H. *Real Life Is Meeting*. London: Sheldon Press, 1942.

————. *The Root of Our Troubles*. London: SCM Press, 1941.

Paton, William. *The Church and the New Order*. London: SCM Press, 1941.

Phillips, Winifred. *We Prayed for Peace—Well!: A Word to Any Who May Feel That God either Ignored Those Prayers or Is Holding the Answer in Abeyance*. London: Walthamstow, 1942.

Pole, W. Tudor. *A Lighthouse Set on an Island Rock*. London: Big Ben Council, 1942.

Pollock, Bertram. *Voices of Sunday*. London: Faith Press, 1943.

Pulsford, Edward J. *Should Christians Fight? An Answer Based on the Christian Sacred Scriptures, in the Light of the Teachings of Emanuel Swedenborg*. London: New Church Missionary and Tract Society, 1940.

Richardson, Alan. *The Message of the Bible in War-Time*. London: SCM Press, 1940.

Roberts, Andrew. *"The Holy Fox": A Biography of Lord Halifax*. London: Weidenfeld & Nicolson, 1991.

Rouse, Ruth, and Stephen Charles Neill, eds. *A History of the Ecumenical Movement 1517–1948*. London: SPCK, 1967.

Rupp, E. G. *Is This a Christian Country?* London: Sheldon Press, 1941.

Salter, F. T. *Keep Smiling! Sixteen Tonic Talks on Religion and Life*. London: Muller, 1942.

————. *An Englishman's Faith: Fifteen War-Time Talks for Comfort and Encouragement to Christian Soldiers*. London: Muller, 1941.

Sampson, Ashley, ed. *This War and Christian Ethics: A Symposium*. London: Blackwell, 1940.

Sangster, W. E. *Ten Statesmen and Jesus Christ: A Christian Commentary on Our War Aims*. London: Hodder & Stoughton, 1941.

Sayers, Dorothy L. *Why Work? An Address Delivered at Eastbourne, April 23, 1942*. London: Metheun, 1942.

————. *Begin Here: A War-Time Essay*. London: Gollancz, 1940.

Sheen, Fulton J. *Philosophies at War*. London: Blandford, 1945.

Short, K.R.M. *Film and Radio Propaganda in World War II*. London: Croom Helm, 1983.

Simpson, William W. *Jews and Christians To-Day: A Study in Jewish and Christian Relationship*. London: Epworth, 1940.

Sinclair, Ronald. *A Religion for Battle-Dress*. London: Mowbray, 1941.

————. *Victim Victorious: A Message for War-Time*. London: SCM Press, 1940.

Steed, Wickham. *Our War Aims*. London: Secker & Warburg, 1939.

Stewart, Douglas. *Personal Religion and the Future of Europe*. London: SCM Press, 1941.

Temple, William. *Some Lambeth Letters.* Ed. F. S. Temple. London: Oxford University Press, 1962.

———. *Christianity as an Interpretation of History.* London: Longmans, Green, 1945.

———. *The Crisis of the Western World and Other Broadcast Talks.* London: Allen & Unwin, 1944.

———. *The Church Looks Forward.* London: Macmillan, 1944.

———. *Towards a Christian Order.* London: Eyre & Spottiswoode, 1942.

———. *One Lord, One People.* London: Lutterworth, 1941.

———. *Citizen and Churchman.* London: Eyre & Spottiswoode, 1941.

———. *Thoughts in War-Time.* London: Macmillan, 1940.

———. *The Hope of a New World.* London: SCM Press, 1940.

———. *A Conditional Justification of War.* London: Hodder & Stoughton, 1940.

———. *A Manual for Prayers in War-Time.* London: Mowbray, 1939.

———. *Letters and Papers of William Temple, Archbishop of Canterbury, 1942–44.* Lambeth Palace Library.

Upton, A. E. *From Chaos to Order: The World Crisis and the Christian Key to Its Solution.* London: Institute of Export, 1943.

van Dusen, Henry P. *What Is the Church Doing?* London: SCM Press, 1943.

Vann, Gerald. *Religion and World Order.* Westminster, England: Dacre, 1945.

———. *Morality and War.* London: Burns, Oates, & Washbourne, 1939.

Vidler, Alec R. *Secular Despair and Christian Faith.* London: SCM Press, 1941.

———. *God's Judgment on Europe.* London:Longmans, Green, 1940.

Voice of the Churches: Representative Leaders and the War. London: Hodder & Stoughton, 1940.

———. *God's Judgment on Europe.* London: Longmans, Green, 1940.

Waln, Nora. *Reaching for the Stars.* London: Cresset, 1939.

Weatherhead, Leslie. *The Church and the New Order.* London: Epworth, 1941.

———. *This Is the Victory.* London: Hodder & Stoughton, 1940.

———. *Thinking Aloud in War-Time: An Attempt to See the Present Situation in the Light of the Christian Faith.* London: Hodder & Stoughton, 1939.

Whale, J. S. *The Old Faith and the New Order.* London: Tinsley, 1942.

Wilkinson, Alan. *Dissent or Conform? War, Peace and the English Churches 1900–1945.* London: SCM Press, 1986.

———. *The Church of England and the First World War,* 2d ed. London: SCM Press, 1996.

Williams, R. R. *The World Church in the World War.* London: SPCK, 1942.

Winnington-Ingram, A. F. *A Second Day of God.* London: Longmans, Green, 1940.

Wolfe, Kenneth M. *The Churches and the British Broadcasting Corporation, 1922–1956.* London: SCM Press, 1984.

Woodward, C. Salisbury, and Harry W. Blackburne. *Clergy in War-Time.* London: Hodder & Stoughton, 1939.

Zimmern, Alfred. *Spiritual Values and World Affairs.* Oxford: Clarendon, 1939.

Index

Ackland, Sir Richard, 128
Acton, Lord John, 106
Adler, Alfred, 124
American Baptist Church, 37
Anderson, Sir John, 39
Angell, Norman, 82
Anglican Pacifist Fellowship, 39–40, 43
Armitage, John, 59, 125
Armstrong, W. H., 37
Atlantic Charter, 104

Baldwin, Stanley, 127
Barclay, George, 13, 14, 60
Barry, F. R., 54, 56, 100, 108
Barth, Karl, 28, 63, 67
Battle of Britain, 12
Baynes, Norman, 58
Belgion, Montgomery, 23
Bell, George, 15, 17–18, 36, 43–44, 101, 116–117
Belloc, Hilaire, 52, 60, 83

Bendiscioli, Mario, 58, 90
Bernanon, George, 117
Berry, Sidney, 9–10, 36, 105
Beveridge, Lord William, 127–128
Bevin, Ernest, 38–39
Bombing, 5, 19; saturation, 41–44
Bottome, Phyllis, 36, 108, 124
Brook, Richard, 79
Bruce, Rosslyn, 2
Buber, Martin, 73
Burke, Edmund, 31
Butterfield, Herbert, 69

Cambridge Union, 5
Cammaerts, Emile, 13
Carey, Walter, 59
Carpenter, S. C., 7, 68
Carrel, Alexis, 111
Cecil, Lord Robert, 3
Chamberlain, Neville, 7, 72, 82, 86
Chesterton, Gilbert Keith, 53, 65
The Christian Pacifist, 25

Christianity and the Social Order, 127, 130

Christianity in the Eastern Conflicts, 56

The Church and the New Order, 103

Churchill, Winston, 19, 36, 44, 82, 98, 103–104, 110–111, 122, 125, 129

Clemenceau, Georges, 53

Cockin, F. A., 10

Colet, John, 23

Collins, L. J., 30

Comford, Alex, 8

Confessing Church, 17

Davidson, Donald, 54, 60, 62, 70, 79

Davidson, Randall Thomas (archbishop of Canterbury), 2, 18, 126

Davies, D. R., 8, 14, 42, 52, 62, 64, 69, 70, 74, 82, 84, 86, 100, 107, 131; career summary, 91–93

Dawson, Christopher, 100, 116, 123

Demant, V. A., 54, 57, 62, 67, 83, 86, 106, 107, 117

Dodd, Charles H., 9

Dostoevsky, Feodor, 62, 69, 107

Douglas, Keith, 17

Drewett, John, 56, 124

Dudden, F. Holmes, 5

Dulles, John Foster, 114

Dunning, T. G., 52, 58, 64, 66, 73, 107, 112

Dusen, Henry van, 103

Economic Consequences of the Peace, 3–4

Eliot, Thomas Stearns, 65, 90, 98, 117, 136

Europe's Catastrophe and the Christian Faith, 13, 33

Europe's Own Book, 109

Faith for Living, 34

Fisher, Geoffrey Francis (archbishop of London), 117, 122

Francis of Assisi, Saint, 33

Franco, Francisco, 4

Frick, Wilhelm, 68

Frisch, Theodor, 54

Gandhi, Mohandas, 26

Garbett, Cyril F., 27

Garlick, Phyllis L., 15

George V (king of England), 5

George VI (king of England), 110

German Christians, 17, 52

Glasgow, George, 52, 81

Gliddon, Paul, 40

God and Nation: A Soldier's Creed, 54

God and the Allies: A View of the Grand Entente, 2

God in a World at War, 11

Goudge, H. L., 25

The Great Illusion, 82

Great War, 1, 3; comparison with World War II, 16–20

Green, Peter, 64

Gupta, Nolini Kanta, 104

Hadham, John, 9, 11, 56, 66, 87, 98, 124

Haigh, Mervyn, 44

Halifax, Lord Edward, 82, 110

Harnack, Adolf von, 4

Harris, Arthur Travers "Bomber," 45

Has the Christian Way Failed?, 30

Henson, Hensley, 60, 100

Hildebrandt, Franz, 17, 34

Hinsley, Cardinal Arthur, 71, 72, 115, 116, 117

Hitler, Adolf, 4, 5, 15, 16, 17, 30, 31, 33, 37, 44, 51, 52, 54, 56, 58, 59, 60, 61, 63, 65, 66, 69, 70, 73, 82, 84, 86, 88, 91, 98, 101, 121, 137

Hoare, L. L., 111

Hobhouse, Stephen, 27, 43

d'Holbach, Baron Paul Henri Dietrich, 3

The Hope of a New World, 130

Houseman, A. E., 12

Howard, R. T., 81

Hughes, A. Price, 80

Huxley, Julian, 64

Idolatry, in national socialism, 57–59

Individualism, in Western thought, 105–106

Inge, William Ralph, 35, 80, 85

Irrationalism, in national socialism, 62–63

Jacks, L. P., 131
Jakubovic, K., 41
Jehovah's Witnesses, 38
Jessop, T. E., 30, 88
Joad, C.E.M., 5, 19, 87
Johnson, Samuel, 38
Jung, Carl, 51

Khaki Election, 3
Keynes, John M., 3, 4, 127, 129
Kirk, Kenneth Escott (bishop of Oxford), 45, 63, 68, 72

Landau, Rom, 51, 52, 74, 97, 100, 123
Lang, Cosmo Gordon (archbishop of Canterbury), 15, 19, 27, 38, 39, 40, 41, 43, 59, 103, 104, 116
League of Nations, 1, 3, 7, 20, 24, 87
Lehrmann, S. M., 64
Lloyd George, David, 3, 4
Lloyd-Jones, Martyn, 10, 13, 84, 86, 130
London Society of Friends, 44
Lowell, James Russell, 8
Lucas, W. W., 28
Luther, Martin, 52

Macnutt, Frederick, 67, 107, 130
Marrin, Albert, 2
Marriott, S. J., 98, 124
Martin, Kingsley, 19
Matthews, W. R., 36, 60, 66, 69, 70, 82, 100, 102, 107, 108, 122, 123
McLaine, Ian, 53
Men Must Act, 34
Methodist Church, 37
Moral relativism, in national socialism, 59–62
Morality and War, 26
Morrison, Herbert, 19
Mosley, Oswald, 71
Mumford, Lewis, 31, 34, 53, 60, 61, 62, 79, 80, 81, 85, 102, 124
Murray, Rosalind, 86
Mussolini, Benito, 4, 31, 51, 70, 121

National socialism, analysis of, 53–72; praise of, 73–74
Newman, John Henry, 105
Nicholls, Hubert A., 41
Nicodim (patriarch of Romania), 44
Nicolson, Harold, 14
Niebuhr, Reinhold, 13, 18, 32, 33, 34, 53, 67, 84, 91, 92, 102, 103, 111, 112, 115
Niemoeller, Martin, 112
Nietzsche, Friedrich, 41, 59, 62, 63, 97
Notes from the Underground, 62

Oldham, J. H., 73, 83, 106
Orwell, George, 18
Otter, Anthony, 9
Oxford Union, 5

Pacifism: defense of, 25–27; history of, 23–25; refutation of, 27–37
Paton, William, 52, 56, 68, 103, 114, 130
Pius XI (pope), 26, 68, 70, 71
Pius XII (pope), 72, 116, 125
Pole, W. Tudor, 111
Pugh, W. B., 114

Quakers, 37

"Race" in Europe, 64
Racism, in national socialism, 64–67
Real Life Is Meeting, 73
Reckitt, Maurice, 24
Reflections on the End of an Era, 91
Roberts, Andrew, 82
Roosevelt, Franklin, 104
Rosenberg, Alfred, 55–57, 65
Rowley, H. H., 114–115
Ruskin, John, 97
Rupp, E. G., 14, 86, 104, 110, 113, 130
Russell, Bertrand, 19
Russell, Gilbert, 12

Salmond, John, 35, 36
Salter, F. T., 12
Sayers, Dorothy, 10, 32, 59, 64, 66, 68, 80, 85, 93, 102, 117, 125, 131
Sheen, Fulton J., 10, 59, 62, 79, 108

Simon, M. P., 40, 41
Sinclair, Sir Archibald, 43, 44
Steed, William, 53, 58, 107
Stewart, Douglas, 61, 68, 80, 83, 84, 85, 86, 109
Studdert-Kennedy, Arthur, 35
The Sword of the Spirit, 72–73
Sword of the Spirit, 116–117

Temple, William, 15, 18, 27, 28, 29, 32, 34, 35, 36, 38, 52, 54, 59, 67, 73, 91, 94, 100, 103, 106, 108, 111, 114, 115; problem of bombing, 41–46; his contribution to reform, 126–130
Thomas Aquinas, Saint, 32, 126
Totalitarianism, in national socialism, 67–69
The Treaty of Versailles: Was It Just?, 87–89

Vatican, 90
Vann, Gerald, 26, 32, 43, 64, 73, 80, 130
van Roey, Cardinal (archbishop of Malines), 44

Vansittart, Sir Robert, 52
Versailles, Treaty of, 3, 4, 5, 87–89
Vidler, Alex, 10, 14, 35, 62, 69, 86, 90, 93, 94

War and the Purposes of God: A Survey of Scripture Teaching, 28
Warman, Guy, 113
Weatherhead, Leslie, 15, 27, 35, 63, 131
Wegg-Prosser, Charles, 71
Wells, H. G., 5
Why the Christian Church Is Not Pacifist, 33
Wilkinson, Alan, 17, 99, 135
Wilson, Woodrow, 1, 4
Winnington Ingram, Arthur (bishop of London), 2, 99
Wood, H. G., 37
The World War: Its Inner Bearings, 104
Wright, C. J., 113

Yeats, William Butler, 89

Zimmern, Alfred, 28, 52, 87, 104, 104

ABOUT THE AUTHOR

A. J. Hoover has been a professor of History for thirty-four years and has taught at Pepperdine University and Abilene Christian University. He has written about several wars and patriotic preaching in both Britain and Germany, and his research has taken him to university libraries in Berlin, Marburg, Heidelberg, Oxford, and Cambridge. This is his third book on clerical nationalism.

ISBN 0-275-96539-2

90000>

EAN

9 780275 965396

HARDCOVER BAR CODE

GOD, BRITAIN, AND HITLER IN WORLD WAR II

The View of the British Clergy, 1939–1945

A. J. Hoover

Foreword by Richard V. Pierard

PRAEGER

Westport, Connecticut
London

Library of Congress Cataloging-in-Publication Data

Hoover, Arlie J.
    God, Britain, and Hitler in World War II : the view of the British
clergy, 1939–1945 / A. J. Hoover ; foreword by Richard V. Pierard.
        p.   cm.
    Includes bibliographical references and index.
    ISBN 0–275–96539–2 (alk. paper)
    1. World War, 1914–1918—Religious aspects.   2. Nationalism—
Religious aspects—Christianity—History—20th century.
3. Nationalism—Germany—History—20th century.   4. Nationalism—
Great Britain—History—20th century.   I. Title.
D639.R4H63   1999
940.4'78—dc21   98–56637

British Library Cataloguing in Publication Data is available.

Library of Congress Catalog Card Number: 98–56637
ISBN: 0–275–96539–2

First published in 1999

Praeger Publishers, 88 Post Road West, Westport, CT 06881
An imprint of Greenwood Publishing Group, Inc.
www.praeger.com

Printed in the United States of America

The paper used in this book complies with the
Permanent Paper Standard issued by the National
Information Standards Organization (Z39.48–1984).

10   9   8   7   6   5   4   3   2   1